William B. Worsfold

The Redemption of Egypt

William B. Worsfold

The Redemption of Egypt

ISBN/EAN: 9783337231538

Printed in Europe, USA, Canada, Australia, Japan

Cover: Foto ©ninafisch / pixelio.de

More available books at **www.hansebooks.com**

The
Redemption of Egypt

By
W. Basil Worsfold, M.A.
Barrister-at-Law

Author of "The Principles of Criticism," "The Valley of Light"
"South Africa," "A Visit to Java," etc.

With Illustrations

London
George Allen, 156, Charing Cross Road
1899

[*All rights reserved*]

Preface

In this book I have endeavoured to give some account of the physical and social characteristics of Egypt, and to exhibit these characteristics in connection with the work of political reorganization and industrial development which is now in progress. The sketches and the information which I have ventured to present to the reader are the fruits of a visit, undertaken for the purpose, during the winter of 1898–99.

In sending this work to the press, I desire to express my thanks to all the many friends who were kind enough to place their information at my disposal, or to assist me in acquiring such information by personal observation. To the following I am especially indebted: Sir Rennell Rodd, C.B., K.C.M.G., First Secretary of Legation; H. E. Yacoub Artin Pasha, Under-Secretary of State for Education; Mr. F. T. Rowlatt, Sub-Governor of the National Bank of Egypt; Mr. W. C. Mackenzie, D.Sc., Director of the School of Agriculture; Coles Pasha, Director-General of Prisons; Mr. Edmund Carver, Chairman of the Egyptian Sugar and Land Co.; Mr. W. O. Joseph, Managing Director of the Fayûm Light Railway Co.; Mr. A. V. Houghton, Headmaster of the Khedivich School and Principal of the Training College; Sir Elwin Palmer, K.C.B., K.C.M.G., late Financial Adviser, and Governor of the National Bank of Egypt; Hassan Oassif Bey, Mudir of the Fayûm; Mr. Reginald Henriques, Secretary (Cairo) to the British Chamber of Commerce; Sir Reginald Wingate, R.A., K.C.B., &c., Director of Military Intelligence, Egyptian Army.

I wish, however, to add that, although I have in no case intentionally misrepresented the views of any of these gentlemen, I am myself solely responsible for the statements or opinions which appear in the book.

The use which I have made both of the admirable reports which are forwarded from time to time by the British Agent to the Foreign Office, and of the official publications of the Egyptian Government, will, I hope, be found to be duly acknowledged in the text.

In the spelling of the modern Egyptian names and words I have, in general, endeavoured to mark the special value of the vowel sounds by the use of the circumflex accent. But, while I have retained this accent in the descriptive chapters, I have omitted to place it on Arabic words which have become practically anglicized by their frequent occurrence in the English reports, when such words—*e.g.*, *kuttab* and *mudir*—have constantly recurred in the political chapters.

In conclusion, I desire to record my indebtedness to Mr. F. T. Rowlatt for his kindness in reading over the proof-sheets of the chapters in which financial and industrial matters are discussed, and for the valuable suggestions by which I have thus benefited.

I also desire to express my thanks to Mrs. Kay, of the Quarter House, Denny, N.B., for her kindness in permitting me to include two of her photographs—placed respectively at pages 226 and 312—among those of my own, which have been used in illustrating the book.

W. B. W.

2 PUMP COURT, TEMPLE, E.C.,
August 1899.

Contents

CHAPTER I

THE SCENE

Water and justice—Egypt is so much of the desert as is flooded by the Nile— The Delta—The Nile banks—The Fayûm—Long servitude of the Egyptians —Sense of justice extinct—Elements of population—Towns and European communities—Characteristics and distribution of these elements—The work of civilization in evidence 1

CHAPTER II

ALEXANDRIA

First sight of Egypt—The mosquito—Literary ideas and realities—No true conception of Egypt obtained through books—First impressions disappointing —Modern aspect of the town—Ptolemaic Alexandria—Plutarch's story of its foundation—Strabo's account—Its quarters, buildings, and characteristics —Causes of its prosperity—Scenes from the life of this Alexandria—Cæsar— Antony and Cleopatra—Berenice—Theocritus' picture of a day in Alexandria —Dr. Botti's account of the Serapeum—The Theodosian column, miscalled "Pompey's Pillar"—Roman Alexandria—The power of the Patriarchs— Athanasius—Theodosius and the origin of the Coptic Church—The Byzantine period—Cyril—Hypatia—Capture of Alexandria by the Saracens— Fate of the Library—Decay of the town 15

CHAPTER III

THE DELTA AND THE COTTON INDUSTRY

Leave Alexandria—First lesson in Arabic—Aspect of the country from Alexandria to Tanta—Reach Mehallet—Centre of the Delta—Cotton provides three-fourths of the Egyptian exports—Growth and characteristics of cotton culture in Egypt—Quality of Egyptian cotton better than American— Margin of price between them—Falling prices—Require continued improvements and economies—Want of rolling-stock on railways—Visit to a cotton (ginning) mill—Methods of cotton cleaning—Ginning—Garbling—

Wages for Arab labour—Output of the mill—Cotton and cotton seed—Uses of cotton seed—Destinations of existing cotton crop—Visit to the town of Mehallet—Village school—Native industries—Weaving and manufacture of linseed cakes—The market—Housekeeping in an Egyptian town . . . 40

CHAPTER IV

THE GOVERNMENT

Four authorities participate in the government of Egypt: the Sultan of Turkey, the Khedive, the Great Powers, England — Origin and nature of the authority of the Sultan—Of the Khedive—Of the international authority—Financial—The *Caisse de la Dette*—Administrative—The mixed administrations—Judicial—The Tribunaux Mixtes—Consular courts—Origin of international judicial authority—The capitulations—The encroachments of the mixed courts on the native—The proposals of the Government to amend the charter of organization—The questions at issue—The authority of the British Government—The successive steps by which the "veiled Protectorate" has grown—First professions of England—Duty of giving advice—Advice must be taken—The offer to withdraw—Justification of position of England—The recovery of the Sudân—Position of England, how altered by the Sudân agreement—Ministries and departments of the Government . . . 57

CHAPTER V

FROM MEMPHIS TO CAIRO

First impression of Cairo—Two Cairos—Mediæval and European—It occupies natural site for capital of Egypt—Memphis—Herodotus' account of Memphis, c. 400 B.C.—Strabo's account—Memphis and Babylon in the age of Augustus—The capture of Babylon by the Saracens, A.D. 638—Fostât—Expansion of Fostât under Tulûn--Foundation of Cairo in 972—Its growth under the Fâtimite Khalifs—The citadel added by Saladin—The tomb-mosques by the Mameluke Sultans—Remains of mediæval Cairo—Respected during British occupation—Preservation of Arabian monuments—Difficulties in the way of exploring mediæval Cairo—Chief groups of buildings . . 73

CHAPTER VI

MEDIÆVAL CAIRO

The Citadel—Built by Saladin—Massacre of the Mameluke Boys—Joseph's Well—The mosque of Mohammed Ali—Æsthetic value of the interior—View of Cairo from the Citadel—Chief streets and buildings of mediæval Cairo—The three gates—El-Futûh—En-Nasr—Ez-Zuwêleh—The Kâdi's House—Reform of the religious courts—A caravanserai—Origin of the

CONTENTS

Bazaars of Cairo—Nâssiri Krosrau's account of the industries of mediæval Cairo—The influence of Persia on Arabic craftsmanship—The Mosque el-Azhar—Condition of the Mohammedan University of Cairo—Signs of reform—"Old Cairo"—The ruins of the Roman station at Babylon—The Coptic Church of Mâri Girgis—Coptic influence on Arabian art—The Mosque of Amr—The site of Fostât—Cairo at sunset 84

CHAPTER VII

THE MOSQUES, AS ILLUSTRATING THE DEVELOPMENT OF ARABIAN ART IN EGYPT

Origin of Arabian art—Byzantine principles—Coptic models—Earliest period, 640-876—Origin and elements of the mosque—The mosque of Tulûn—Second period, 876-972—Fâtimite period, 972-1171—Mosques of El-Azhar, &c.—Development of "colonnaded" mosque—Persian influence—First example of Arabian portal at El-Akmar—Stucco decoration and woodcarving—Eyyubite period, 1171-1250—Introduction of (cruciform) college-mosque—Influence of Crusades—Development of "stalactite" pendentives—Period of Turkoman Mamelukes, 1250-1382—Use of Gothic forms in mosques of period—Development of lesser arts in Cairo—Introduction of dome—Creation of characteristic Arabian façade—Richness of internal decoration and furniture—Use of marble—Absence of distinctive Arabian column—Period of Circassian Mamelukes, 1382-1517—Completion of evolution of mosque—Kuttâb and Sebil added—Perfection of exterior form—Mosques of period—Include "Tomb-Mosques"—Tombs of the Khalifs—Sunset from Windmill Hill 108

CHAPTER VIII

THE EDUCATION SYSTEM

European Cairo—Absence of public buildings—Civilizing influences—System of education—Vernacular schools or kuttabs—Primary schools—Secondary—Special schools and colleges—School of law—Engineering—Technical schools—Training colleges for teachers—Total attendance in Government schools, and cost of education—Policy of Government in respect of teaching of French and English—"Linguistic free-trade"—Results of this policy—Proportion of boys learning French or English—Relationship of the educational machine to population of Egypt—Reform of the kuttabs—Commencement of national education—Various attempts to improve the kuttabs—The results already obtained—Opinions of Artin Pasha—Prospects of education—Narrowing the interval between the educated official and the ignorant masses—The progress of women's education—Visit to the School of Agriculture—Practical work in the fields—Cost of students to the state—The Khedivieh school—Fasting and school work—Difficulty of maintaining social influence on boys after they have left school—A provincial school—Eton jackets 143

CHAPTER IX
LAW AND ORDER

Inherent defect of the Mixed Tribunals—Reasons for retaining them—Commercial community favourably disposed to them—Amendment of Bankruptcy Law required—English language should be recognized—Compromises—System of Native Tribunals—Personnel of judges must be raised—Improvement of administration—Committee of judicial control—Extension of summary jurisdiction—Amendments of criminal law—The Prosecutor-General's department—The Parquet—Improved relations between the Mudirs and the police—Results of these reforms shown by criminal returns—Improvement of the prisons—New buildings required—Defects of the old system—Reform introduced by Coles Pasha—Visit to the prison at Gizeh—Organization of prison labour—Classification of prisoners—Food—General impressions 170

CHAPTER X
SOCIAL CAIRO

Gezireh—The Anglo-Saxon playground—Unobtrusiveness of English in Cairo—Army of Occupation forms an exception—The Khedive—Chief figure in social life—The Khedivia—Mother of Khedive takes precedence of wife—Life of English residents—Race meetings—Gymkhanas—Opera House—Position of native women—Presentation to *Vice-Reine Mère*—Description of ceremony—Participation of Egyptian men in social life of the English—Of Egyptian women—Calls upon European ladies—Native servants—Difficulty of language 185

CHAPTER XI
THE BARRAGE AND THE IRRIGATION SERVICE

Story of the Barrage—System of irrigation different in Upper and Lower Egypt—Importance of the Barrage—Designed by Mougel Bey in 1843—Rosetta branch completed in 1863—The whole structure abandoned in 1867—Moncrieff organizes irrigation service in 1883—Anglo-Indian engineers—Temporary repair of Barrage—Effect of this—Permanent repair undertaken—Source of its insecurity—The remedy—The design put into execution by Colonel Western and Mr. Reid—Method and difficulties of work—Accomplished in 1890—Effect upon cotton crop of Delta—Completion of irrigation system of Lower Egypt—Perfect organization of irrigation service—Attempt to employ Egyptians as inspectors—Present appearance of Barrage—Consolidation of the piers and foundations now effected—Construction of subsidiary weirs—Efficiency and stability of Barrage secured—Drainage of cultivable area of Egypt now in progress 196

CONTENTS

CHAPTER XII

THE PYRAMIDS

The museum at Gizeh—Egyptian statues—Conventional attitudes—Type of face revealed—Coptic sculptures—Egyptian art "barbaric"—Visit to the Pyramids of Gizeh—Absence of romance—The Sphinx—Enormous bulk of Pyramids of Cheops and Chephren—Origin of the Pyramids—Immortality of the soul—Herodotus's account—View from the plain—Merits and defects of Pyramids as essays in architecture—Æsthetic significance—Due to size—Power of association—Remains of Memphis—Sakkâra—Apis tombs—Mastaba of Thy—Heliopolis—Plato's residence there—Strabo's account—Revision of the calendar due to priests 213

CHAPTER XIII

RAILWAYS, SUGAR, AND FINANCE

From Cairo to Luxor by rail—Defective administration of railways—Its causes and results—Proposals to remedy this—Visit to a sugar-mill at Beliâneh—Work of the Egyptian Sugar and Land Company—Irrigation and sugar-crushing—The pumping station—The sugar factory—Processes employed—Crushing—Cleansing—Evaporation—Separation of sugar crystals from molasses—Sugar culture in Egypt—The Daïra administration—Private mills—Amount of private capital invested—Methods of the Daïra factories—Economy in working—Fall of prices—Destination of sugar export—Development of private enterprize probable—The Daïra administration to be wound up in 1905—Extension of area available for sugar cultivation by Nile reservoir—Effect of fall of prices in cotton and sugar—Egyptian finance—Sir Elwin Palmer's views—Both industries safe—Other prospects of expansion of revenue 235

CHAPTER XIV

LUXOR

Arrival at Luxor—Egyptian weather—Site of Thebes—The capital of the New Empire—Its monuments—Strabo's account of Thebes—The Colossi of Memnon—Explanation of the phenomenon—Advantages of Luxor—Wind and dust—Strabo's description of the Egyptian temple—His criticism—Comparison with the Greek temple—The deficiency of design in the Egyptian temple—Its significant features—Its vast size—The Pylon—The Polystyle Hall—The Egyptian Column—The Polystyle Hall at Karnac—The temple of Luxor—Sordid surroundings of the temples—The temples on the west bank—The Valley of the Tombs of the Kings—The Ramesseum —View of Luxor 251

CHAPTER XV

ASSUÂN

From Luxor to Assuân—The first cataract—Elephantine—Syene—Philæ—Strabo's visit—His account of the Nilometer—Position of Syene under the tropic—The passage of the cataract—Journey to Philæ—Relation of Egypt with the desert tribes under the empire—The Christians of the Thebaid—Visit to the quarries above Assuân—To the Nilometer—The Convent of St. Simeon—Harbour of Assuân *en fête*—Philæ—The Temple of Isis—The Conception of the goddess—Introduction of worship into Greece and Italy—Roman buildings at Philæ—Captain Lyons' survey—The Nile reservoir—Scene on the east bank of the Nile—Dimensions of the dam—Other works for the irrigation of Upper Egypt—The dam at Assiût—Terms of the contract for construction—Deferred payment—International control makes this arrangement necessary—Estimated gain to Egypt from reservoir, &c.—Number of workmen employed at Assuân 275

CHAPTER XVI

LOCAL GOVERNMENT AND THE CONDITION OF THE FELLÂHÎN

From Assuân to the Fayûm—Scene of the Nile reservoir of ancient Egypt—Herodotus's account of Lake Moeris—Strabo's account—Fertility of the district—The Labyrinth—The Mudîr of the Fayûm—Local administration in Egypt—Representative institutions established by organic law—Legislative Chamber—General Assembly—Municipalities—Provincial and Town Councils—The Mudîr central figure in provincial administration—Hassan Bey—His duties and functions—Relations of Mudîr and Parquet—Industrial development of the provinces—Light railways—In the Delta—The Fayûm Light Railway Co.—Native Board of Management—Construction of markets in provincial towns and villages—Aspect of the Fayûm—The Fellâh—In the fields—At home—The indebtedness of the Fellâhîn—Proposals to remedy this evil 295

CHAPTER XVII

THE DEVELOPMENT OF THE SUDÂN

The loss and recovery of the Sudân—Now depopulated and devastated by Mahdist tyranny—Condition of Sudân in 1882—Stewart's report—Present condition—Darfûr and Kordofân not yet recovered—Administration of provinces already occupied—Dongola province—Sir William Garstin's report on Sudân—Description of Khartûm—The Blue Nile and the White Nile contrasted—Egypt's immediate interest centres in the marsh area around

CONTENTS

Lake No—The weed barrier called "sudd"—Factors in the annual Nile flood—Effect of the sudd on the water-supply of Egypt—Enormous loss of water by evaporation in the marsh area—Possibility of diminishing this loss by preventing the river from "spilling" the water-supply of the Great Lakes—Clearance of sudd first operation—Climate of Sudân and its depopulation are obstacles to industrial development—Railway construction—Line from Wâdi Halfa to Khartûm—Proposed line to connect the Nile Valley with the Red Sea coast—Best route *viâ* Gedâref and Kassâla—The "granary of the Sudân"—Little scope at present for private enterprize—Reasons for this—Pumping stations—Telegraph construction—The Gordon College 317

List of Illustrations

COLOURED

THE CITADEL OF CAIRO	.	*Frontispiece*
CAIRO FROM GEZÎREH	.	*To face page* 186
THE PYRAMID OF CHEPHREN		,, ,, 220
THE PYRAMIDS OF GÎZEH	.	,, ,, 224

FULL PAGE

EMÎR EL-GÂI YUSEFI MOSQUE FROM SÛK ES-SELLÂHA	,, ,,	74
LOOKING SOUTH FROM END OF THE STREET EL-NAHHÂSÎN	,, ,,	82
THE BÂB EL-FUTÛH	,, ,,	92
THE BÂB EN-NASR		94
THE BÂB EZ-ZUWÊLEH	,, ,,	96
ENTRANCE TO OKELLA IN STREET EL-GAMÂLÎYEH	,, ,,	98
TOMBS OF THE KHALÎFS	,, ,,	114
SANCTUARY OF MOSQUE EL-TELAYEH	,, ,,	122
MÛRISTÂN OF KALÂÛN	,, ,,	126
INTERIOR OF MOSQUE EL-GHÛRI	,, ,,	136
MOSQUE OF KAÏT BEY	,, ,,	140
THE DAMIETTA BARRAGE	,,	204
THE RAMESSEUM	,,	254
THE APPROACH TO KARNAC	,, ,,	257
THE TEMPLE OF RAMSES III. AT KARNAC	,, ,,	263
THE TEMPLE OF LUXOR	,, ,,	264
THE POLYSTYLE HALL AT KARNAC	,, ,,	266
PHILÆ	,, ,,	276
THE TEMPLE OF ISIS	,, ,,	284
MEDÎNET EL-FAYÛM	,, ,,	309

LIST OF ILLUSTRATIONS

IN THE TEXT

	PAGE
Headquarters of the Army of Occupation, Alexandria	19
Shore of the Great Harbour	21
Site of the Canopic Gate	25
So-called Pompey's Pillar	33
Site of the Pharos	39
Kafr ez-Zaiyât Station	43
Camels with Cotton	50
Bâb el-Azab	85
The Central Court of the Citadel	87
Guard-tent of the Seaforths	89
Cairo from the Mokattam Hills	91
Street of Bâb el-Wezîr	93
Bêt el-Kâdî	96
Khân el-Khalîl Bazaar	99
Interior of Court of El-Azhar	102
Mosque of Amr	105
Interior of Court of Mosque of Tulûn	112
Interior of El-Hârim	118
El-Akmar	119
Doorway of Sultan Hasan Mosque	120
Mastaba of Mosque el-Muaiyad	121
Engaged Pillar	122
Decoration of El-Telayeh	123
Tombs of the Mamelukes	125
Arches in Mosque of Kalâûn	127
Gothic Doorway in En-Nâsir	128
East Façade, Sultan Hasan Mosque	130
Sanctuary of Sultan Hasan	131
Pulpit at El-Muaiyad	132
Plaster Work at En-Nâsir	133
Pillars at Mosque of Kalâûn	135
Kulleh Base (and Capital)	136
Stalactite Capital	137
Corner of Emîr Gâi el-Yusefi Mosque	138
Dome of El-Muaiyad	139
Decorated Capital	140
Prize Cattle	165
Prisoners Making Mats	182

LIST OF ILLUSTRATIONS

	PAGE
Travelling Winch	208
Menûfîyeh Canal and Lock	209
West End of Rosetta Barrage	211
Pyramid of Medûm	215
Group of Arabs	226
Step Pyramid of Sakkâra	228
Mariette's House	229
Entrance to Mastaba of Thy	231
Obelisk at Heliopolis	233
Feeding Sugar Mill with Cane	242
Colossi of Memnon	254
Avenue of Krio-Sphinxes	258
Temples at Medînet Habu	259
Temple of Poseidon at Paestum	261
Pylon of Temple of Luxor	264
Bud Capital	265
Calix Capital	266
Clustered Papyrus Shaft	267
Statue of Ramses II.	268
Shrine of Alexander the Great	269
Altar to Augustus	270
Chamber Transformed into Church	271
Temple of Dêr el-Bahri	272
Valley of the Tombs of the Kings	273
The Nilometer at Assuân	281
Convent of St. Simeon	283
Capitals at Temple of Isis at Philæ	285
The Kiosk	286
Roman Gateway	287
Steam Cranes at Nile Reservoir	289
Site of the Nile Reservoir	291
Sakîyeh on the Nile	293
Native Police	305
Native Plough	310
An Arab Shepherd	312
Gathering Palm Fibre	313

THE
REDEMPTION OF EGYPT

CHAPTER I

THE SCENE

Water and justice—Egypt is so much of the desert as is flooded by the Nile—The Delta—The Nile banks—The Fayûm—Long servitude of the Egyptians—Sense of justice extinct—Elements of population—Towns and European communities—Characteristics and distribution of these elements—The work of civilization in evidence.

NUBAR PASHA is credited with saying, some time before his death, that all that Egypt wanted was "water and justice." In this pregnant remark we can find a summary of the physical and social conditions which make Egypt differ from other countries, and cause it to be in a special sense a country apart. Egypt, then, wants water because it is a rainless desert, where the earth draws its supplies of moisture not from its own sky, but from the clouds which gather two thousand miles away over the mountains of Abyssinia and of Central Africa. This abundance is conveyed by a single channel, the river Nile, which pours its waters for more than a thousand miles without tributary stream, or increment of any kind, from the Atbara to the Mediterranean. Where the waters of the Nile can be laid upon the earth, there, and there only, does Egypt cease to be the desert; there, and there only, is the face of the earth green and not brown, can crops be grown and trees planted, flocks and herds find pasture, and man erect his dwellings and pursue the arts of civilized life. Egypt, then, is so much of the area of the desert of North-East Africa as is either flooded or irrigated by the waters of the Nile. It was with this fact writ large before him that Herodotus cast his memorable phrase—Egypt is the gift of the Nile.

Of what, then, does this gift consist? First, of the fields on either side of the Nile, from Assuân to Cairo; second, of the triangular district at the river's mouth, known as the Delta; and thirdly, of the little area called the Fayûm, once lake-land, but now reclaimed, and irrigated, like the rest of cultivable Egypt, by the water of the Nile. Of these, the first—the valley of the Nile—varies in breadth from one to twenty miles, and consists of the plain enclosed between the low ridges of hills west and east, called respectively the "Lybian" and the "Arabian" hills. This area, as thus understood, gives a green riband edging the white waters of the Nile for some 500 miles from Cairo to Assuân, or 600 if we allow for the curves of the river, and, together with the Fayûm, constitutes what is called Upper Egypt. A few miles to the south of Cairo the Nile divides into two main branches, of which one runs in a north-westerly direction to Alexandria, and the other in a north-easterly direction to Damietta. Beyond and between these two main streams, numerous branches and canals form a network of channels which carry, and have carried for many years in the past, the waters of the Nile throughout the Delta. This area, formed to a large extent of successive deposits of Nile mud, and thus supplied with an abundance of Nile water, is called Lower Egypt; and it is Lower Egypt which is the chief seat of population, and which yields the largest supplies of cotton, the most important product of modern Egypt. These districts, together constituting habitable Egypt, are the "gift of the Nile"; but there is another district which owes its existence solely to the great commercial scheme which has especially brought Egypt into connection with the western powers of Europe. That scheme is, of course, the Suez Canal, which, connecting as it does the waters of the Mediterranean with those of the Red Sea and of the Indian Ocean, forms an integral portion of the ocean highway which leads from Europe to the countries of the Far East, and in particular to British India and the Australasian colonies. At both the Mediterranean and Red Sea entrances to the Suez Canal there are considerable towns, which owe their existence solely to the realization of Ferdinand de Lesseps' great enterprize; but these towns are so much of the nature of European settlements, and depend upon conditions that are so entirely different from the natural conditions of the rest of Egypt, that their existence scarcely limits the truth of Herodotus' description even to-day.

What makes inhabited Egypt, therefore, cease to be a part of the north-eastern corner of the great desert of Africa is the presence of the waters of the Nile; and it is in exact proportion to the extent in which the inhabitants of the Nile valley and of the Delta have been able to fertilize their fields with these waters that the prosperity of Egypt has increased or diminished. To extend and perfect the irrigation system, first of the Delta, and then of Upper Egypt—or, in Nubar Pasha's words, to give Egypt water—is to make Egypt alike populous and prosperous, and the energy of the Egyptian Government, since the English occupation in 1882, has been primarily concentrated upon this all-important object.

After water comes justice. Water is necessary for the very existence of the Egyptians. Justice is necessary for their social and political development; in other words, to make them a nation. In order to understand the extent to which the inhabitants of the Nile valley have been deprived of justice—how, in fact, they have come to lose at once the sense of justice in their dealings with each other, and the power to claim it from others—it is necessary to glance backwards at the story of Egypt in the past. It is unnecessary to speak of the remote era at which this story commences, for the antiquity of Egypt enters so much into any conception of the country that all civilized peoples have found in the Pyramid a truthful symbol of the mingled unprogressiveness and antiquity which has characterized Egypt since the birth of literature. The quality of antiquity, therefore, is inherent in any conception of Egypt; what we have to notice is, that for roughly 2500 years the people of Egypt, that is, the people who tilled the fields of the Delta and the banks of the Nile, have been governed by alien rulers, and placed under the tutelage of alien races. From the time of Amasis, the last of the ancient kings of Egypt, the succession runs from Persia to Greece, from Greece to Rome, from Rome to Arabia, from Arabia to Constantinople. It is true that a large proportion of the present inhabitants of Egypt are themselves the descendants of the victorious armies which overran Egypt in the seventh century of the Christian era; but the Arab population which was thus introduced into the Nile valley and the Delta rapidly sank to the level of the native inhabitants, and the rulers of Egypt from the date of the Mohammedan conquest to the time when, in the sixteenth century, Egypt became a province of the Turkish Empire, were in fact a series of alien princes whose authority was maintained by mercenary troops enlisted for the most part in Eastern Europe and Asia Minor. With the tradition of so long a period of servitude, it is not surprising that the sole conception of law which existed in the minds of the native inhabitants of Egypt up to the date of the English occupation was the will of the stronger, nor that even now, after fifteen years have passed, the idea of an equal administration of justice in the Western sense should be so unfamiliar that the possession of equal rights arouses only a faint appreciation. To the Fellâh of fifteen years ago justice was a difficult conception, an ideal as impossible of attainment as the proverbial moon which excites no tears, because none but a child or a lunatic would cry for it. To create in such a population the temper of mind which would enable it to recognize and appreciate an even-handed administration of the law, and a proportionate distribution of the burden and cost of government, is a problem as difficult as it is interesting. Nevertheless this problem, difficult as it is, has been approached by the Egyptian Government, directed and inspired by the English advisers. The precise degree of success which has already been attained will appear in the sequel; for the present it is sufficient to note that a resolute endeavour is being made to supply this second want by the readjustment of the taxes and the reconstruction of the native courts, and that this effort will not cease until so much of justice as is involved in an equitable distribution of financial burdens and a capable and impartial administration of the law has been placed within the grasp of the humblest of the Egyptian populations. When this object has been attained, more, much more, remains to be done. To reform the laws and reconstruct the courts is a comparatively easy task. To create the habit of mind and the moral atmosphere which can alone enable the people themselves to appreciate and claim the benefits thus placed within their reach, and to carry the spirit of justice into dealings too minute to form the subject of any external control, is a task which can only be accomplished gradually by the continuous application of the deeper processes of social reform. To-day many customs and habits that are insanitary, anti-social, and uneconomic prevail among the inhabitants of Egypt. These customs cannot be replaced until time has elapsed and knowledge has grown; for the change from ignorance to enlightenment upon which the moral development of such a nation can alone be built is one which necessarily demands and requires a long period for its realization. To expect any signs of this change would, therefore, be to anticipate the future.

With these central facts—the rainlessness of Egypt, and the degradation of its inhabitants arising from their long-continued servitude to alien rulers—before us, we can proceed to consider in outline the character, pursuits, and geographical disposition of the varied elements which together form the Egyptians of to-day. According to the latest census, the population of Egypt numbers 9,734,000 persons. Of this total the great majority, say 9,000,000 persons, are either Arabs or descendants of the original inhabitants of the Nile valley who have become practically identified in language, custom, and religion with their Arabian conquerors. These Arabs profess and practise the Mohammedan religion—a circumstance which at once gives a certain social solidarity to the mass of the inhabitants of Egypt, and renders the introduction of Western reforms the more difficult. Second in point of numbers, though following at a long interval, are the Copts. This element numbers some 600,000; and the Coptic element, which represents to a greater extent than any other the descendants of the ancient Egyptians, continue to practise the Christian religion which their ancestors embraced at the time when Egypt, in common with the other provinces of the Roman Empire, deserted the pagan gods for the worship of Christ. In addition to the differences of social custom which this difference of faith entails, the Copts are as a body better educated and wealthier than their Mohammedan neighbours, with whom, however, they are in other respects closely identified. The Copts have an inherited aptitude for figures, and this characteristic, together with their superior education in general, enables them to furnish a proportion of clerks for merchants' offices and for the public services, altogether disproportionate to their numbers. They also furnish a large number of the "craftsmen"—the goldsmiths, embroiderers, and weavers—of the towns. As evidence of their superiority in wealth, it may be mentioned that the greater proportion of the capital provided for the first industrial enterprize controlled by a native board of management—the Fayûm Light Railway Company—was provided by Coptic capitalists of Assiût. To the Arabs and Copts we must add the small section of Turks, Armenians, and Syrians, who, although not racially connected with the bulk of the Egyptian population, may for practical purposes be considered as forming part of the "native" population of the country. Of these the Turks, who are mainly connected with the old governing oligarchy, are wealthy. The Armenians and Syrians are merchants, or the employés of merchants; and sometimes they are to be found occupying positions in the public service. The most distinguished member of the Armenian community in Egypt, and perhaps the most enlightened of the native politicians, was Nubar Pasha, whose words have been already quoted. Altogether these "Non-Egyptian Ottoman subjects," as they are officially styled, number only 40,000.

But the permanent inhabitants of Egypt do not consist solely of its native population. From the Middle Ages onwards —not to go back to remoter periods, when first the Greeks and afterwards the Romans colonized the Delta and the valley of the Nile—there have been colonies of Europeans in Egypt; and from the beginning of the present century communities of Greeks, Italians, and French have found a field for commercial and professional enterprize under the régime of Mohammed Ali and his successors. Of late years Germans and English have also swollen the numbers of the European population. To-day the numbers of the respective nationalities who are represented in Egypt are these: Greeks, 38,175; Italians, 24,467; French, 14,155; Austrians, 7117; Russians, 1400; Germans, 1277; and "other countries"—a term which includes Americans and Belgians—4585. The British community in Egypt amounts to 19,557; but of these some 5000 consist of the soldiers, with their wives and families, who form the Army of Occupation, while a considerable proportion of the remainder is made up of the numerous English officials who practically control and direct the various departments of the administration. Until lately an equal proportion of the French total also consisted of the same official class; but the increase of British influence since the occupation in 1882 has naturally had the effect of increasing this element of the British community at the expense of the French. It must be noted also that the British total includes 6463 Maltese and 614 British Indians, while the French total includes similarly 3901 French colonial subjects from Algiers and Tunis. Roughly speaking, the Greeks find employment in the lesser branches of commerce, as clerks under employers of English or French nationality, as money-lenders, and retail shopkeepers. There are, however, a considerable number of Greeks who follow the profession of the law, and plead before the mixed tribunals and the native courts. The bulk of the Italians are people of the working class; and in particular this nationality provides a large proportion of the masons and other artizans, whose services have been required in the erection and construction of the public buildings, public works, and private residences built on European models, required in the development of the country, and the extension and improvement of the towns, which have accompanied the general progress of the last fifteen years. To-day the large majority of the European workpeople employed in the construction of the great reservoir at Assuân are Italians. In addition to the large number of officials of French nationality who are still employed in the various departments of the Egyptian Government, a considerable proportion of the more important industrial enterprizes, such as sugar and cotton mills, are controlled and managed by Frenchmen, and this nationality is well represented among the better class shop-keepers of Cairo, Alexandria, and other large towns. The numbers of the other nationalities are scarcely large enough, with the exception of the British, of whom we shall speak presently, to require a separate description; and it will be sufficient to add that the Germans and the Americans are mainly, though not exclusively, employed in commerce. The German clerk in Egypt is as much in evidence as elsewhere; and while the inns of the small towns are generally kept by Greeks, the hôtels built for the reception of the visitors and tourists who annually flock to Egypt, are usually managed by Germans.

The British community consists of officials, merchants, directors of companies, and other persons engaged in the management of industrial enterprizes; of engineers, doctors, and other professional men; of the military officers employed in the Egyptian army and police; and lastly, of the officers and men of whom the Army of Occupation for the time being consists. The great majority of these Englishmen in Egypt are to be found in Cairo or Alexandria, but throughout the whole of Egypt, wherever administrative reform or industrial enterprize is in progress, Englishmen, and sometimes English families, are to be seen. The work of the English officials in the respective departments of the Government will be referred to in more than one of the chapters which follow ; since, broadly speaking, an account of the progress of Egypt is a record of what individual Englishmen of this class have accomplished during the last fifteen years. But this progress could not have been accomplished had not the resources of the country been fostered by private enterprize. This private enterprize has been mainly directed towards the development of the cotton and sugar industries; but in addition to these main sources of national wealth a number of industrial enterprizes, more or less directly concerned with these industries, have been projected throughout Egypt. These auxiliary enterprizes are the construction of tramways, light railways, markets, and generally, the provision of new means for the convenience of the producing classes both in town and country, and the improvement of the old means already at their disposal. The great bulk of the capital required for these enterprizes has hitherto been provided or collected by foreigners, but a large proportion of the Europeans entrusted with the supervision or management of them are Englishmen. Of these resident English the more wealthy make it their custom to return to England at intervals of two or three years, for longer or shorter periods of recreation ; and the wives and families of the men of this class return to England during the three or four hot months, June to October, of each year. For the climate of Egypt is so hot and so dry, that Englishmen can never look forward to a permanent residence in that country, in the sense in which they look forward to a permanent residence in Australia, South Africa, or Canada. This circumstance differentiates the British residents from the Italian, Greek, and French; for these latter, especially the Greeks and Italians, can and do make a home in Cairo or Alexandria, while the British can never expect to be anything more than birds of passage. Nevertheless, as in India, so in Egypt at the present day, the work of controlling and organizing the native population is in the hands practically of Englishmen.

It has been necessary to speak with some fulness of the European population in Egypt. Although it is numerically small, it forms an element of great importance, not merely from the fact that the Egyptians have now been placed under European control and organization, but also because the mere existence of these European colonies has been, and is, one of the most fertile sources of the present administrative difficulties of the Egyptian Government. For, strange as it may seem, the European resident, however closely he may be identified by length of residence or identity of interests with the Egyptians in whose country he has made a home, does not owe allegiance to the Egyptian Government. If accused of a crime, he is tried by the consular representative of his own country, while in the case of a civil dispute he sues for justice before an international tribunal, which derives its authority, not from the local government, but from treaties made and enforced by the Great Powers of Europe. It is not necessary to relate the origin of this anomalous and vexatious condition of affairs now. So much as is necessary for the reader to know on this subject will be given in a subsequent chapter: but it is necessary that he should realize at the outset that the European residents in Egypt—small in numbers, but important both politically and commercially—are subject neither in their persons nor in their property to the native government. This circumstance, and the fact that a portion of the national wealth, together with the annual revenue which accrues from it, is actually held in mortgage by Europe, have together created an additional and unusual obstacle to the progress of administrative reform; they also increase the merit of efforts, which are destined eventually to triumph, in spite of these unprecedented difficulties.

The object of the present chapter, which is to present to the reader in the simplest form those essential facts which underlie any discussion of the circumstances and conditions of Egypt in the present day, will not be fulfilled without an attempt to indicate in rough outline the geographical disposition of the various elements of the inhabitants of Egypt which have been mentioned. The Arab population, which outnumbers all the other elements put together in the proportion of fifteen to one, is most dense in the Delta, where the greater productiveness of the soil, due to the early extension of irrigation works, has long encouraged the growth of population. At the northernmost point —the apex—of the Delta, some ten miles before the Nile divides into the two chief branches, which with other lesser channels form its mouth, lies the city of Cairo, with a population of some 600,000 inhabitants. Second in importance to Cairo, lying a little westward of the Rosetta mouth of the Nile, is Alexandria, the chief port and commercial centre of Egypt. In both these towns, which are linked by an excellent railway service, there are considerable European populations. Alexandria, in fact, bears the appearance of a European town, built in the Italian or French style, rather than that of an Egyptian. Cairo is sharply divided between the mediæval town of minarets and narrow, winding, unpaved streets, and the modern town of handsome squares and broad, tree-lined streets, which is furnished with all the accompaniments and conveniences of a European town of the first rank. Besides these towns there are European inhabitants and European quarters at Port Saïd, Ismaïlia, and Suez, all of which are ports on the Suez Canal. Besides the Mediterranean ports of Rosetta and Damietta, and, of course, Alexandria, the Delta possesses some half-dozen large inland towns; that is to say, towns whose inhabitants, numbering from 60,000 to 20,000, are almost exclusively native, and where as yet the only European buildings are mills and factories, with the few necessary European residences required by the managers of such works. Altogether the population of Lower Egypt—that is, of the Delta, Cairo, and the Suez Canal—is 5,676,109. In Upper Egypt the population spreads on either side of the Nile, in a density which varies with the width of the cultivable area which lines the river banks from

Cairo to Assuân, where Egypt ends and Nubia begins. None of the towns of Upper Egypt approach the proportions of Cairo or of Alexandria; nevertheless there are considerable centres at Assiût, which has a population of 42,076, and lies just half-way between Cairo and Assuân; at Minyeh, a centre of the sugar industry, at Keneh, the centre of the manufacture of the porous water-bottles, called *kulal*, without mentioning Luxor and Assuân, the two towns long familiar to tourists by reason of the temple ruins found in their immediate neighbourhoods. The most thickly populated district after the Delta is the Fayûm, which lies some fifty miles to the north of Cairo, westward of the Nile valley, from which it is separated by a stretch of desert. The fertility of this area, which has been reclaimed gradually from the waters of the lake known to the ancients as Lake Mœris, exceeds that of the Delta, and the population is proportionately large. Medinet, the chief town of the Fayûm, has a population of some 30,000 inhabitants, while that of the entire district is not less than 370,000. The Copts are mainly to be found, as we should naturally expect, in parts of Upper Egypt remote from the great centres of Mohammedan influence in the North. At Assiût there is a considerable Coptic element, and from here southwards in the towns of Tahta, Girgeh, Esneh, and at Luxor, the chief centre for the tourists who annually visit the vast ruins which bear witness to the greatness of ancient Egypt, they abound, although they are scarcely distinguishable in manners or dress from their Mohammedan neighbours. Beside the settled Arab population—the fellâhîn of the country districts, and the craftsmen, traders, and servants of the towns—there is a migratory population of Bedouin and other desert tribes which, making their home in the spacious wastes that stretch east and west of the Nile valley, visit the towns at intervals, and mingle for longer or shorter periods with their more settled but less independent kinsmen. It is interesting to note that this Bedouin population has largely increased during the years of the British occupation, and that a greater proportion tend to become " settled " each year.

The settled Bedouin inhabitants now number more than 500,000. The total population of Upper Egypt is 4,058,296.

To-day from Assuân, where the Nile waters break over the shallows and rocks of the first cataract, to Alexandria and Port Saïd, the iron road has been laid, and the tireless locomotive bears its freight of men and materials. Neither the heat of the sun overhead nor the dust of the desert delays its course; nor does it pay any regard to the wonderment of the naked children of nature whose privacy it thus invades. And up and down the iron road white men have gone, taking with them their corrugated iron, their machinery, and their tinned meats, and all the other weapons with which the battle of civilization is fought. And so the traveller who visits Egypt for the first time, traversing its length from the golden shores of the Mediterranean to the borders of Nubia, is surprised to-day to find tall chimneys breaking the level of the landscape wherever he goes. In town and country alike the west jostles the east. In the midst of streets filled with a mêlée of camels, donkeys, and loosely-clad Arabs, he is startled by a section of police, marching in single file, with their sergeant at their head. The faces of these uniformed figures are dark, but their bearing unmistakably recalls the model of London. So, too, in the country, the landscape is Oriental, but the tall white-brick shafts which rise above the line of palm-trees are unmistakably western. The countenance of the desert is scored by the parallel lines of the iron way, and Father Nile, the parent of Egypt, wears western trappings in the iron bridges, with their rigorous lines, which span his waters. Here are the outward and visible signs of that fifteen years of progress achieved in the land of the immovable pyramid, which constitutes, as it has been truthfully called, a record of development unexampled in the history of civilization. To realize this progress it is not enough to see Egypt as it is now, we must know something of what Egypt has been in the past, and something of the character of the race which inhabit it. It is from the accidental words of persons long resident in the country that we gain the clearest idea of the greatness of the change which the English occupation has brought. "Before the English came," said one of this class, not an Englishman, to the writer, "the pashas and the rich men paid no taxes, or very little; the poor men paid taxes on everything. Every woman in Egypt has a bit of gold, often her sole wealth. I have seen poor women made to give up their bits of gold—made by blows of the kúrbash. The English have changed all that." The English occupation, by extending the protection of the law to the peasant, has already made such gross manifestations of injustice impossible; but many years must pass before even the powerful ministers of civilization which England has introduced can create the spirit of justice in the people themselves. The great reservoir at Shellâl, with its ancillary canals, will speedily give Egypt "water"; but the Egyptians must give themselves "justice."

CHAPTER II

ALEXANDRIA

First sight of Egypt—The mosquito—Literary ideas and realities—No true conception of Egypt obtained through books—First impressions disappointing—Modern aspect of the town—Ptolemaic Alexandria—Plutarch's story of its foundation—Strabo's account—Its quarters, buildings, and characteristics—Causes of its prosperity—Scenes from the life of this Alexandria—Cæsar—Antony and Cleopatra—Berenice—Theocritus' picture of a day in Alexandria—Dr. Botti's account of the Serapeum—The Theodosian column, miscalled "Pompey's Pillar"—Roman Alexandria—The power of the Patriarchs—Athanasius—Theodosius and the origin of the Coptic Church—The Byzantine period—Cyril—Hypatia—Capture of Alexandria by the Saracens—Fate of the Library—Decay of the town.

ALEXANDRIA gives no sign to the approaching traveller. On this low coast the narrow pillar of the lighthouse—a poor substitute for the colossal Pharos—is the first object to meet the eye of the forward watch upon the steamer's bow. And then the breakwaters, docks, and houses of the town itself rise from the sea. The Alexander of the Ptolemies, the sovereign city that ruled the world, first with undisputed authority, afterwards as the rival of Imperial Rome, is dead and buried. The Alexandria of the Middle Age, that took the spices and gold of the East with one hand and passed them on to the West with the other, is also dead, but its bones have not yet been decently covered. Modern Alexandria is the creation of Mohammed Ali, whose parentage the city acknowledges by the equestrian statue in its central square. Thanks to the rioters whom Arabi's rebellion let loose, the streets and houses of this Alexandria are more regular and convenient than the date of its original foundation—some seventy or eighty years ago—would warrant. Around the European town the native quarters stretch like an untidy fringe; and here, where the Alexandria of the Middle Age survives, there is not indeed an Arab town, but a town where Arabs live. There are 270,000 of them, but they are packed away so closely in their rookeries, or lie so close to the soil in their huts, that they make far less show than the 50,000 Europeans, who spread themselves and their property ostentatiously in streets and squares, warehouses, docks, and railway stations.

It was four o'clock in the afternoon of December 4, 1898, when I first saw the white line of buildings dividing the sea from the sky, which is all that tells the modern traveller that he is approaching Alexandria. At this time my knowledge of Egypt was contained in four words—Pyramids, Nile, Cairo, and Khartûm; but before this day ended I had to add a fifth—mosquito. The *Thames*, in which we had left Venice on the preceding Tuesday, had been delayed by head winds; and when we took on board our pilot, there was only just so much of daylight left as would serve to let him take us over the harbour bar in safety before night fell. As the custom-house officials signified their intention of only passing hand luggage after dark, we and all of our fellow-travellers, who were not compelled by urgent business to land that night, postponed our disembarkation until the morning. That was the opportunity of the Alexandrian gnat. He had the good taste—perhaps he lacked the energy—not to disturb the vision of the star-lit canopy, which overhung the dark shadows and twinkling lights of the shipping around us, and the distant gleam refracted from breakwater, wharfs, and houses that marked the circle of the harbour. But when I had retired to my cabin, he came with an abundant company through the open port, and all night long he cheered me with his music and his kisses. And so I added a fifth word to my Egyptian vocabulary.

When I say that my knowledge of Egypt was contained in these four words, and that before I had set foot on the Egyptian shore, I had to add another term of a quite different order, I fear that my remarks may be misunderstood, unless I add a word of explanation. Let me say at once, then, that I had read my guide-book, that I had read too more than one standard work, both historical and descriptive, including publications of the year. But I found that the preconceived ideas thus formed in no way corresponded to the actual impressions which I received from contact with the realities themselves. The magnitude of the space which Egypt has occupied in literature, the number and variety of the appeals which it makes, seem to have united in producing a literary glamour which obscures rather than reveals the true Egypt. The antiquarian buries himself in the darkness of the tombs; and there, in closely scanning the hieroglyphics and sculptures which cover their walls, he becomes blind to the external effects of colour and atmosphere which hold the artist, and dumb to the articulate cries of the Present, which absorb the politician. He measures the value of a building, a sculpture, or a relief, not by relation to any standards of artistic merit or practical utility, but by the assistance which it affords him in reconstructing the past. His Egypt is the Egypt of the Pharaohs and the Ptolemies, and the Nile Valley is for him simply the most fruitful field for antiquarian research that the world affords. The artist overlooks the most obvious of material deficiencies, and the most flagrant of moral defects, in a country which provides him with a subject at once picturesque in itself and stimulating to the imagination. His eye is filled with minaret and dome, with calyx capitals, broad pylons, and stately colonnades; with the graceful curve of the yard from which the Nile boat hangs its sail, with the airy plumage of the palm, and the still Nile reflecting rosy cliffs beneath an opal sky. And with his vision thus filled with the ideas of beauty, he forgets the flies and filth of the towns, the dust-heaps which surround the temple ruins, and the incessant cry for bakshish of the picturesque Arabs. The mind of the politician and the economist is occupied with the urgent needs of the present; his gaze is attracted by the depraved morality and arrested intelligence of a once noble race; he is curious about the constitutional anomalies, and the administrative inefficiency of the composite Egyptian Government, and the hundred and one problems that have been solved, or await solution, by the men who are now engaged in the redemption of Egypt. As he contemplates the splendid spectacle of the Anglo-Saxon race engaged in this task, he becomes enthusiastic for reform, and in his appreciation of the possibilities which the future holds he omits from his account all mention of the past, and even fails to notice the artistic significance of these very material and moral deficiencies which he burns to see removed.

There was another reason why I had been unable to obtain a true conception of Egypt through the medium of books. Since the English occupation events have moved rapidly. In particular, the swift advance which had carried the English and Egyptian flags successively to Dongola, Berber, and Khartûm, had exceeded the most sanguine anticipations of the political prophets. With the echo of the acclamations that followed the "stricken field" of Omdurman still ringing in my ears, it seemed strange to read how all thought of reconquering the Sudân had once been abandoned, and how recently Wâdi Halfa had been the southern limit of the Khedive's authority.

Once free of the docks with their motley crowd of Arabs and dragomen, the traveller finds himself to all intents and purposes in a European town. The stucco houses, the smart shops, the electric tramways repel him. He resents the great *Place*, with its neat gardens, its theatre, and its *Bourse*. He silently protests against the hôtel with its European servants and equipment: in this commonplace air of comfort he yearns in vain for a flavour of the East. It does not compensate him to know that Alexandria is the commercial centre of Egypt, that its European population—mainly consisting of Greeks and Italians—is greater than that of Cairo, that the Appeal Court of the Tribunaux Mixtes sit here, that it is the headquarters of the British Chamber of Commerce, and that its seaside suburb, Ramleh, is almost as British as Brighton. Where, he asks, is the Pharos, the Museum, the Library, Cleopatra's Palace, the harbour in which Cæsar swam, holding his manuscript above his head, the Serapeum, the Sungate and the Moongate, the Mole seven furlongs long that joined the island of Pharos to the mainland, and separated the waters of the eastern and western harbours, and the lake harbour, where the Nile boats lay that rivalled in numbers and size the sea-going galleys and corn-ships that crowded the docks beneath the shadow of the Pharos?

It is some time before he realizes that in this very Khedivial hôtel he is in the centre of the Ptolemaic city. A stone's throw

HEADQUARTERS OF THE ARMY OF OCCUPATION.

from the hôtel door are the sites of the Museum, the Library, and the Gymnasium. The *Rue de Rosette*, where he read the legend, "Headquarters—Army of Occupation," in uncompromising English, is the actual line of the great Canopic street which ran for three miles, traversing the town from west to east. On the shore of the now disused "new harbour," making due allowance for the encroachments of the land, he distinguishes the points severally occupied by the Timoneum of Antony, the theatre, the headland of Lochias, crowned by the palace of the Ptolemies, with the Temple of Artemis hard by. He follows the *Rue de Rosette* westwards to the point where it is crossed by the *Rue de la Colonne*, and passing southwards he finds himself within ten minutes where the widowed column—the sole remnant of the ancient city—stands sentinel above the ruins of the Serapeum. Gradually he makes his Strabo fit the Alexandria of to-day, he reads his Plutarch with renewed interest, and in place of the " commercial centre" of the occupation there comes the fair vision of the Ptolemaic capital. He sees no longer the stucco houses and the Arab huts, the smart shops of the Europeans, and the sordid dust-heaps of the Arabs, but that ocean of white roofs and glittering pediments which spread from the barren plain of the Necropolis at his feet to the leafy groves of Eleusis on the west; and beyond the palaces and temples of Bruchium, across the blue space enclosed by the white arms of the Heptastadium and the promontory of Lochias, the marble Pharos once more flashes in the sunlight.

Plutarch, in his life of Alexander, tells a pretty story of the founding of the town. "And if what the Alexandrians say, upon the faith of Heraclides, be true, Homer was no bad auxiliary, or useless counsellor, in the course of the war. They tell us, that when Alexander had conquered Egypt, and determined to build there a great city, which was to be peopled with Greeks, and called after his own name, by the advice of his architects he had marked out a piece of ground, and was preparing to lay the foundation; but a wonderful dream made him fix upon another situation. He thought a person with grey hair, and a very venerable aspect, approached him, and repeated the following lines:

'High o'er a gulfy sea the Pharian isle
Fronts the deep roar of disemboguing Nile.'—POPE.

Alexander, upon this, immediately left his bed, and went to Pharos, which at that time was an island lying a little above the *Canobic* mouth of the Nile, but now is joined to the continent by a causeway. He no sooner cast his eyes upon the place, than he perceived the commodiousness of the situation. It is a tongue of land, not unlike an *isthmus*, whose breadth is proportionable to its length. On one side it has a great lake, and on the other the sea, which there forms a capacious harbour. This led him to declare that Homer, among his other admirable qualifications, was an excellent architect, and he ordered a city to be planned suitable to the ground, and its appendant conveniences. For

SHORE OF THE GREAT HARBOUR.

want of chalk, they made use of flour, which answered well enough upon a black soil, and they drew a line with it about the semicircular bay. The arms of this semicircle were terminated by straight lines, so that the whole was in the form of a Macedonian cloak.

"While the king was enjoying the design, on a sudden an infinite number of large birds of various kinds rose, like a black cloud, out of the river and lake, and, lighting upon the place, ate up all the flour that was used in marking out the lines. Alexander was disturbed at the omen; but the diviners encouraged him to proceed, by assuring him it was a sign that the city he was going to build would be blessed with such plenty as to furnish a supply to those that should repair to it from other nations."[1]

Three centuries later, when the line of the Ptolemies had achieved a splendid *dénouement* in the mutual ruin of Cleopatra and Antonius, and Egypt had become a province of the Roman Empire, Strabo visited Alexandria. His careful notes enable us to form an accurate idea of the character which the town presented at this period. He notices the physical and political conditions which unite to make it "the greatest commercial centre of the world." He sketches the plan of the town, and describes its principal buildings. He traces the canals which unite the sea to the lake, and the lake to the Nile; and he describes the positions of the western suburbs of Nicopolis, Eleusis, and Canopus.

The plan of the town, he says, resembles a mantle in form, whereof the two long sides, being thirty furlongs, are washed respectively by the waters of the Mediterranean and by those of the lakes Mareotis and Maria, while the two short sides, being seven or eight furlongs, stretch from the sea to the lake. The whole of the space thus enclosed is cut up by streets which horses and chariots can traverse, while from east to west and from north to south there run two principal streets intersecting each other at right angles, which are more than a hundred feet in breadth. The royal quarter, which occupies one-fourth or one-third part of the entire area of the town, is filled with monumental buildings; for each king, he says, has added in turn his contribution to the splendid erections of his predecessors. Nevertheless, these buildings harmonized with each other, with the buildings of the harbour, and with the general mass of which they were the centre. From the town to the island of Pharos there stretched the Great Mole, which separated the western harbour of Eunostus

---

[1] Plutarch, "Alexander" (Langhorne's translation).

from the "Great Harbour," at whose entrance stood the Pharos, and whose shore was lined with temples, palaces, docks, and arsenals. It was seven furlongs in length — hence its name, the Hepta-stadium — and besides giving access to the island of Pharos, it originally served as an aqueduct, a service which was now no longer required of it, for after Cæsar had depopulated the island in the Alexandrian war, only a few sailors had made their homes there. At either end, passages for ships passing from the one harbour to the other had been left, and these passages were spanned by bridges. The Pharos stood on a rock on the eastern extremity of the island. It was "a many-storied tower of white stone and marvellous construction." It was erected by Sostratus of Cnidos, a royal favourite, "for the salvation of navigators," in the words of the inscription. Opposite the Pharos was the headland of Lochias, which advanced so far from the mainland as to leave only a narrow and dangerous entrance to the harbour. At its extremity was the palace of the Ptolemies, with its groves and terraces stretching to the water's edge, and beyond them the artificial harbour reserved for the royal galleys. Opposite this latter was the little island of Antirrhodus, upon which also were royal buildings, with a smaller harbour. On the shore opposite lay the theatre, and from a point slightly westwards protruded the headland upon which the temple of Poseidon was built; and from this headland Antony had carried forward a mole into the middle of the harbour, at the end of which he had constructed his Timoneum. The significance of this name is explained by Strabo. After his defeat at Actium, Antony resolved, like Timon of Athens, to withdraw from the world, since he had been deserted by all his friends. The Cæsarium lay above the temple of Poseidon, and from this point westwards to the Hepta-stadium stretched the wharfs and docks. On the other side of the Hepta-stadium, in the harbour of Eunostus, was a large artificial dock called Cibotus, or the Chest; and from this point a canal ran southwards, joining the western harbour with Lake Mareotis.

Rhacotis, the Egyptian quarter, lay on either side of this canal, and beyond it to the west stretched the Necropolis. At the south-western corner of the city, but within the curve of the canal, was the Serapeum and other ancient fanes, which in Strabo's time had come to be deserted for the newer and more splendid sanctuaries erected in the western suburb of Nicopolis, the City of Victory, founded in commemoration of the final triumph of Augustus over Antony and Cleopatra. Besides the buildings already mentioned as lining the shore of the Great Harbour, Strabo mentions other conspicuous edifices which adorned the purely Greek Alexandria of the royal quarter. He says nothing of the library which had been burnt when Cæsar destroyed the Egyptian fleet in the Great Harbour ; nor does he tell us what had become of the remnant of the 900,000 scrolls which it had then contained. Afterwards, as we know, they and the subsequent additions which constituted the second library were transferred to the Serapeum. Possibly at this time they were housed in the sister building of the Museum. This latter institution he describes as being endowed by public funds and governed by a priestly official, who was appointed formerly by the sovereign of Egypt, and in his day by the emperor. The features of the building itself which he mentions were an external colonnade, an inner hall for lectures and discussions, and a large house in which the scholars resided, and took their meals at a common table. The most splendid of the remaining buildings was the Gymnasium, with porticoes of more than a furlong in length, past which ran the great Canopic street in its passage throughout the city from the Necropolis on the west to the Canopic Gate on the east. In the centre of the royal quarter was the Hall of Justice standing in a wooded space, and southwards the Paneum, a conical eminence encircled by a gradually ascending pathway, from the summit of which a prospect was obtained over the whole city. Outside the Canopic Gate lay the Hippodrome, and beyond it, on the sea-shore, the suburb of Nicopolis, which he describes as scarcely less populous than the city itself. He does not describe the position of the Lake Harbour, but he tells us that its wealth exceeded that of the Ocean Harbour, for the trade of Egypt, carried down the Nile and led thence by numberless canals, concentrated at this point. He mentions, however, the Canopic Canal which joined the lake to the mouth of the Nile, so-called, and to Schedia, the point on the river, thirty miles distant from Alexandria, where the state barges were anchored,

SITE OF THE CANOPIC GATE.

and a custom-house was established to collect the dues upon the goods and merchandise which were carried up or down the river. This canal, he says, you find on your right hand as you leave the Canopic Gate, and on its bank is Eleusis, a large and extensive pleasure resort; and from this point, he continues, the Canopic Canal runs parallel to the sea-coast, from which it is separated by a narrow tongue of land. And here, on the coast beyond Nicopolis, was the Zephyrium, the headland which bore the temple of Arsinoë-Aphrodite, where Berenice hung the lock which she had vowed in payment for the safety of her lord.

Alexandria was favoured in its climate, because the winds which blew over the two seas—the Mediterranean and the Lakes—between which it lay tempered the heat of the Egyptian summer. The source of its commercial prosperity lay in the fact that the trade of India and Ethiopia passed through it. It was this transit trade, he notices, which yielded double dues, both import and export, that made the revenues of Egypt so prolific; and Alexandria was thus not only the port of Egypt, but also the *entrepôt* where the west and east exchanged their wares. Curiously enough he omits to make any mention of the Jewish community, whose influence and wealth contributed so largely to the commercial importance of Alexandria. They lived in their own quarter, westward of the royal city; and we know from Josephus that they were placed on an equality in respect of political privileges with the rest of the citizens by Cæsar, in return for the support which they rendered to him in the Alexandrian war. These privileges were confirmed subsequently by the Roman emperors, and were enjoyed by them until they were expelled by Cyril in the fifth century of our era. Strabo also writes of the Roman system of government then recently established. The Roman army of occupation was divided into three divisions, of which one was stationed at Alexandria, the second at Syene, on the borders of Ethiopia—the modern Assuân—while the third was disposed at Babylon, a point on the eastern bank of the Nile opposite Memphis, and elsewhere throughout the intervening country. The government of Alexandria was carried on by four officials, the Governor, who was of patrician rank, the Recorder, the Chief Judge, and the Chief of the City Police, all of whom filled offices which had previously existed under the Ptolemaic kings. In speaking of this and of other arrangements for the government of the country, he dwells with pride upon the benefits which had resulted to Egypt from the establishment of an orderly and regular administration, and an equitable system of taxation, much in the same way as a modern traveller might speak, in noticing the effects of the English occupation to-day.[1]

From this description we can form a tolerably accurate conception of the external characteristics of the Alexandria of the Ptolemies, which for three centuries—332–30 B.C.—was the capital of Egypt, the court of the Lagidæ, and the centre of Greek art and thought. The resources of the Nile Valley and the Delta, the profits of the Eastern trade wrested from the Phœnicians, and the decline of Greece, formed the materials out of which an absolute monarchy could create a society at once learned, cosmopolitan, and luxurious. All that remained of Eastern and Egyptian learning, all that survived of Greek genius, all the promise of the sciences then coming to the birth, were attracted by "the magnet of Alexandria, where scientific appliances and collections were inexhaustible, where kings composed tragedies and ministers wrote commentaries on them, and where pensions and academies flourished."[2]

Here in the shadow of the colonnades and groves of the museum, or in quiet chambers of the royal palaces that looked over the shimmering plain of water to the glorious Pharos, the lords of thought worked and wrote. Here Eucleides laid down with faultless precision the "Elements of Geometry"; Archimedes, inventor of the screw, applied his mathematics to the common uses of life; Manetho traced the dynasties of the ancient kings of Egypt; Eratosthenes read alike the secrets of the stars and the story of the past; Aristarchus, the founder of criticism, reaped the harvest of literature, and placed the masters in the class of the best; Ptolemy, the astronomer, mapped out alike the heavens and the earth. Here, too, Theocritus, Callimachus, and Apollonius Rhodius sang: and let the faint perfume of dead flowers breathe from the closed vase of Greek song.

We may be sure that in this Alexandria life was never commonplace. Some passages are so rich in human interest that literature has made them part of the common stock of knowledge

[1] Geographica, xvii. C. 791–C. 801.   [2] Mommsen, Bk. III. ch. viii.

from which our minds are furnished. Was ever fortune tempted to do her worst as Cæsar tempted her when he suffered Cleopatra's charms to keep him in dalliance, while the king's minister, Pothinus, and the general Achillas, raised the turbulent commons of Alexandria in revolt, and spread sedition among the Roman garrison? Pompey's death had left him master of the world: but now the master of the world was shut up with a handful of legionaries in the royal palace by the harbour. Had Cæsar's daring been less reckless, or his command of the arts of warfare less perfect, he would have perished before the relieving force of Mithridates had reached the Nile. As it was, the blackened ruins of the great library and the charred remains of the priceless scrolls collected within its walls were witness of the desperate expedients by which alone Cæsar could preserve his life. Twenty years later Alexandria witnessed the last fling of the rival of Augustus and the Egyptian queen—no longer the "inimitable lovers" but the "companions in death." Were there ever such revels as these? when Antony and Cleopatra, doffing their robes of state, wandered at will, like common wantons, through the moonlit streets? And was there ever such a death as Cleopatra's? The magic of her living presence was supreme—"to return to her was a greater object than to conquer the world." The spell of her death scene is no less potent. "They found her quite dead lying on her golden bed, and dressed in all her royal ornaments. Iras, one of her women, lay dead at her feet, and Charmion, hardly able to support herself, was adjusting her mistress's diadem. One of Cæsar's [Octavianus] messengers said angrily, 'Charmion, was this well done?' 'Perfectly well,' said she, 'and worthy a descendant of the kings of Egypt.' She had no sooner said this than she fell down dead."[1]

Pompey the Great, Cæsar, Antony, Augustus, Cleopatra, and the boy king Ptolemy—here is a cast to act a tragedy, and when the tragic interest is highest Alexandria is the scene.

The story of Berenice is less intense, and its interest is of a

[1] Plutarch, "Antony" (Langhorne).

different order. A few days after her marriage, so runs the fairy tale, Ptolemy Euergetes, her lord, set forth with his army to take the field against the Assyrians. In a transport of grief Berenice made a vow to Aphrodite that she would give her a lock of hair, if only the goddess would bring back her lord to her arms. Ptolemy returned safe and victorious, and Berenice in payment of her vow cut off her golden tresses and placed them within the temple of Aphrodite on the headland of Zephyrium. The next day the tresses were gone. The king and queen were grievously alarmed; but Conon, the mathematician, assured them that the hair had been carried by divine power to heaven that so it might shine among the stars. The original poem of Callimachus, the laureate, has perished: but before it was lost Catullus gave it in Latin to the Roman world. And so the pretty fiction of Conon and Callimachus has become a fact; and Berenice's lock, set in the soft Elegiacs of the Roman master, shines in the firmament of poetic thought.

> "Scilicet in vario ne solum limite coeli
>   Ex Ariadneis aurea temporibus
> Fixa corona foret; sed nos quoque fulgeremus
>   Devotae flavi verticis exuviae.
> Uvidulam a fletu, cedentem ad templa Deum, me
>   Sidus in antiquis Diva novum posuit.
> Virginis et saevi contingens namque Leonis
>   Lumina Callisto juncta Lycaoniae
> Vector in occasum, tardum dux ante Booten,
>   Qui vix sero alto mergitur Oceano.
>
> . . . .
>
> Non his tam laetor rebus, quam me abfore semper,
>   Abfore me a dominae vertice discrucior;
>
> . . . .
>
> Tu vero, regina, tuens cum sidera Divam
>   Placabis festis luminibus Venerem
> Sanguinis expertem, non votis esse tuam me,
>   Sed potius largis effice muneribus.
> Sidera cur retinent? utinam coma regia fiam:
>   Proximus Hydrochoi fulgeret Oarion."

But interesting as is the life of the Palace and the Porch, literature has preserved for us another aspect of life in Alexandria.

In his fifteenth Idyll Theocritus has told us how two women of the people spent a day in the metropolis. They do not live in palaces, but tell the nurse to take care of the children, and be sure to keep the street door locked when she is left behind on a day like this: for it is a festival day and the streets are crowded with sight-seers. Gorgo and Praxinoë—for so they are called—are from Syracuse: and the sights of Alexandria have for them the charm and novelty of a metropolis. To-day they are bent upon seeing the image of Adonis (which has been decorated by Queen Arsinoë, the consort of Ptolemy Philadelphus), and hearing the "hymn to Adonis" sung by a celebrated professional singer. Gorgo has come to fetch her friend, and we meet her on the door-step of Praxinoë's house. When she has entered, the two friends discuss the defects of their husbands, and their own new dresses, and other such matters precisely in the manner of to-day. Then they set off for the palace where the festival is being held. They find the streets packed with crowds of people, and Praxinoë has a narrow escape of being run over by the rearing horse of one of the Royal Horse Guards. Eventually they reach the palace gates: but here the dialogue must speak for itself:—

"*Praxinoë*. Tremendous! Take hold of me, Gorgo; and you, Eunoe, take hold of Eutychis! tight hold, or you'll be lost. Here we go in altogether. Hold tight to us, Eunoe! Oh, dear! oh, dear! Gorgo, there's my scarf torn right in two. For heaven's sake, my good man, as you hope to be saved, take care of my dress!

"*Stranger*. I'll do what I can, but it doesn't depend upon me.

"*Praxinoë*. What heaps of people! They push like a drove of pigs.

"*Stranger*. Don't be frightened, ma'am, we are all right.

"*Praxinoë*. May you be all right, my dear sir, to the last day you live for the care you have taken of us! What a kind, considerate man! There is Eunoe jammed in a squeeze. Push, you goose, push! Capital! We are all of us the right side of the door, as the bridegroom said when he had locked himself in with the bride.

"*Gorgo*. Praxinoë, come this way. Do but look at that work, how delicate it is! how exquisite! Why, they might wear it in heaven.

"*Praxinoë*. Heavenly patroness of needlewomen, what hands were hired to do that work? Who designed those beautiful patterns? They seem to stand up and move about, as if they were real; as if they were living things and not needlework. Well, man is a wonderful creature! And look, look, how charming he lies there on his silver couch, with just a soft down on his cheeks, that beloved Adonis—Adonis, whom one loves even though he is dead!

"*Another Stranger*. You wretched women, do stop your incessant chatter! Like turtles you go on for ever. They are enough to kill one with their broad lingo—nothing but *a, a, a*.

"*Gorgo*. Lord, where does the man come from? What is it to you if we *are* chatter-boxes? Order about your own servants! Do you give orders to Syracusan women? If you want to know, we came originally from Corinth, as Bellerophon did; we speak Peloponnesian. I suppose Dorian women may be allowed to have a Dorian accent.

"*Praxinoë*. Oh, honey-sweet Proserpine, let us have no more masters than the one we've got! We don't the least care for *you*; pray don't trouble yourself for nothing.

"*Gorgo*. Be quiet, Praxinoë! That first-rate singer, the Argive woman's daughter, is going to sing the *Adonis* hymn. She is the same who was chosen to sing the dirge last year. We are sure to have something first-rate from *her*. She is going through her airs and graces ready to begin."[1]

During the period that Egypt was governed from Rome— 30 B.C. to the partition of the Empire between Honorius and Arcadius in A.D. 385—Alexandria held a turbulent and enterprizing community. From contemporary writers we know that

[1] As translated by Matthew Arnold in his "Essays on Criticism."

its inhabitants included 300,000 citizens in addition to an equal number of slaves, and its circumference measured fifteen miles in length. The wealth of Arabia, of the east coast of Africa, and the Indies, continued to pass through its harbours on its way to supply the luxurious needs of Imperial Rome. Among the manufactures in which its people were employed was the weaving of linen, the blowing of glass, and the preparation of the papyrus. Alike in their aptitude for the arts, and in their turbulent and excitable character they were the Parisians of the ancient world. "The people of Alexandria," says Gibbon, "united the vanity and inconstancy of the Greeks, with the superstition and obstinacy of the Egyptians. The most trifling occasion, a transient scarcity of flesh or lentils, the neglect of an accustomed salutation, a mistake of precedency in the public baths, or a religious dispute, such as the sacrilegious murder of a divine cat, were at any time sufficient to kindle a sedition among that vast multitude, whose resentments were furious and implacable."[1] On one occasion the several quarters of the city waged war against each other for a period of twelve years. It was then—during the anarchy into which the Roman world was dissolved by the captivity of Valerian in A.D. 260—when its temples and palaces were converted into fortresses which the several nationalities sought only to destroy, that the Ptolemaic Alexandria was ruthlessly defaced: and in this general devastation Bruchium, the royal city of the Ptolemies, with the monumental buildings which it contained, was the first to be destroyed.

But apart from the wounds inflicted by these internecine conflicts, the importance of Alexandria declined from the foundation of a rival centre of Greek thought in the Eastern capital which Constantine established on the shores of the Bosphorus in A.D. 324. Moreover, during all this period Christianity had been slowly but surely acquiring its supremacy over the conduct and thought of the Græco-Roman world; and although the forces of paganism found a last stronghold in the Serapeum of Alexandria, the

[1] "Decline and Fall," vol. i. chap. x.

disputes of the philosophers had already been replaced by the speculations of theology, and the brown monks from the convents and retreats of the desert had become objects as familiar and characteristic in the streets of Alexandria as the students of the

So-called Pompey's Pillar.

museum. The final triumph of the Christians of Alexandria over their pagan neighbours, represented by the destruction of the temple of Serapis in A.D. 391, is marked by the tall column, so long miscalled Pompey's Pillar, which antiquarians have identified as a monument erected to commemorate this event, in the closing years of the reign of Theodosius, or in the time of his son Aurelian. But the internecine conflicts of its own citizens were not the only events to devastate the city. Caracalla, in the course of his insane progress through the eastern provinces of the Empire (A.D. 213), ordered a general massacre of the Alexandrians, the progress of which he watched and directed from the Serapeum. The Great Library had disappeared in the reign of his predecessor, Septimius Severus; after Caracalla's visit to Egypt the ancient museum was no longer in existence.[1] In A.D. 296 Dioclesian reduced Alexandria after a siege of eight months, in which it was wasted by fire and sword. From these events there resulted not only the destruction of the chief buildings of the Ptolemaic city, but the partial depopulation of the quarter in which they stood; and in course of time the neighbourhood of the temple of Serapis, which in Strabo's time had been abandoned for the newer and more splendid temples of the eastern quarters, became once more the focus of the city's life. The antiquarian researches of Dr. Botti, the curator of the museum at Alexandria, and the excavations made by him round the base of the Theodosian column, have enabled us to trace the relative positions and characteristics of the group of buildings which came to be erected there, and which formed collectively the Capitol, or Forum, of the Alexandria of the late Roman and Byzantine periods. These buildings, which do not of course include those edifices which were erected before or during the Ptolemaic period, are (1) the Claudium, or School of Law, established by Claudius I. on the western flank of the hill now called Hamûd-es-Sañri: (2) Colonnades surrounding the base of the hill, out of which opened the second library and museum, enclosing a Serapeum and Iseum. These buildings were erected in the reigns of the Flavian Emperors, and of Trajan and Hadrian; (3) a Column in honour of Serapis, erected in the reign of Antoninus. This collection of buildings is described by two writers of the fourth century, Aphthonius and Rufinus; the former speaks of them as the Acropolis of Alexandria,

[1] Botti *Fouilles à la colonne Théodosienne*, Alexandrie, 1897.

and comparable to the Acropolis of Athens; the latter, who was himself present at the destruction of the temple of Serapis, describes the colossal statue of Serapis, the walls of the sanctuary covered with plates of silver and of gold, and the profusion of its columns of marble and of precious stones, with other details of the lately destroyed edifice. It stood in the centre of a square court surrounded by colonnades. This court, which was approached by a staircase of a hundred steps, formed the crown of a square mass of buildings, of which the basement rested upon vaults.

Speaking of the suppression of paganism throughout the Empire by Theodosius, and the consequent destruction of the heathen temples throughout the Roman world, Gibbon has told the story with all the fulness of its picturesque and dramatic details.[1] Not only was the temple itself destroyed, and the colossal statue dragged through the streets and burnt in the amphitheatre, but the new library was also pillaged. According to Dr. Botti, the former column of Serapis was now re-erected upon a base which had formerly belonged to a column previously erected in honour of one of the Roman Emperors, to commemorate the triumph of the Christians over the worshippers of Osiris and of Isis. This column, which the visitor knows under the mistaken name of Pompey's Pillar, Dr. Botti calls the Theodosian Column.[2]

During this century—the fourth of our era—the power of the Church continued to increase: and the Archbishop, afterwards styled the Patriarch of Alexandria, wielded an influence superior to that of any civil authority. Once more the stream of Alexandrian life was mingled with the central current of the world's history. The battle of the Trinity was fought at Alexandria, and the struggle of Athanasius for the doctrine of the divinity of Christ is as heroic and momentous as the conflict of Cæsar and Pompeius for the supremacy of the Empire. Although the doctrine of the Trinity had been ratified by the Council of Nice in A.D. 325, the cause of the Arians revived under the Emperor

---

[1] Vol. ii. chap. xxviii. [2] Botti, ib., p. 138.

Constantius, and George of Cappadocia was thrust into the seat of Athanasius by the forces of Sebastian. The long administration of Athanasius (A.D. 326–373), says Gibbon, "was a perpetual combat against the powers of Arianism. Five times was Athanasius expelled from his throne, twenty years he passed as an exile or a fugitive; and almost every province of the Roman Empire was successively witness to his merit and his sufferings in the cause of the Homoousion, which he considered as the sole pleasure and business, as the duty, and as the glory, of his life. Amidst the storms of persecution the Archbishop of Alexandria was patient of labour, jealous of fame, careless of safety; and although his mind was tainted by the contagion of fanaticism, Athanasius displayed a superiority of character and abilities which would have qualified him far better than the degenerate sons of Constantine for the government of a great monarchy." [1] Two centuries later —in A.D. 538—the Patriarch Theodosius was removed by Justinian because he refused to recognize the decision of the Council of Calcedon (A.D. 451); but the succession of "orthodox" Patriarchs, maintained by the arms of the Emperor of the East in the patriarchal throne of Alexandria, did not avail to secure the submission of the great majority of the Christians of Egypt, nor prevent the election of rival Patriarchs, supported by the voluntary contributions of their followers in lieu of the official stipends appropriated by the orthodox prelates. And to this day the Christian Church of Egypt is governed by the successor of Theodosius, and the members of that Church, under the name of Copts, or Egyptians, alone afford a link by which the inhabitants of the valley of the Nile can be identified with the Egyptians of antiquity.

During the Byzantine period, that is to say, from the partition of the empire to the invasion of Egypt by the Saracens (A.D. 395–638), Alexandria retained its commercial importance as an *entrepôt* between the East and the West: but its prosperity was seriously diminished by the expulsion of its Jewish community

[1] Vol. i. chap. xxi.

by the Patriarch Cyril in A.D. 415. At the time of this event, the Jews of Alexandria, whose presence had been welcomed, and whose political position had been established, alike by the Ptolemies and the Roman Emperors, numbered some 40,000 persons. The violent and unconstitutional means employed by Cyril to effect his object constitute a stain upon his character, while from an administrative point of view, the policy to which it gave effect was equally injurious and indefensible. The purging of the city alike from the taint of Judaism and of Paganism which Cyril accomplished during the period when he assumed the functions of civil magistrate was accompanied by a dramatic episode, which has made a deeper impression upon the world than his more far-reaching injustice against the Jews. In spite of the growth of Christianity, Alexandria still retained at this time its position as a school of profane learning, and the second Library and Museum established near the ruins of the Serapeum was still frequented by philosophers and students. The most famous of the teachers of this period was Hypatia, the daughter of Theon the mathematician, who lectured both at Athens and at Alexandria upon the philosophy of Plato and Aristotle, and upon the geometry of Apollonius and Diophantus. Her beauty, her popularity, and above all her reputed influence with Orestes the Prefect, drew upon her the hatred of the Christian authorities and made her the victim of fanatical violence. The horrible details of her death, or rather martyrdom, in the cause of Greek philosophy, are only too well established, and they have been made the basis of Charles Kingsley's novel, "Hypatia." But the curt narrative of Gibbon is more impressive than the picturesque detail of the novelist. "On a fatal day, in the holy season of Lent, Hypatia was torn from her chariot, stripped naked, dragged to the church, and inhumanly butchered by the hands of Peter the reader, and a troop of savage and merciless fanatics. Her flesh was scraped from her bones with sharp oyster-shells, and her quivering limbs were delivered to the flames. The just progress of inquiry and punishment was stopped by seasonable gifts: but the murder of

Hypatia has imprinted an indelible stain on the character and religion of Cyril of Alexandria." [1]

What remains to be told of the story of Alexandria can be condensed into a few sentences.

On December 22, A.D. 640, after a siege of fourteen months, Alexandria opened its gates to the forces of Amr Ibn-el-Às, the victorious general of the Khalif Omar. "I have taken," he wrote to his master, "the great city of the West. It is impossible for me to enumerate the variety of its riches and beauty, and I shall content myself with observing that it contains 4000 palaces, 4000 baths, 400 theatres or palaces of amusement, 12,000 shops for the sale of vegetable food, and 40,000 tributary Jews. The town has been subdued by force of arms, without treaty or capitulation, and the Moslems are impatient to seize the fruits of their victory." [2]

The fate of the Library is involved in mystery; in the absence of any contemporary account, the story of Abulpharagius has obtained credence. According to the author of the Dynasties, who wrote, it must be remembered, six centuries after the event in question, Amr was inclined to spare the scrolls for which the learned grammarian, John, surnamed Philoponus, had interceded, but when he had referred the matter to the Khalif, Omar replied, "If these writings of the Greeks agree with the book of God they are useless, and need not be preserved: if they disagree they are pernicious, and ought to be destroyed." In accordance with this sentence the scrolls, so the story runs, were served out to feed the fires of the 4000 baths of the city, and so vast was the mass of literature that six months elapsed before it was exhausted.

Under the Mohammedans Alexandria retained its commercial importance, in spite of the foundation of the Arab capital of Egypt, first Fostát and then Cairo, near the site of Memphis, at the apex of the Delta, until the Eastern trade was diverted from its ancient pathway by the discovery of the maritime route to India by

[1] Vol. ii. chap. xlvii. [2] Eutychius, *Annales*. ii. 316. as quoted by Gibbon.

Vasco da Gama in 1497. From the time when the Turks and Moors ceased to be the commercial intermediaries between Europe and the East, the importance of Alexandria slowly declined, and at the time of Napoleon's invasion of Egypt, when in 1798 the

TURKISH FORT ON THE SITE OF THE PHAROS.

city became once more the scene of an international conflict, its population had decreased to some 5000 inhabitants. The revival of Alexandria, which, as we have already seen, was due to Mohammed Ali, may be said to date with the construction of the Mahmûdîyeh Canal in 1819.

CHAPTER III

THE DELTA AND THE COTTON INDUSTRY

Leave Alexandria—First lesson in Arabic—Aspect of the country from Alexandria to Tanta—Reach Mehallet—Centre of the Delta—Cotton provides three-fourths of the Egyptian exports—Growth and characteristics of cotton culture in Egypt—Quality of Egyptian cotton better than American—Margin of price between them—Falling prices—Require continued improvements and economies—Want of rolling-stock on railways—Visit to a cotton (ginning) mill—Methods of cotton cleaning—Ginning—Garbling—Wages for Arab labour—Output of the mill—Cotton and cotton seed—Uses of cotton seed—Destinations of existing cotton crop—Visit to the town of Mehallet—Village school—Native industries—Weaving and manufacture of linseed cakes—The market—Housekeeping in an Egyptian town.

COTTON is to Egypt what coal is to England or wool to Australia. If we had forgotten—or not yet completely realized—that modern Egypt draws its income not from corn but from cotton, we were soon reminded of the fact. On the wharfs of Alexandria the bales of cotton, piled into vast oblong masses, were as prominent an object as the loose-robed Arabs; and in the town cotton prices and the cotton crop were in the mouths of every one, for the Delta is the chief seat of the cotton culture, and cotton provides three-fourths of the total exports of Egypt. When, therefore, Mr. Carver, whose acquaintance we had made on the *Thames*, suggested that we should pay a visit to his cotton-mill before we went on to Cairo, we gladly accepted the invitation; for I had come to Egypt not only to see mosques and pyramids, but also mills and plantations.

There was nothing to keep us in Alexandria. We had followed the *Rue de Rosette* to its eastern extremity, where, passing the handsome houses in which the wealthier Greeks and Italians live, we had found the remains of the Rosetta Gate, which is said

THE DELTA AND THE COTTON INDUSTRY 41

to occupy the site of the famous Canopic Gate of antiquity. We had driven through the mean dwellings of the native quarter, past the wilderness of white tombs which forms the Mohammedan burial-place, and climbed thoughtfully over the excavated masses of masonry at the base of the Theodosian column, and seen all that remains of the *forum* of Alexandria. We had paid a brief visit to the museum of Græco-Roman antiquities, and we had paced the desolate shore of the great harbour, and noticed the crowd which poured daily from the Ramleh railway station into Alexandria, over the ground once covered by the palaces of the Ptolemaic kings. Apart from the dusty palms that struggled everywhere to resist the tide of stucco, the sayces, with their gay sashes and gold-embroidered jackets, who ran before the smart European carriages in the *Rue de Rosette*, and the flaming leaves of the *poinsettia* in the shaded garden of the hôtel, were the sole objects we had found to put the thought of the East in our minds.

We left Alexandria by the nine o'clock express for Cairo, by which we could travel as far as Tanta, where we had to change carriages for our destination—Mehallet el-Kebîr. In the same compartment were an American gentleman and his wife. They had spent more than one winter in Egypt, and they were kind enough to give us our first lesson in colloquial Arabic. *Yalla!* "go on," was sufficient to check the undesired attentions of the Arab vendor—there was a crowd of them round the carriage window—and, if that proved ineffectual, we were to say *Imshi!* "go away"; and if this failed, we were to have recourse to the peremptory monosyllable *rûhh!* with a fine roll of the "r." Notwithstanding our newly acquired knowledge, it was reassuring to hear the guard, who came to look at our tickets, address us in perfectly intelligible English. Punctually at the hour the train rolled out of the station, and when we had got free of the town and the waters of Lakes Mariût and Abukir, the landscape showed level with green patches of Indian corn and clover, and brown fields of cotton stubble—brown because the snowy harvest had been gathered, and only the grey sticks and withered leaves remained in the fields. To the north of the railway ran the Mahmûdiyeh Canal, by means of which Alexandria was once more connected with the Nile, and the barren country around once more received supplies of fertilizing water. It was the first step in the restoration of the town, accomplished early in the century by Mohammed Ali; and until the construction of the railway this waterway was the sole means of communication with Cairo and the rest of Egypt. Even now we could see the curved yards of the Nile boats, and the heads and loads of the camels on the path below its high banks, showing how largely it was still used for the transport of merchandise and produce. Now and again we passed villages of brown, square huts, with roofs of loose stubble and sticks. Some of these primitive dwellings were circular in form, like the huts in the Kaffir kraals of South Africa, except that they were built of mud bricks instead of straw; and almost always there was the dome and square body of a little mosque, resplendent with whitewash, standing a little apart from the rest of the village, and often surrounded with a collection of gravestones as white as itself. The only trees that we noticed at first were the palms; but afterwards, as we got away from the coast, there were tamarisks and thorns, and here and there lebbek trees with their solid roof of foliage. Everywhere irrigating canals and channels had been cut, and the fields were dotted with the blue shirts of the Arab men and the darker dresses of the women. We saw the primitive ox-plough, drawn laboriously by the patient oxen through the furrows of red earth, and the primitive waterwheel, the sâkiyeh, driven by the same patient beast, ceaselessly revolving over the water-pits, and emptying its clumsy jars into the water channels.

Several considerable towns and villages—notably Damanhûr, the ancient Horus, one hour from Alexandria—had been passed before we saw the Nile. It was the Rosetta branch, and we swept over it by the great iron bridge into Kafr ez-Zaiyât. Twenty minutes later—at eleven—we saw the dome and

THE DELTA AND THE COTTON INDUSTRY 43

minarets of the great mosque of Tanta, where in August of each year vast crowds of pilgrims assemble from the Levantine countries and the north coast of Africa to celebrate the nativity of the popular Mohammedan saint, Seiyid el-Bedawi. The town itself, by virtue of its 60,000 inhabitants, is the third in Egypt. It is the point where the Alexandria and Damietta lines converge for Cairo: and here we changed into the Damietta train, which

KAFR EZ-ZAIYÂT STATION.

deposited us within the hour at Mehallet el-Kebir. Before the train drew up we had caught the welcome of an English face, and we stepped down to shake hands with Mr. S——, the manager of the mill, who had come to meet us.

We were now in the very centre of the Delta, within a few miles of the most productive soil in Egypt; and the tall chimneys that broke the level of the landscape told us that the wealth of Egypt was being garnered by European skill and European energy.

It needs only a few figures to reveal the importance of the cotton industry to Egypt. Although the geographical area of Egypt covers some 400,000 square miles, its habitable area is expressed (in round numbers) by the diminutive total of 13,000 square miles; and of this area one-fourth is covered by the stream of the Nile and its attendant lakes, and one-sixth by the innumerable canals which fertilize the soil. In other words, the Delta and the Nile Valley afford together some five and a half million acres [1] of cultivable land, of which the larger half belongs to Lower Egypt—practically the Delta—and the best of this land is appropriated to the cultivation of the cotton plant, which is grown in the Fayûm as well as in the Delta. In the government plantations, that is to say, on the estates which are worked by the Domains Administration, and on those of the most enlightened private owners, the land is put under cotton crop only once in *three* years; but in no case is a crop taken from the land more often than once in *two* years. Yet the value of the cotton crop so far exceeds the value of all other crops, that of the £12,000,000 [2] worth of exports which Egypt annually produces, £9,000,000 are due to this industry. The sugar industry, which ranks next in importance, provides an export of from half to three-quarters of a million pounds in value. The amount of cotton grown in Egypt has advanced from 2,792,184 kantars—the kantar is 99 lbs.—in 1881 to 5,879,479 kantars in 1896-7; but during the same period the average price of the kantar has fallen from rather more than three Egyptian pounds (£E3.143) to rather less than two (£E1.734). This fall in value has been met, in part at least, by the adoption of improved methods of cultivation and preparation. Thus in the Domains Administration,

[1] In 1897 land tax was paid on 5,328,601 *feddans*. The feddan is 1 acre 6 square perches, *i.e.* slightly larger than the English acre.—*Tableaux Statistiques, 1881-1897. Le Caire, 1898.*

[2] The exports of Egypt range from £E12,982,508 (the Egyptian pound equals £1 and 6d.) in 1881 to £E12,321,219 in 1897. The lowest year is 1886, with £E10,129,620; the highest was 1891, with £E13,878,638. All through this period the *quantity* of produce grown has steadily increased, but the fall in prices has reduced the *value.—Tab. Stat.*

where the best and most economic methods are employed, it has been found possible to increase the nett profit per feddan in spite of the adverse market. Taking the periods 1879 to 1887, and 1888 to 1897, as a basis for comparison, the Commissioners are able to report that a yield of 2.77 kantars of cotton, selling at £E2.53, in the former period has been replaced by a yield of 4.36 kantars. And although this increased yield sold at only £E2.06, owing to the fall in price, yet it gave a nett return per feddan which was £E1.69 in excess of the nett return of the previous period. Similarly increased yields of cotton seed and of cotton wood were secured; and thus, by economies and improvements, the total return per feddan on the Government estates was raised from £E8.61 in the former period to £E10.57 in the latter.[1]

One important result of the steady expansion of the Egyptian cotton crop in the face of the decline in value must be noticed, because it touches the very foundation of Egyptian finance. The large increase in the supply has caused the margin of price between Egyptian and American cotton to contract. The Egyptian cotton is (with the exception of a small amount produced in the South Sea Islands) the finest in the market, and as such it is used for the finest cotton cloth and for cambric. It commands, therefore, a price in advance of the American cotton; but, on the other hand, the American cotton, by virtue of its vastly larger output, controls the market. Not only does a fall in the value of American cotton produce an equivalent fall in the value of the Egyptian, but the more expensive Egyptian article cheapens more rapidly from its largely increased production than the American. Nevertheless, the Egyptian industry is secure, in spite of falling prices, so long as its produce commands a larger price than that of its rival; but the extent of its security is measured by the margin of price which separates the produce of the respective countries. The nature of this margin, and the degree in which it affects Egypt, will appear from the fact that in January 1897

[1] *Domaines de l'État Égyptien* . . . *Compte Général des Opérations*, &c. Paris, 1898.

American and Egyptian cotton were selling respectively at 4d. and 5⅝d. per pound, showing a difference of 1⅝d. in favour of Egypt: while at the end of the year the prices were 3¼d. and 4 7/16d. respectively, that is to say, the margin had contracted from 1⅝d. to 1 3/16d.[1]

At the same time, the demand for Egyptian cotton at this reduced price has increased. Russia in particular has bought more freely since the fall in prices. And here, again, there is a significant fact to be noticed. In spite of the economies which have been noticed above, the main factor in the increased output is the extension of the area under cultivation, and this extension means in Egypt an increased supply of water. The improvements already effected in the irrigation of the Delta will be discussed in a subsequent chapter, and it is therefore unnecessary to say more in this place than that it is intended to increase the already largely increased water supply of the Delta by additional works which are already in course of construction. Both in this vital matter, and in the encouragement which is being given to the construction of agricultural railways, due provision is being made by the Public Works Department for that further extension of the cultivated area which is necessary for the continued prosperity of the cotton industry under its present conditions. But in considering the future of the cotton industry, it is useful to recall the past. Cotton cultivation was introduced by Mohammed Ali as early as 1821, but it only assumed importance under the stimulus of the civil war in America, which for the time being deprived the Lancashire mills of their American supplies. The abnormal prosperity which this event brought to Egypt was of course short-lived, but it served, nevertheless, as an excuse for the fatal extravagances of Ismâil. The present prosperity of the industry has been secured by genuine and permanent improvements in the condition of the area available for such cultivation, and by economies in preparation. Nevertheless, during the whole period that these improvements have been in operation—that is

[1] "Annual Report of British Chamber of Commerce." Alexandria, 1897.

to say, from the time when, in 1886, English influence became predominant in the government of the Khedive—the industry has been confronted with a fall in prices so considerable, that while its output has been doubled, the value of that output has remained practically stationary. While, on the one hand, not to have lost ground under circumstances so unfavourable is evidence of the successful co-operation of the Government with private enterprize, yet the fact itself serves to show how economic conditions entirely beyond the control of an administration may hinder, or even completely obstruct, the best directed efforts. "The value of the exports [of Egypt] in 1898," says Lord Cromer in his last report,[1] "was £E11,805,000, as compared to £E12,321,000 in 1897. The decrease, amounting to £E516,000, was almost wholly due to the fall in the price of cotton. The quantity of cotton exported in 1898 was 270,000 kantars greater than in the previous year, but this was accompanied by a diminution in the value to the extent of £E464,000.

"Sugar fell off both in quantity and value. There was also some decrease in the exports of rice, beans, wool, molasses, and hides. On the other hand, onions, wheat, flour, and henna showed a fair increase."

But to return to Mehallet.

While we were engaged in depositing our luggage under the care of an official, Mr. S—— left us for a moment in quest of trucks. The Egyptian railways had got into an unsatisfactory condition. It was not the fault of the Railway Administration, but that of the *Caisse de la Dette*. In their jealous regard for the interest of the bondholders, the Public Debt Commissioners have again and again refused to sanction the expenditure of funds, which would otherwise have been available for works of public utility. It is a short-sighted policy, for these works would have yielded a return many times as great as the value of the interest on the capital which has been thus locked up. And so, in plain words, the railways had been starved. Their earnings to

[1] "Egypt," No. 3 (1899).

the utmost penny had been eagerly seized by the Commissioners to pay the interest on the Privileged Debt, and no adequate provision had been made for maintenance and expansion. The result had been that, in spite of an increased traffic and increased earnings, the permanent way and buildings had been neglected, and the rolling-stock had become hopelessly dilapidated and insufficient. Here was a case in point. Mr. S—— wanted to send off his bales of cotton, but there were no trucks to take them, and before a fresh supply could be obtained from Alexandria the steamer might, or might not, have left the docks.[1]

But Mr. S—— was, I suppose, accustomed by this time to such incidents. At any rate he showed no signs of discomposure when he joined us again. The mill was close to the station, and a few steps brought us into an ample yard, through which he led us among mountains of great sacks, with the whirl and rush of machinery in our ears, past panting Arabs and lumbering camels, to a deep veranda upon which his office opened. It appeared that our chief business, which was to go through the mill, was to be postponed until after luncheon; and so while J—— went into the house to make the acquaintance of Mrs. S—— I remained seated on the veranda by the office door to gather such information as would enable me to understand what I should afterwards see.

The mill, Mr. S—— told me, had been acquired by Messrs. Carver & Co., its present owners, in 1869; but it had been built then for some years. An old Arab, whom Mr. S—— called up and questioned, said that he remembered the big chimney being unfinished in 1861. It was not, of course, a cotton mill in the Lancashire sense. They received the cotton as it came from the fields, and prepared it for exportation. More exactly it was a "ginning" or "cotton-cleaning" mill; their business was to

[1] The Commissioners have since made considerable grants to the Railway Board for the purchase of rolling-stock and rails; but the same principle of "penny-wise and pound-foolish" still characterizes their action in other respects (*e.g.* in the case of the Nile Reservoir now under construction at Assuân). See also chapter xiii. p. 239.

separate the cotton from the seed, and to clean these products
and forward them in sacks and bales to Alexandria, for shipping to
England, or to some other country, where the cotton-spinning and
cotton-weaving were done. No, he said, with a smile, he was not
new to the work; he had been connected with the place for a long
time, as his father had been manager before him. There were
five ginning mills in the place, but this did more work than any
of the others. The first thing, he continued, is to get a supply
of good cotton from the growers. The cotton crop is sown in
February or March, and it is harvested in the following September or October. It is sown generally in the Delta once in two
years, though it is better to grow it every third year. During
the intervening time the land is sown with beans, or clover, or
some cereal. Thus half of each estate is under cotton every year,
with the exception of those belonging to wealthy proprietors,
where only one-third is laid down with cotton, and from these, of
course, a better yield is obtained. We have our agents in the
various districts, who keep us informed of the prospects of their
respective crops from year to year. We see samples of the several
crops on the various estates, and we then examine those crops
which we think most likely to suit our purpose, as they lie in the
stores. When we have made our selection, we send our own bags
for the grower to fill; and we make our own arrangements for
conveying the bags to the factory. Sometimes they come in the
canal-boats, sometimes, but not often, by rail, and when the stores
are close to the mill they are brought by cart. Yes, he said, as
he caught my inquiring glance, they often come that way too.

In the middle of our talk a line of camels had swung through
the factory gate, and they were proceeding with that indescribable
mixture of pride and clumsiness, which only a well-laden camel
can assume, into the centre of the yard. We left the veranda
and went to see them being unloaded. At a sign from their
drivers they had lumbered—there is no other word for it—on to the
ground; and there they lay round the weighing machine waiting
patiently while the two huge sacks, which formed their respective

loads, were uncorded and wheeled off to increase the size of the mountains of cotton through which they had threaded their way.

Yes, said Mr. S——, the camel will carry these two bags, which weigh from four to five kantars each — roughly from four to five hundred pounds — for thirty miles a day. These camels are making three journeys a day of ten miles there and back: the shékh gets five piastres — about a shilling — for each journey, and he pays the drivers four piastres — tenpence — a day.

CAMELS WITH COTTON.

These men are Bedouins, as you see; they live for the greater part of the year in the desert, and only come to the Delta in the autumn to do this carrying work. The cotton crop, as it comes from the fields in these bags, is on an average one-third cotton and two-thirds seed — that is, by weight.

As we turned away from the camels and walked back to the house for lunch, Mr. S—— added, "As the work of the factory is, roughly, to prepare the cotton crop for exportation, we are only busy for half the year, that is, from the end of September to the end of March or the beginning of April. During the rest of the year all that we have to do is to put the machinery and the factory buildings into repair, and to handle any small deposits of cotton that are occasionally held over in the growers' stores. And now," he said, as we reached the foot of a flight of steps leading to a balcony above, " you will be glad to think of something else for a little while."

I suppose it is that the background of rude or semi-barbarous surroundings throws into relief the moral and physical advantages of the Anglo-Saxon ; but whether or not this be the explanation, I am at least certain that I have few pleasanter reminiscences than those which are afforded by the occasions on which I have enjoyed the hospitality of the Englishman abroad. I have met him on an African farm, on a New Zealand sheep station, and on a Javan coffee plantation ; and I have found him always alike, the kindest of hosts and the most competent of cicerones ; and I have rarely left his house without feeling a sense of satisfaction in the thought of the enormous part which was played by my countrymen in the work of civilisation throughout the world. To-day our luncheon party consisted of Mr. S—— and his assistant, Mr. H. C——, Mrs. S—— and her sister, and our two selves. Although Mehallet is a town of over 30.000 inhabitants the S——s were the only English, and almost the only Europeans in the place ; and this made the little refinements of the table equipage, the sense of home—so grateful after weeks of hotel life—the more surprising. The only strange viand that the table afforded was the chalk-white buffalo butter. It differed more in appearance than in taste from the ordinary butter of the cow ; but it was many weeks before we met with it again, during our visit to the Fayûm.

When lunch was over we threaded our way once more through the masses of cotton bags across the yard to the mill. The first process is the separation of the cotton from the seed. This process is called " ginning," and in the gin-room at Messrs.

Carver & Co.'s mill there were sixty-four gins, driven by steam-power, ranged in two rows on either side, and between them rails were laid the length of the room on which ran an ordinary railway truck. The machines were served by Arab boys or girls, and they each turned out from 900 to 920 kantars of cotton in a day of twelve and a half hours. The gross amount of stuff handled in the gin-room per day was about 2700 to 2760 kantars—in round numbers 2360 cwts. or 120 tons. And in the whole season, on an average a gross weight of 360,000 kantars, yielding about 120,000 kantars—or 5200 tons —of cotton, passes through the gins. The Arabs who bring the supplies of cotton from the fields and handle it at the factory, are paid at the rate of four piastres[1] a day. The cotton thus separated from the seed is carried in truck loads to the press-room adjoining the gin-room. Here it is made up into bales by means of hydraulic presses.

The seed which has been separated by the gins is "garbled." The object of this process is to gather the cotton which still adheres to the seeds after they have been collected from the gins. For this purpose the seed is passed through a perforated cylinder, revolving by steam-power, from which the seed itself drops through the perforations into collecting boxes, while the cotton thus freed from the seed passes out at the end of the cylinder.

Any seed to which cotton fibre still remains after garbling, is submitted to a further and final process of cleaning. This final cleaning is accomplished by an American saw gin, called the Scarto gin. The seed is finally made up into sacks ready for exportation.

By these repeated processes the cotton fibre and the cotton seed are separated without any loss of either. They are all

---

[1] The piastre (strictly the piastre tarif in distinction from the piastre current, which is now used only in transactions between natives) is one-hundredth part of the Egyptian pound. It is worth 2½d.; and 97½ piastres are equivalent to the English pound sterling. The Egyptian pound, as already noticed, is worth £1, 0s. 6d. of English money.

THE DELTA AND THE COTTON INDUSTRY 53

closely watched to avoid waste; and even the sweepings from the floors of the sheds are made up into sacks and sold to native buyers. The value of the Egyptian cotton, as being the finest in the market, has already been noticed. The cotton seed, all of which is exported, with the exception of a small quantity which is kept for sowing purposes, yields a pure oil which is especially valuable because it can be flavoured and so used for table purposes. Most of this oil is, however, sold for lubricating machinery. A further product which the Egyptian cotton seed yields is the seed cake which is used by the English farmer for feeding his cattle.

As to the destination of the Egyptian cotton export; if we take a ten years' survey we find that about half of the cotton bales which leave the wharfs of Alexandria find their way to English ports. About one-sixth of them go to Russia, and one-eighth to Marseilles and Spain; while the rest, with the exception of small quantities which reach America and Bombay, are sent to Trieste and Italy. Almost all the seed is taken by England— Hull in particular takes one-half of the whole Egyptian export, and the balance is sent to Marseilles and other Continental ports.[1]

[1] The following shows the exact figures for the year 1896-97. It is fairly typical (except for a rapid increase of the American purchase):—

Cotton Exports (in Bales).

1st Sept. to 31st Aug.	United Kingdom	Marseilles and Spain	Trieste	Italy	Russia	America	Bombay	Total
1886-97	343,822	88,445	80,674	51,522	130,958	51,056	4,179	750,656

Cotton Seed (in Ardebs = 5 bushels, 1 peck, 1½ gallons).

1st Sept. to 31st Aug.	Hull	London	Sundry Ports Direct	Liverpool	Marseilles	Other Continental Ports	Total
1896-97	1,678,920	521,223	806,859	159,696	276,858	107,285	3,550,881

—From "*Report of British Chamber of Commerce,*" 1897.

When the busy time is over, all the employés, with the exception of the one or two European mechanics, are dismissed. The manager of the mill and his assistant, and the chief engineer, take the opportunity of paying a visit to Alexandria or Ramleh, or they run over to Europe for a holiday.

After we had left the mill and returned to the house, J—— went with Mrs. S—— and her sister for a walk into the town, while I stayed behind to sketch and write notes on the veranda. They were accompanied on their expedition by an Arab servant, an escort which was required not so much to protect them from annoyance, as to pilot them through the narrow and devious streets. One of the first places they visited was the kuttâb, or village school. In the dim light, J—— descried the schoolmaster sitting cross-legged upon a mat, with two rows of tiny children, ranged sideways in front of him, in the same attitude on the ground. The master himself was weaving a mat, and the boys and girls were plaiting straw, an occupation which both parties were able to combine with the business of education. This consisted, so far as the children were concerned, in the recital of passages from the Kurân, in which they were repeatedly prompted by the master, accompanied by a more or less energetic swaying of their bodies from the hips backwards and forwards. From the school they passed on to inspect some of the native industries of the town. The chief of these, the weaving of shawls and handkerchiefs by hand from silk thread, J—— was unable to see, as on this occasion these workshops were closed; but the cotton-weaving—towels, counterpanes, curtains, &c.—was going forwards busily. The looms were driven by foot-power, and one man worked both treadle and bobbins with the help of a boy who was seated by his side.

A more curious sight was afforded by the manufacture of linseed cakes. In a dark and dirty chamber, half stable and half factory, a buffalo was walking patiently round and round, turning a round stone over a square one, and thus crushing the seed into a pasty mass. In an adjacent room brown Arabs were filling wooden vats with this paste, from which the oil was drained off into a well sunk in the floor. Others filled the primitive presses of wicker-work with the solid substance that remained in the vats, and finally ranged the round cakes from the presses on the floor to dry. Between the two chambers there was a place of prayer, and the voice of a devout Mohammedan mingled with the sound of the grinding-stones.

The streets were about eight feet wide, and innocent of any pavement other than was afforded by the trodden earth. The houses, with their projecting mushrebiyeh windows, and the mosques—of which there were 300 in the town—were alike in a dilapidated and often ruinous condition; for, as Mrs. S—— explained, the Egyptians do not repair their buildings. They let them fall to pieces from decay, and then build new ones. On their way to the market, which they next visited, Mrs. S—— pointed to the gaudy paintings which appeared here and there on the front of a house. These paintings, she said, which consisted of rude imitations of foliage, showed that the inhabitant had accomplished a pilgrimage to Mecca. Other objects which attracted J——'s attention were some gaudily painted wooden boxes outside a shop. "Gaudily" is scarcely sufficient, for these boxes, which were about as large as a cabin trunk, were streaked or spotted with all the colours of the rainbow. They were "bride boxes," and Mrs. S—— added that no native girl could be married in Egypt unless she possessed one of these hideous cases in which to bestow her trousseau. In the market there were men and women sitting cross-legged on the ground, with their wares—coloured jars, silk and cotton shawls and handkerchiefs, fruit, and sweetmeats—in front of them. Unlike the itinerant vendors of Cairo and Alexandria, they took no pains to attract the attention of the European visitors, although they showed no reluctance in displaying their goods when they were asked to do so.

As they returned to the factory, Mrs. S—— discussed the question of provisions from the point of view of European housekeeping. The price of meat, she said, was low, and poultry was thrown in with it, almost as a bakshish. Vegetables were very scarce, but on the other hand fruit was plentiful, and very cheap when it was in season. There was plenty of game, that is to say, snipe and quail, to be had; milk and bread were cheap, but groceries were procured direct from England, since it was cheaper to pay both carriage and duty than to buy them at Alexandria.

A pleasant cup of tea preceded our return to the station. It was the more acceptable because of the heat, which, without being oppressive, was equivalent to a warm day in the English summer. Then, when we had said our adieux to our kind hosts, we took our seats in the train for Tanta, where we were to join the evening express to Cairo.

CHAPTER IV

THE GOVERNMENT

Four authorities participate in the government of Egypt: the Sultan of Turkey, the Khedive, the Great Powers, England—Origin and nature of the authority of the Sultan—Of the Khedive—Of the international authority—Financial—The *Caisse de la Dette*—Administrative—The mixed administrations—Judicial—The Tribunaux Mixtes—Consular courts—Origin of international judicial authority—The capitulations—The encroachments of the mixed courts on the native—The proposals of the Government to amend the charter of organization—The questions at issue—The authority of the British Government—The successive steps by which the "veiled Protectorate" has grown—First professions of England—Duty of giving advice—Advice must be taken—The offer to withdraw—Justification of position of England—The recovery of the Sudân—Position of England, how altered by the Sudân agreement—Ministries and departments of the Government.

THE administration of Egypt at the present day is conducted by officials and departments whose authority is derived from more than one source. This divided authority is the outcome of circumstances so unusual that it is impossible to characterize the government of Egypt by any of the brief and recognized descriptions which can be employed in the case of less abnormal administrations. Although the paramount power rests at the present time in the hands of England, Egypt is neither a British colony nor a protected state in the sense of being a British possession. Technically, again, Egypt remains a part of the Ottoman Empire, since the sovereignty of the Khedive, and the authority, therefore, of the Khedive's ministers, consists of powers defined and conveyed by the firmân or decree issued by the Sultan in June 1873. On the other hand, both the authority of the Sultan as suzerain and the independence of the Khedive as sovereign, under the terms of this firmân, have been practically superseded by an international control exercised by the Great Powers of Europe; and while, by virtue of the military occupation effected in 1882, Great Britain has to a very large extent assumed the rights and duties collectively exercised by the Great Powers, international tribunals and international departments, which derive their authority from the collective action of the Great Powers, still remain in existence.

There are, therefore, four distinct authorities which play more or less energetic parts in the government of Egypt as it is to-day. First, there is the Sultan of Turkey, possessing the rights of suzerain; second, the Khedive, or hereditary sovereign of Egypt; third, there are the Great Powers of Europe exercising a general control over the Khedive's government, and administering special departments by means of international commissions and boards; and fourth, there is the British Government holding the country with its troops, and virtually directing the entire executive by means of "advisers," who control the policy and action of the several ministers of whom the Khedive's government is from time to time composed.

Before we discuss the government of Egypt, as it is carried on to-day, it is necessary for me to indicate briefly the origin of each of these separate authorities. As I have already mentioned, Egypt became a province of the Turkish Empire in the sixteenth century; and the authority of the Sultan of Turkey originated by right of the conquest, which was achieved in the year 1517, by the Osman Sultan Selim I. The sovereignty thus acquired was subsequently legalized by the action of Mutawakkil, the last representative of the Abbaside Khalifs, who then formally transferred the religious rights and hereditary prerogatives of the Khalifate to the then Osman Sultan. It is by virtue of this cession that the Sultan of Turkey has since been recognized as the religious head by the majority of the followers of Mohammed throughout the world. The religious authority of the Sultans of Turkey remains to this day undiminished, but their power in Egypt has been modified by the establishment of Mohammed Ali and his family as hereditary rulers of Egypt. Mohammed Ali, who succeeded in making himself master of Egypt and afterwards of Syria, between the years 1805 and 1839, would have achieved the entire independence of Egypt had not the European Powers, acting upon the initiative of England, forced upon him an arrangement under which he was compelled to sacrifice part of the fruits of his successful revolt. Under the firmân of investiture, which was issued in 1841 as the result of this intervention, Syria was restored to the Ottoman Empire, and Egypt was placed under the suzerainty of the Sultan. At the same time the immediate sovereignty of Egypt was conferred upon Mohammed Ali and his heirs, who thus became the hereditary rulers of Egypt. In 1867 the title of Khedive or Viceroy[1] was conferred upon Ismaïl, and this concession was followed by the firmân of 1873, under which the precise relationship of the Khedive to the Sultan was defined. The authority of the Sultan in Egypt is confined, therefore, to the exaction of the duties which the Khedive owes to him under this arrangement, and to restricting the Khedive from doing anything which he is forbidden to do by the terms of the suzerainty. The most important of these duties is the annual payment of a tribute amounting to about £700,000, and the chief restriction which the suzerainty exercises upon the independence of the Khedive is to prevent him from maintaining more than a certain number of ships of war. So long, therefore, as the Khedive conforms with certain technical formalities, forwards this sum of £700,000 each year to Constantinople, and refrains from creating a navy, the authority of the Sultan is practically inoperative in Egypt.

The authority of the Khedive is naturally that of an independent sovereign of the despotic eastern type, except so far as it is thus restricted by the suzerain rights of the Sultan of Turkey, and by treaty obligations previously incurred by the suzerain power, and therefore binding upon Egypt in common with other provinces of the Ottoman Empire. An authority of this kind

---

[1] *Khidêwi-Misr* is the actual form of the title.

was exercised by Mohammed Ali and his successors virtually up to the time when Ismaîl was deposed and the dual control was established, that is, on June 26, 1879. Three years previous to this date the Great Powers of Europe commenced to intervene in the government of Egypt by the establishment of the Mixed Tribunals and the Caisse de la Dette, and since that time European control has increased both in its range and its effectiveness. These successive steps, which will be duly noted, have terminated in the present state of affairs, in which the Egyptian government is practically vested in English officials; but, nevertheless, the Khedive and the Khedive's ministers theoretically remain in possession of this complete and despotic authority at the present moment, and to this day every act of the government of Egypt is technically based upon the authority of the Khedive.

Next, there is the authority of the Powers. Although, as I have already mentioned, the control of England has to a large extent superseded that formerly exercised collectively by two or more of the Great Powers, a general restraint is still exercised upon the financial policy of the government by the international board called the Caisse de la Dette, and at the same time certain departments of the administration are carried on by commissioners or boards, which similarly derive their authority from the collective action of the Great Powers. There is, moreover, an international court called the Tribunaux Mixtes, which has a restricted criminal, and full civil jurisdiction over the foreigners, who, as I have already stated, are exempt from the jurisdiction of the local courts. The international authority is, therefore, partly financial, partly administrative, and partly judicial.

The Caisse de la Dette, which is the instrument of the financial authority of the Great Powers, was originally constituted by a Khedivial decree of May 2, 1876, thus following the Tribunaux Mixtes by three months. As thus originally constituted, the Caisse was a committee of bondholders appointed to receive certain revenues which had been assigned by Ismaîl's government under diplomatic pressure for the payment of the interest due on the Egyptian debt. At this time the scope of the commission was so limited that the British Government neglected to propose a commissioner, and the Caisse was originally composed of three members representing respectively France, Austria, and Italy. Since then the importance of the Caisse, or Public Debt Office, has greatly increased, and at the present time the board consists of six commissioners, representing respectively England, France, Austria, Italy, Germany, and Russia. At the same time the functions of the commissioners have been extended, since they are no longer merely a committee of the bondholders, but have added to their original duty of receiving the revenues assigned to the service of the Debt, those of financial representatives of the respective interests of the several Powers by whom they are appointed.

The administrative authority of the Great Powers is exercised by the Railway Board, and the two commissions which respectively manage the Daira Sanieh and Domains Estates, known collectively as the Mixed Administrations. Each of these administrations is theoretically controlled by the representatives of three nationalities, England, France, and Egypt, with equal powers. As the result of this arrangement the railways and telegraphs, and the management of what are practically the "Crown" lands of Egypt—two important departments of the administration—remain under international control. Of these the Railway Board was constituted in 1876, and the Daira and Domains Commissions respectively in 1877 and 1878.

The origin of the international authority, both financial and administrative, is to be found in the breakdown of the Khedive Ismaïl's government, which resulted in the virtual bankruptcy of Egypt. In compounding with her creditors—first in the Goschen-Joubert settlement of 1876, and then in the more complete inquiry which resulted in the Law of Liquidation of 1880[1]— Egypt was not only compelled to assign certain definite revenues and certain properties to the payment of the interests on the various loans which had been advanced to her by Europe, but

[1] Modified by the Convention of London, 1885.

she was also compelled to insure the productiveness of the sources of income which she thus assigned by placing the more important of them under European management. Twenty years ago, when the Khedive's government was absolutely incompetent, this course was not only justifiable but necessary; but to-day, when every department of the Khedive's government has been rendered efficient through the exertions of the English advisers and officials, the existence of these mixed administrations is an unnecessary and injurious interference with the administrative freedom of the Egyptian Government.

The Tribunaux Mixtes, which form the chief instrument of the judicial authority of the Powers, were instituted, as already stated, in February 1876. They form a court having exclusive authority in civil cases in which the parties are of different nationalities, i.e. between two foreigners of different nationalities, or a foreigner and a native: they have also power to decide cases in which the title to real estate is involved where the parties are both of the same nationality, and a limited criminal jurisdiction which is concerned mainly with the discipline of their own proceedings, and certain small offences against police regulations. They consist of a Court of Appeal, which sits at Alexandria, and of Courts of First Instance, sitting respectively at Alexandria, Cairo, and Mansourah; and both the Court of Appeal, and the Courts of First Instance, have a parquet or criminal staff attached to them. The bench of the several courts is composed of judges of various nationalities, with a large majority of Europeans over natives. As this International Court exercises, to a large extent, the authority previously exercised by the Consular Courts of the various Powers, it was necessary to obtain the consent of all the fourteen Powers concerned before the law upon which this international jurisdiction is based could be framed by the Egyptian Government. That the negotiations thus required were effected, and the innumerable local difficulties which stood in the way of so important a change were overcome, is mainly due to the perseverance and adroitness of Nubar Pasha.

In addition to the Tribunaux Mixtes the judicial authority of the Powers is directly exercised by means of the Consular Courts, which alone possess—with the slight exception above noticed—criminal jurisdiction over the respective subjects of the several Powers concerned.

The origin of the international administrative authority was, we saw, to be referred to the incapacity of the Egyptian Government to manage its financial affairs. The origin of the international judicial authority, exercised through both the Tribunaux Mixtes and the Consular Courts, must be traced to a period long anterior to the bankruptcy of Egypt under the Khedive Ismáil. From the fifteenth century onwards, treaties, or rather concessions, were made by the Ottoman Government with the various Powers of Europe, which regulated the conditions under which foreigners were permitted to reside within the limits of the Empire. The original intention of these treaties, which are known collectively as the "capitulations," was to permit of the settlement of Christian traders by protecting them from the religious fanaticism of the Mussulman populations. With this object in view three main privileges were conferred upon foreign residents by the respective capitulations granted to the several European and American Governments—immunity from taxation, inviolability of domicile, and freedom from the jurisdiction of the local courts. The duty of recognizing these privileges was transmitted by the Porte to the Government of Egypt, as exercised by Mohammed Ali and his successors, with the result that a concession originally necessary for the existence of Christian traders in a Mussulman community has been converted into a means of unfairly avoiding the burden of taxation and of escaping from the authority of the law. And in Egypt to-day, where, as we have already seen, the various European communities form an element of great importance, the existence of the treaty obligations embodied in the capitulations forms a constant source of friction between the Egyptian Government and the representatives of the Powers, and in itself constitutes one of the gravest of those administrative difficulties in which the situation abounds.

It remains to add that of late years the international judicial authority has tended rather to increase than diminish. The medium through which this increase of authority has been acquired is the Tribunaux Mixtes. By giving an extended interpretation to certain articles in its charter of organization, this International Court has encroached upon the sphere of the native tribunals, and has usurped an authority which can properly be vested only in the executive. Under these circumstances the Egyptian Government have proposed to modify the articles in question, with a view of preventing these encroachments; and in the meanwhile, that is to say, whilst the necessary negotiations between the representatives of the Great Powers are proceeding, the courts have been prolonged for a period of one year only. And here it is necessary to explain that the existence of these courts depends upon the agreement of the Powers and the Egyptian Government. The law, under the terms of which they were instituted, provided only for their establishment for a period of five years, namely from 1876 to 1881. They have been subsequently renewed for periods of one year in 1881, 1882, and 1883: and for periods of five years in 1884, 1889, and 1894; and now (in 1899) they have been renewed again for one year only, under the special circumstances stated above.

As the position of the Tribunaux Mixtes is a question of great importance, it will be useful for me to state as succinctly as possible both the nature of the encroachments of which the Egyptian Government complain, and the measures by which they propose to remedy the evil.

The encroachments are twofold in character. First, the judges of the courts have held, whether rightly or wrongly we need not discuss, that they are authorized by Article 11 of the Charter of Organization under certain circumstances to control the administrative acts of the Government. The most notorious instance of the application of this interpretation is the decision given by the Court of Appeal in December 1897. On that occasion it was held that the action of the Public Debt Commissioners in applying a part of the General Reserve Fund to the defrayment of the cost of the Sudân expedition was *ultra vires*; the further point, however, whether a decision of the Commissioners must or must not be unanimous, was left undecided. In order to prevent the repetition of a similar interference with the discretion of the Caisse, or with the freedom of the executive in general, the Government propose to amend the Article in question by the insertion of words which unmistakably embody the principle, that "acts of sovereignty, and all steps dictated by political motives, were not intended to come within the jurisdiction of the Courts," and that any general administrative measure is beyond their cognizance.

Second, Article 9, which reserves all civil and commercial causes "between natives and foreigners, and between foreigners of different nationalities," for the exclusive jurisdiction of the Tribunaux Mixtes, has been interpreted to include all cases in which any "mixed interest" is affected. As the Egyptian Government consider that this interpretation enables the court to encroach unfairly upon the sphere of the native courts, it is proposed to similarly amend this article by a distinct assertion of the principle, that "the question of jurisdiction should be determined solely by the nationality of the parties really engaged in the suit, without reference to the mixed interests which might be indirectly involved."

As no alteration can be effected in the constitution of the Tribunaux Mixtes without the consent of the (fourteen) Powers, the question can only be decided by diplomatic action, and negotiations for the proposed amendments in the Charter of Organization are now (1899) in progress.[1]

At the same time, the Egyptian Government having in view

---

[1] For a full statement of this question, see Lord Cromer's Reports for 1898 and 1899, *sub voce* "Mixed Tribunals." The expressions quoted in the text are taken from this source.

the possibility of the Powers refusing to consent to these amendments, and of a consequent return to the "ancien ordre de choses," that is to say, a revival of the civil jurisdiction of the consular courts, are rightly endeavouring to make the native courts as efficient as possible. Not only are the native courts, properly so called, being strengthened by the introduction of competent English judges in the place of the more unsatisfactory native or European judges, as these latter retire from time to time, but the religious courts, the "Mehkemeh Sheraieh," in which questions of personal status such as marriage, divorce, and succession are decided, in accordance with the Mohammedan law as contained in the Kurân, have at length been reformed.[1] The value of the reforms effected in the native courts is too well understood to require any comment here, but it may be added that the Mehkemeh Sheraieh are institutions which combine the functions of the Chancery Division of the High Court with those of Somerset House. The goal at which the Egyptian Government aim is, of course, to render the Egyptian tribunals, both civil and religious, so efficient that foreigners may be reasonably asked to submit their disputes to the decision of the local courts; in other words, to make the international court and the consular jurisdiction as unnecessary as it is anomalous.

Lastly, there is the authority of the British Government. It is interesting to notice the successive steps, as revealed by the Blue Books, by which the *de facto* supremacy—the veiled Protectorate, as it has been called—has grown. First, there was the partnership with France—the financial settlement of Goschen and Joubert in 1876, the Dual Control of 1879. Then there was the "Occupation" in 1882. France recoiled before the tremendous responsibilities created by the rebellion of Arabi, and the task of restoring order devolved upon England alone. The British fleet operated with the one purpose "of protecting His Highness

---

[1] In spite of the opposition of the Legislative Council, fomented by Mukhtar Pasha, the Sultan's Commissioner in Cairo, this reform was effected by a Khedivial decree in May last (1899). See also p. 96.

the Khedive and the people of Egypt against the rebels."[1] The British troops, under Lord Wolseley, were sent to Egypt "with the sole object of re-establishing the authority of the Khedive."[2] These declarations of the Government were perfectly sincere, for any purpose other than that of a temporary occupation would have been instantly repudiated by the nation. But after Alexandria had been bombarded, and Arabi's army had been broken at Tel-el-Kebir, England found herself with a country on her hands. A statesman expert was despatched, and on the lines of Lord Dufferin's report, reforms were initiated. Then it was that Her Majesty's Government notified to the Powers that they had accepted the responsibility which circumstances had laid upon them, and had assumed "the duty of giving advice" to the Khedive's Government, "with the object of securing that the order of things to be established should be of a satisfactory character, and possess the elements of stability and progress."[3] The transition from "responsibility" to "control" was rapid. A year after England had assumed the duty of "giving advice," Lord Granville wrote to Lord Cromer, then Sir Evelyn Baring: "In important questions, where the administration and safety of Egypt are at stake, it is indispensable that Her Majesty's Government should, so long as the provisional occupation of the country by English troops continues, be assured that the advice which, after full consideration of the views of the Egyptian Government, they may feel it their duty to tender to the Khedive, *should be followed.*"[4]

Three years later, England was formally called upon to make good her professions of disinterested action. In the interval much had happened. The London Convention of 1885—secured by the persistency of England—had lightened the financial burden laid upon Egypt by the Law of Liquidation in 1880;

---

[1] Letter of Admiral Seymour to the Khedive, under date July 22, 1882.
[2] Proclamation of General Wolseley, under date August 19, 1882.
[3] Despatch of Lord Granville to Powers, January 3, 1883 [C. 3462].
[4] C. 3844.

Anglo-Indian engineers had taken in hand the irrigation system of the Delta, and the repair of the Barrage had been commenced; the Egyptian army had been reorganized; the Corvée had been mitigated, though not as yet abolished; and the more conspicuous administrative iniquities had been removed. Nevertheless, when the Sultan asked the British Government to fix a date for the evacuation of Egypt, England was prepared loyally to fulfil her engagement, with such modifications alone as the march of events and the interests of the Egyptian people required. "The British Government," Lord Salisbury wrote,[1] "must retain the right to regard and uphold the condition of things which will have been brought about by the military action and large sacrifices of this country. So long as the Government of Egypt maintains its position, and no disorders arise to interfere with the administration of justice or the action of the executive power, it is highly desirable that no soldier belonging to any foreign nation should remain upon the soil of Egypt, except when it may be necessary to make use of the land-passage from one sea to another. Her Majesty's Government would willingly agree that such a stipulation should, whenever the evacuation had taken place, apply to English as much as to other troops; but it will be necessary to restrict this provision, as far as England is concerned, to periods of tranquillity. England, if she spontaneously and willingly evacuates the country, must retain a treaty-right of intervention, if at any time either internal peace or external security should be seriously threatened. There is no danger that a privilege so costly in its character will be used unless the circumstances imperatively demand it."

And an arrangement upon these lines was actually concluded by the respective representatives of England and Turkey. The British troops were to remain for three years longer in the country, and the Egyptian army was to continue for two years

---

[1] To Sir Henry Drummond Wolff, the British Plenipotentiary then at Constantinople for the purpose of these negotiations. Under date January 15, 1877 [C. 5050].

more under the direction of British officers. England, however, retained in effect a right to re-occupy the country, if its " internal peace or external security" should be threatened. At the same time it was further agreed in a protocol that a proposal for the abolition of the capitulations, and for the establishment of a " local and uniform jurisdiction and legislature," should be jointly addressed by the signatories to the Great Powers. Owing to the opposition of France, supported by Russia, the Sultan refused to ratify the Convention which his plenipotentiary had signed. It is not necessary to point out how this peevish and short-sighted opposition has since recoiled upon the head of its author. All that need be said here is, that those Englishmen who think it right to assume an apologetic air, when they refer to the continued presence of England in Egypt, are either ignorant of the facts, or misinterpret the principles of international morality upon which such censures are based. *Vigilantibus non dormientibus lex subvenit*—"the law helps those who keep awake, not those who lie asleep," is a principle which applies with even greater force to the relationships of nations than to those of individuals. When Egypt was in a state of anarchy, France stepped aside, the rest of Europe never lifted a finger, the Sultan—the suzerain authority—had neither the will nor the power to restore the Khedive's Government, still less to reform the abuses under which the mass of the people of Egypt laboured. In the name of common sense, therefore, what principle of public or private morality could be invoked which would require England to resign the reward of her efforts, or even justify her in abandoning the necessary and beneficent task of redeeming Egypt?

Lastly, after ten years of strenuous and successful effort—effort which embraced financial and administrative reform, the improvement of the condition of the people, and the development of the industries of the country—came the recovery of the lost provinces, the destruction of the forces of Mahdism at Omdurman, and the virtual assumption by England of the government of the

Sudán. With the signature of the "Agreement between Her Britannic Majesty's Government and the Government of His Highness the Khedive of Egypt, relative to the future administration of the Soudan," "done in Cairo the 19th January 1899," the position of England in Egypt has been indirectly, but none the less materially, modified. The nature of this modification will appear sufficiently from the following significant facts. In the first place, the text of the agreement was published in the *Journal Officiel*, that is, the Egyptian Government *Gazette* —not in French, but in English and Arabic. In the next place, the suzerainty of the Sultan was ignored; and lastly, any claims to extra-territorial privileges which might be based upon the capitulations, or the existence of the international courts, are distinctly repudiated. The justification for this failure to recognize either the rights of the Sultan as suzerain, or the rights of foreigners based upon treaty obligations incurred by the suzerain authority, lies in the fact that these provinces had in effect been abandoned by Turkey and re-conquered at the sole and exclusive cost of England and Egypt. And it is scarcely necessary to add, that the Power in whose representative the administration of the Sudán is virtually vested, controls the waters of the Nile and holds Egypt in the hollow of her hand.

It is not my intention to speak here of the details of the reforms which have already been effected during the period of the English occupation. Such information as I have been able to gather on these points will be given in connection with those opportunities of observing the process of redemption which occasion has from time to time presented in the course of my stay in Egypt. It remains, however, for me to complete this brief account of the Government of Egypt by a sketch of the departments, by which the work of administration is at present carried on. Apart from the international administrations which have been already mentioned—the Public Debt Office, the Daira Sanieh, the Domains, and the Railway and Telegraphs Board—there are six ministries, each of which, directed nominally by a native minister, but actually by the English "adviser" (or an equivalent official), is provided with a number of high officials, of whom the great majority are Englishmen. These ministries are: first, the Ministry of the Interior, which includes the important Sanitary Department, of which Sir J. G. Rogers is Director-General, and the Police. An essential part of the work of this ministry is the control and direction of the general system of Local Government, in which the Mudirs form so important a feature. Second, the Ministry of Finance, to which Mr. J. L. Gorst is attached as financial adviser, in succession to Sir Elwin Palmer, now Governor of the National Bank of Egypt, and in which the Post-Office is included. Third, the Public Works Ministry, in which Sir W. Garstin sits as Under-Secretary of State, and which includes the Irrigation Service — a service of vital importance to the prosperity of Egypt — and the Survey Department. Fourth, the Ministry of Public Instruction with Artin Pasha as Under-Secretary, and Mr. Douglas Dunlop, as Inspector-General. Fifth, the Ministry of Justice, with Mr. MacIlwraith as Legal Adviser, in succession to Sir John Scott, and Mr. Corbet as Procureur-Général. And lastly, there is the Ministry of War, the real business of which is, of course, almost entirely performed by the English officers who command the Egyptian troops. Speaking generally, while the great majority of the highest positions in the Civil Service are occupied by Englishmen, or by other Europeans, the great mass of the rank and file, both of the officials in the departments and of those in the local services, are Egyptians. The policy of the Egyptian Government in this matter is sufficiently expressed by the phrase, "English heads and Egyptian hands."

It is characteristic of the situation that I have written thus far of the Egyptian Government without any word of Lord Cromer. Officially styled the British "Agent and Consul-General" — or in full the "Minister Plenipotentiary, Agent, and Consul-General," — he is the representative of the British Government; and as the decisions of the British Government are rightly based upon the opinions of "the man on the spot," he is in a sense the real ruler of Egypt. In the Sudán Agreement it is Lord Cromer's signature that stands written in pledge of the faith of Her Majesty's Government. If the advice of a British expert is disregarded, if an obnoxious minister must be dismissed, or a Khedive deposed—then the British Agent appears; at other times he is as unobtrusive as his official residence is modest. But whether the sky be fair or foul his motto is always *Festina lente*.

CHAPTER V

FROM MEMPHIS TO CAIRO

First impression of Cairo—Two Cairos—Mediæval and European—It occupies natural site for capital of Egypt—Memphis—Herodotus' account of Memphis, c. 400 B.C.- Strabo's account - Memphis and Babylon in the age of Augustus —The capture of Babylon by the Saracens, A.D. 638 - Fostât—Expansion of Fostât under Tulûn—Foundation of Cairo in 972—Its growth under the Fâtimite Khalîfs—The citadel added by Saladin—The tomb-mosques by the Mameluke Sultans—Remains of mediæval Cairo—Respected during British occupation—Preservation of Arabian monuments—Difficulties in the way of exploring mediæval Cairo—Chief groups of buildings.

LIKE the first view of St. Peter's at Rome, the traveller's first impression of Cairo is one of disappointment. He had cherished the place so long in his mind as the well-head of Oriental life; he had read the "Arabian Nights" once more after twenty years; he had noted with pleasing anticipation the long sections devoted to "street scenes," "Arabian buildings," and "Mohammedan customs" in his guide-book—in short, he had forgotten nothing, every mosque was to have its minaret and dome, every woman to wear her *yashmak*, every man to have pointed toes to his slippers, and to sit astride of a gaily caparisoned mule, in an atmosphere cooled by fountains, and perfumed by attar of roses. But this vision was dispelled when the train drew up alongside the platform of the railway station, and he saw his friend waiting for him in a straw hat and a tweed suit, which would not have been unbecoming at Henley. Of course he does not forget his Arabian Nights and his guide-book at once. On the contrary, he notices, with great satisfaction, one or two unmistakable minarets, which he passes as he drives from the station to his hôtel, or to his friend's house at Kasr-ed-Dubara, and he buys a fly swish from an Arab at the gate. Moreover, after he has gone round the links at

Gezireh two or three times, and played about as much lawn tennis and croquet in a week as he would have played in a season at home, he confides to his friend that he would like to see the Bazaars, or the Mosque of Sultan Hasan, or the Tombs of the Khalifs. His friend, however, who is a resident, does not encourage him. It is not much good, he tells him, to go to the Bazaars unless he wants to buy something, and as for the mosques he must first get a ticket. Of course he can easily drive to the Tombs of the Khalifs, but it is very hot, and yes—he must have a ticket before he goes there, too. "My dear fellow," he ends, "perhaps I am nervous, but I have been down with fever twice" —he looks the picture of health in his Norfolk jacket and knickerbockers—"and you may take my word for it, the less you go into that part of the town the better. *Here*, thank Heaven, we are tolerably clean and airy, but the native streets have not been swept since the days of Saladin." Then the visitor listens to some statistics of the sanitary—or rather insanitary—condition of the old town, with a vivid account of the cholera in '95. In the end his friend promises to ride out with him to the Pyramids, where they can have a good lunch at the Mena House Hôtel.

Nevertheless it is all there, even to the plash of fountains and attar of roses. The fact is that there are two Cairos, which, lying side by side without any visible division between them, hold two populations whose lives are absolutely distinct and dissimilar.

According to the latest returns, Cairo has a population of some 600,000 inhabitants. Of these, the great bulk are closely crowded in the network of narrow streets of which the old town is composed, while the remainder occupy the spacious streets and squares lying to the west and north. The city lies on the east bank of the Nile, between the desert at the foot of the Mokattam Hills and the river. Roughly speaking it extends for two miles east and west, and for three miles north and south. If the rectangular space thus indicated be divided by a line drawn diagonally from the railway station on the north to the Citadel on the south, it will roughly separate European from mediæval Cairo. To the

Emîr el-Gâi Yusefi Mosque from Sûk es-Sellâha

east of this line 500,000 brown-skinned Arabs are living in the quaintest and most delightful, but, at the same time, the dirtiest and most dilapidated of streets. Seen from the Citadel, this Cairo presents the appearance of a mass of level roofs, out of which countless minarets and domes rise skywards. To the west of this line are the palaces, public buildings, the wide tree-lined streets, and the gardens of the European quarters. Here, in these infinitely less picturesque, but infinitely more sanitary, streets and squares, the bulk of the 20,000 or 30,000 Europeans live, together with the Egyptian grandees and their households. Seen from the roof of one of the numerous palaces erected on the east bank of the Nile, this Cairo looks like a vast garden intersected with white roads bordered by lebbek avenues, and variegated by patches of bright-hued flowering shrubs, in the midst of which the white walls and roofs of the houses glitter in the sunshine. Northwards, the Nile widens and encircles the island of Gezireh, of which the southern extremity is linked to the city by the Great Nile bridge; and it is the road which is carried by this bridge that leads the traveller across the island, and then over a second and lesser bridge to the west bank of the river, and thence to the Pyramids of Gizeh. At a point scarcely ten miles below the city, distinguished by the Arabs as the "Cow's Belly," and marked for the modern traveller by the imposing towers and arches of the Barrage, the Nile divides into the two branches which, flowing respectively to Rosetta and Damietta, form the Delta.

The position which Cairo occupies is the natural site for the capital of Egypt. Lying at the junction of the Nile valley and the Delta, and in closest proximity to the head of the Gulf of Suez, which gave access by sea to Arabia, India, and the east coast of Africa, and by land to Syria and Persia, it presents a union of advantages attained by no other spot. Memphis, the capital of ancient Egypt, was here; and although Memphis subsequently yielded to Thebes in the south, and Alexandria on the Mediterranean, it retained enough of its past greatness to hand on its tradition of supremacy—and perhaps its name—

through Babylon and Fostât to Cairo, its mediæval successor. To-day the ruins of Memphis can be traced for twenty miles along the west bank of the Nile from Gizeh to Sakkâra. The dwellings of the living were built among the fertile low-lying fields which lay between the river and the desert. At the back of this green fringe, never more than five miles in breadth, rose a low sandy ridge, and upon, and behind, this barren ridge they built the city of their dead; and while the palaces and temples of Memphis have gone, the pyramids which stretch from Gizeh to Dahshûr remain to this day the mightest tombs in the world.

It is from Herodotus, who visited Egypt during the Persian domination in the fifth century before the Christian era, that we get a glimpse of the natural surroundings of ancient Memphis.[1] The narrow strip of land which formed its site was won from the Nile, and westwards of the city the level country, over which the great river spread its water at will, bore the appearance of a lake. The works to which Memphis owed its existence—the construction of an embankment to the south of the city, which thrust the river from its ancient course at the foot of the Lybian or western ridge to its present course which skirts the opposite Arabian Hills, and the drainage of the swampy country to the north by an artificial reservoir or lake—was ascribed to Mena by the priests of Hephæstus (Ptah), to whom he owed his information. And he adds that the embankment, which formed this bend of the Nile above the city, was carefully watched, and repaired every year by the Persian authorities at the time of his visit; since, but for its protection, the whole of Memphis would be in danger of being washed away.[2]

When Egypt expanded southwards and commercial relationships were established, through the Red Sea ports, with India

---

[1] Memphis is the Greek form of the Egyptian name, which is said to be *Men-nofer* (station-good = the "well-founded"). The Coptic form is *Memfi* or *Menfi*, itself a corruption of the Egyptian. In the Bible Memphis appears as *Moth*—translated Memphis, Hos. x. 6; and *Noth*, Jer. ii. 16, &c.

[2] Book ii. 99. εἰ γὰρ ἐθελήσει ῥῆξαι ὑπερβῆναι ὁ ποταμὸς ταύτῃ, κίνδυνος πάσῃ Μέμφι κατακλυσθῆναί ἐστι.

and the east coast of Africa, the centre of government moved
southwards to Thebes; and again, when Egypt was governed by
the Ptolemies, and the influence of Greece became supreme,
Alexandria, which looked across the Mediterranean to Athens
and Antioch and Syracuse, became the centre of the national
life. Nevertheless, even in the age of Augustus, when Egypt
had been incorporated into the system of Rome, Memphis stood
in the first rank of the provincial towns of the Empire. It was
at this epoch—400 years after Herodotus—that Strabo visited
Egypt. When he passed southwards from Alexandria he found
Heliopolis "completely deserted,"[1] but Memphis "was a great
and populous city, second only to Alexandria." It lay on an
incline which sloped from the high grounds on which were built
the temples and palaces, to the level of the plain where the mass
of its houses stood. Here it was edged by groves and lakes;
and again to the northward it was encircled by water. Its population, like that of the surrounding district, was formed of people
of more than one nationality: the palaces of the royal quarter
had become isolated and deserted buildings, but the temples
were as yet maintained, although he notices that the Sphinx
avenues of the Serapeum, which was especially exposed to the
sand-storms of the desert, were partially or entirely embedded
in sand. Besides the temple of Serapis he mentions those of
Apis, which is "identical with Osiris," of Hephaestus, and of
Aphrodite or Selene. Opposite the northern end of Memphis,
on the east bank of the Nile, was Babylon, a fortified post which
had originally been peopled by a colony of Babylonians, but was
now occupied by one of the three divisions of the Roman army
in Egypt. Here he notices the aqueduct with its machinery
for raising water from the Nile, which supplied the Roman encampment, and notices the view of the Pyramids in the midst of
Memphis on the opposite bank.[2]

When the Saracens invaded Egypt in the 17th year of the

---

[1] *Geographica*, C. 805.   [2] C. 807, 808.

Hegira, and 638th of the Christian era, Amr, after the initial conquest of Pelusium, led the forces of the Khalif Omar upon Babylon. "The banks of the Nile," says Gibbon, "in this place of the breadth of 3000 feet, were united by two bridges of sixty and of thirty boats, connected in the middle stream by the small island of Rouda, which was covered by gardens and habitations. The eastern extremity of the bridge was terminated by the town of Babylon and the camp of a Roman legion, which protected the passage of the river and the second capital of Egypt. This important fortress, which might fairly be described as a part of Memphis or Misrah was invested by the arms of the lieutenant of Omar; a reinforcement of 4000 Saracens soon arrived in his camp; and the military engines, which battered the walls, may be imputed to the art and labour of his Syrian allies. Yet the siege was protracted to seven months, and the rash invaders were encompassed and threatened by the inundation of the Nile. Their last assault was bold and successful; they passed the ditch, which had been fortified with iron spikes, applied their scaling-ladders, entered the fortress with the shout of "God is victorious!" and drove the remnant of the Greeks to their boats and the isle of Rouda. The spot was afterwards recommended to the conqueror by the easy communication with the gulf and the peninsula of Arabia; the remains of Memphis were deserted, the tents of the Arabs were converted into permanent habitations, and the first mosque was blessed by the presence of fourscore companions of Mahomet."[1]

Around this mosque, which is said to mark the spot where, a few hundred yards eastward of the walls of Babylon, the tent of the conqueror had been pitched, grew up the first Arab capital of Egypt, thus named Fostât, or the Tent.[2] Two centuries later Ahmed ibn Tulûn, the son of an enfranchised slave, was appointed governor of Egypt by the Khalif of Bagdad. A year later, A.D. 869, he renounced his allegiance, and became Sultan of

---

[1] Gibbon, iii. chap. li.   [2] Literally, "*Skin* tent."

Egypt, thus founding the short-lived dynasty which bears his name. Under his administration Fostât expanded northwards; and at Askar there arose a palace surrounded with gardens, by the side of which was an open space for tournaments and games of arms. In 876 he built on the hill of Kalat-el-Kebsh, or "the Castle of the Ram,"[1] the great mosque which bears his name. A century later (972), when the Fâtimite dynasty was established in Egypt, Gôhar, the General of Muizz, caused a new capital to be constructed still further northwards of Fostât and encircled it with walls. In the centre of this town, which was called El-Kâhira, or "the Victorious,"[2] was erected a palace for the Khalif and barracks for his guards. The Fâtimites traced their descent from Fâtima, the daughter of Mohammed, and "Ali," her husband and cousin, the son of Abu Taleb. In the divisions which subsequently arose from the dissensions which followed the death of the Prophet, the Fâtimites, who recognized Ali as his true successor, were stigmatized as *Shiites*, or heretics, by the orthodox followers of the Abbaside Khalifs. With the establishment, therefore, of the Fâtimite Khalifs at Cairo, both the religious and temporal supremacy of Bagdad was terminated, and a new and splendid era was opened up for Mohammedan Egypt. The capital was the first to benefit by the new order of things; in addition to the magnificent city walls, parts of which are still standing to this day, mosques and public buildings were erected for the first time on a scale commensurate with its dignity. The materials for the embellishment of Cairo were taken in part from the ruins of Memphis; and yet, notwithstanding this work of demolition, which continued for several centuries, so vast were the proportions of the ancient capital of Egypt that its ruins

[1] According to a Mohammedan legend the hill is that upon which Abraham sacrificed a ram, after he had proved his readiness to offer up his son Isaac.
[2] *Cairo* is, of course, a corruption of El-Kâhira. The native name of the city is in full *Masr el-Kâhira*. *Masr*. or *Misr*, the Hebrew *Mazor* (dual misraim = the two Egypts)—possibly connected with *Memphis*—is used by the natives to indicate both the capital and the country of Egypt. *Masr el-Atika* is Old Cairo, i.e. the remains of Fostât and Babylon. *Masr el-Bahri* is Lower Egypt.

continued to excite the wonder and admiration of travellers two centuries after the birth of its mediæval successor.

The foundations of the material greatness of the Arabian capital of Egypt were laid during the two hundred years of the Fâtimite period. It remained only for Salâh-ed-Dín, in 1166, to crown the western spur of the Mokattam Hills with the massive battlements and towers which still frown upon an obsequious city, and for the military dynasties of the Turcoman and Circassian Mamelukes [1] to create the groups of tomb-mosques which lie in the desert respectively to the south and east of the town. The rest of the architectural wealth of Cairo was provided by the individual contributions of successive Sultans, and to this accumulation of religious and secular buildings no significant addition was made after the year 1517, when Egypt lost its independence once more and became a province of the Turkish Empire. The remains of the buildings thus erected constitute what I have called collectively mediæval Cairo. In noticing the position which the native and modern quarters respectively occupy, it will be remembered that we found these latter lying between the remains of mediæval Cairo and the Nile. The reason of this is not far to seek. Although the waters of the Nile had at the date of the foundation of Cairo been more effectively confined than they were in the remote period when Memphis was the capital of Egypt, yet the eastern bank was still so imperfectly protected against inundation that it was impossible for the mediæval city to approach its edge. With the advent of European engineers this danger was finally averted, and the space thus placed at the disposal of Mohammed Ali was used for the construction of the new Cairo. I speak of these older quarters of the town designedly as "mediæval Cairo," because they still present to the eye what

---

[1] The word *mamlûk* means "bought slave." The Mamelukes were purchased in the slave markets of Georgia, the trans-Caspian regions, and the Caucasus, and sold by the Syrian merchants to the Khalifs and their Sultans, by whom they were trained to form a body-guard. These mercenary troops became the chief military resource of the Khalifs, and ultimately ruled in the place of their masters.

is to all intents and purposes the external appearance of the mediæval capital.

This priceless inheritance from the past has been sedulously respected during the period of the British occupation. Not only has the old town been left practically untouched, but provision has been made for preserving the more valuable of its buildings by careful and judicious restoration. The efforts of the Committee for the Preservation of the Monuments of Arabian Art have been restricted by the limited funds which were available for such a purpose; but notwithstanding this difficulty, some of the most significant of the religious and secular buildings have already been more or less completely restored, while others are in course of restoration. Moreover, funds have at length been provided for the erection of a museum of Arabian art in the square of the Palace Mansûr Pasha, through which the great street of Mohammed Ali runs to the Citadel. In this new building, which is actually under construction, the small but representative collection which illustrates the development attained by the Arabian craftsmen of the Middle Ages in the lesser arts of wood carving, metal work, glass work, enamelling, plaster work, and the engraving of freestone and marble, will be adequately and conveniently disposed.[1] At the same time, while the fullest facility is afforded the visitor for inspecting these interesting buildings, suitable regulations have been framed with a view of preventing any abuse of the privilege, or any cause of annoyance to the Mohammedan population.

But however determined the traveller may be to investigate the interesting field of research afforded by mediæval Cairo, he will find certain practical difficulties which stand in his way. In the first place, the streets are dirty and evil-smelling: the roadways, being unpaved, and consisting in great part of accumulated deposits of filth, are swept by clouds of dust—

[1] At present this collection is housed in a temporary building within the walls of the Mosque el-Hâkim, in an exceedingly interesting but somewhat inaccessible quarter of the old town.

this dust being particles of dried filth—while at the same time they are packed by a composite mass of Arabs, camels, and donkeys. In the second place, in the entanglement of these narrow and crooked streets, with their ceaseless stream of noisy and restless humanity, he will not find it easy, even with the assistance of maps and guide-books, to discover the objects of his search. It is quite true that a certain number of the more prominent buildings are visited every day in the season by crowds of tourists. There is no difficulty in finding these, but once outside the beaten track—and many of the most interesting remains of mediæval Cairo are not included in the itinerary of the guides, nor even mentioned in the guide-books—and he will find that a considerable amount both of time and patience must be expended before his object is obtained. Perhaps I may be allowed to illustrate this difficulty by an example drawn from my own experience. The mosque of El-Akmar is one of considerable significance in the history of Saracenic art, yet when I wished to find it, I received no assistance from guide-book or map. I then made inquiries from a competent authority, and received from him what seemed at the time to be very precise directions. Nevertheless, I must have passed the spot indicated half-a-dozen times at least before I descried its ruined minaret behind a block of equally ruinous shops and houses, and I made three successive attempts before I succeeded in making my sketch, so difficult was it to secure the required conditions of light and the necessary freedom from disturbance in the narrow and crowded street of El-Nahhâsin.

For nearly six weeks during the months of December and January scarcely a day passed without my visiting one or other of the ancient quarters of the town. I shall not attempt to give the reader any account of these separate journeys, but I shall present him, in as few words as possible, with some of the broad results of these walks in Cairo, in the hope that my notes, which have at least the merit of being based upon a practical experience, may be of service to him in undertaking similar excursions. In

Looking South from end of the Street el-Nahhâsin
(Minarets of Mûristân of Kalâûn, and Barkûkîyeh)

a sense, every street, almost every house, affords material for
a study. But there are certain remains which can be usefully
considered in groups. The first and most important of these
groups, both intrinsically and because it offers a tolerably complete chain of historical sequence, is the mosques; and these, with
the exception of the mosques of Mohammed Ali and El-Azhar,
I shall reserve for a separate chapter. Second is the group of
military constructions, which includes the gates of the town walls
of the Fâtimite period and the Citadel of Saladin. Third, there
are two or three buildings which do not come under either of
these heads, but which possess an interest either individually or
because they are typical of the class to which they respectively
belong. Lastly, there are the mingled remains of Babylon and
Fostât, which are distinguished as *Masr el-Atîka*, or Old Cairo.

CHAPTER VI

MEDIÆVAL CAIRO

The Citadel—Built by Saladin—Massacre of the Mameluke Beys—Joseph's Well—The mosque of Mohammed Ali—Æsthetic value of the interior—View of Cairo from the Citadel—Chief streets and buildings of mediæval Cairo—The three gates—El-Futûh—En-Nasr—Ez-Zuwêleh—The Kâdi's House—Reform of the religious courts—A caravanserai—Origin of the Bazaars of Cairo—Nâssiri Krosrau's account of the industries of mediæval Cairo—The influence of Persia on Arabic craftsmanship—The Mosque el-Azhar—Condition of the Mohammedan University of Cairo—Signs of reform—"Old Cairo"—The ruins of the Roman station at Babylon—The Coptic Church of Mâri Girgis—Coptic influence on Arabian art—The Mosque of Amr—The site of Fostât—Cairo at sunset.

We made our way to the Citadel on the first morning that was at our disposal after we had reached Cairo. We had been told that the best way of getting a general idea of the city and its surroundings, was to climb to the battlements of Saladin's fortress, and gaze upon the view which they afforded. Our early days in Cairo had been occupied with social matters, which kept us in the European quarters, and we had as yet seen little or nothing that was characteristic of the Arabian capital of Egypt; but now, as we passed up the slight incline where the long street of Mohammed Ali joins the Rumêleh Square, we found walls on either side of us so vast that we craned our necks in vain to catch sight of their crests. To the left was the massive shell of the unfinished Rifaiyeh mosque, which covers the family burial-place of the ex-Khedive Ismaïl; to the right the titanic flank of its vast original, the ancient fane and tomb of Sultan Hasan. For the first time we felt that we were in Cairo—in a centre of El-Islâm equal in significance to Constantinople, Damascus, and Morocco. As we entered the square, the Citadel spread itself before us. Above the towers and battlements of "the fortress of the mountain,"[1] raised by Saladin's faithful minister, the eunuch Bohar ed-Din, seven centuries ago, a great dome rose easily from a square mass of grey stone, between two slender minarets. The giant bulk of the fortress, gateway, walls, battlements, and towers, stood plain in the clear light; but the

BAB EL-AZAB.

dome and the minarets of Mohammed Ali's mosque were veiled in a blue haze, which seemed to lift them into the sky above our heads.

We ascended the curving stairs which led to the gate El-Azab, and passing beneath its vaulted roof climbed to the central space, the summit of the spur, around which the buildings of Saladin's royal residence were grouped. The road, which was

[1] Kala el-Gebel.

narrow and uneven, ran between high walls. This passage, closed at either end, was the trap in which the Mameluke Beys were caught by Mohammed Ali on March 1, 1811. Of the 480 who obeyed the summons all were shot down, with the exception of one, Amin Bey. There are two accounts of the manner in which he effected his escape. According to the romantic account, he leapt his horse through a broken parapet of the wall to the moat beneath, springing from the saddle before the animal crashed upon the ground forty feet below the battlements. The historical is more sober: it tells us that Amin was late, and being warned by the sound of firing as he approached the Citadel, turned his horse's head and galloped in hot haste from the walls. It was a violent and bloody remedy—this massacre of the last representatives of the Circassian Guards—the girdle (*halka*) that had first encircled and then strangled the person of the Khalif; but it delivered Egypt from the most shameless of her foreign oppressors.

Saladin's palace, erected on the crown of the hill in the centre of the circle of walls and towers, has gone, and in its place stands the alabaster mosque of Mohammed Ali. Northwards, and below the mosque, is the open space to which we climbed. The eastern side was occupied by the battered wall of the old mosque of the Sultan Kalaûn, built by his son En-Nâsir in 1317; northwards, and below, was an inner line of walls pierced by two gates, of which one led to the great Bâb el-Gedîd—the new gate—now the chief entrance to the Citadel, and the second gave access to the barracks where the Seaforth Highlanders were housed. The west side was also closed by a wall through which a third gate led to the Western Battery. In the centre of this bare, stony space was the guard-tent, with a group of Highlanders, whose flashing weapons and bright kilts gave a touch of colour and movement to the scene.

First we retraced our steps, past the northern and eastern façades of the mosque of Kalaûn, to the broken door which admits the stranger to the mighty shaft which Saladin sunk to supply his fortress with water. Passing through a dark passage cut in the rock, we descended, with the assistance of two Arabs with lighted candles, until we stood in a gallery. As we grasped uneasily the wooden rails, which alone protected us from the black depths below, we looked down into the huge square shaft that pierced through the limestone rock to the soft sand, 280 feet below. The actual well—Joseph's Well it is called—was here; we could see a glimmer of light reflected from the water, but we felt no desire to descend the gruesome passage which

THE CENTRAL COURT OF THE CITADEL.

led down the shaft, and investigate it more closely. In spite of the protests of our guides, we hurried past the disused sâkiyeh, by which the water was raised, and emerged thankfully into the light of day.

The name requires a word of explanation. The famous Kurdish mercenary, who made himself master of Egypt on the death of the feeble Adid, the last of the line of Fâtimite Khalifs, is known in history as Saladin: but his actual style and title was Saleh ed-Din, Yûsuf ibn Eyyûb—Joseph the son of Job.

Saviour of the Faith. According to the tradition, an ancient well was discovered during the construction of the Citadel, and this well, reconstructed and improved by the great square shaft, was called "Joseph's Well" in honour of its restorer. At the same time the original well has been identified by a Jewish legend as the well in which Joseph was cast by his envious brethren, when they journeyed to the ancient capital of Egypt to seek for corn. And thus the name has a double significance.

The third of the three gates of the Citadel, the Bâb el-Gebel, or the Mountain Gate, so called because it leads directly to the Mokattam Hills, lies at the end of a narrow passage, which turns northwards from Joseph's Well. It is the smallest of the three, and stands in the angle of the eastern walls. As we stood on the sandy path beyond the gate we were astonished to find how near the red cliffs of the range, crowned by the Turkish fort, seemed from this point, and to note how far the lofty battlements of the Citadel stretched eastward.

Returning by the same uneven paths, we found ourselves once more in the bare space below the alabaster mosque. We entered by the east corner of the courtyard, donning the clumsy slippers which the attendants offered us. On all four sides there were colonnades with alabaster pillars, and the dome which covered the fountain of purification—the Hanefiyeh—in the centre, rested upon columns of the same material. This alabaster —used so freely for the internal and external decoration of the building that it has given it the name of the "alabaster" mosque —was brought from the quarries of Benisuéf. The mosque was commenced by Mohammed Ali on the site of the old palace, which was destroyed in 1824; but it was not completed until 1857, in the time of Said Pasha, Ali's fourth son. The tomb of Mohammed Ali lies just to the right of the entrance which leads from the outer court to the domed interior. It is covered by a splendid piece of drapery, and enclosed within a massive screen of gilt bronze. In a sense this mosque, as being the burial-place of the founder of the present dynasty, is the official place of worship of the Khedive, and as such it is visited by him in state on the great festivals recognized by the Mohammedan religion. On these occasions the Khedive enters by a separate door, which is in the centre of the north façade, and occupies a seat of state within the Prayer Recess.

The mosque of Mohammed Ali is too recent a building to possess any historical importance; but it is not by any means wholly barren of æsthetic significance. Its architect was Yúsuf

GUARD-TENT OF THE SEAFORTHS.

Boshna, a Greek of Constantinople, who reproduced in it the form of the Nuri Osmaniyeh mosque, which is itself one of a group of mosques at Constantinople based upon the model of Constantine's Cathedral, the church—now the mosque—of St. Sophia. While the actual building is marred as a piece of architecture by the frigidness of a literal copy, it is none the less admirable as the crown and completion of the ancient pile of buildings in the centre of which it rears its gracious dome and slender minarets.

The plan of the mosque is very simple. The anterior court to the west, and the domed interior to the east, are both quadrangles of almost equal size, except for the fact that the colonnades which surround both alike are placed inside the former—the anterior court, and outside the latter—the domed interior. The quadrangle of the interior, which is thus slightly smaller than that of the courtyard, is broken only by the Prayer Recess, which is carried forward from the eastern side. Four massive columns, advanced about one-fifth inwards, carry the central dome. At each corner of the quadrangle four lesser domes rise between the central columns and the outer walls. The spaces uncovered by the central dome and these four lesser domes are filled by half domes, which fall from the base of the central dome to the level of the outer walls. The projecting Prayer Recess on the east side is covered by two-thirds of a separate dome, which springs from the half dome on the east. Seen from the outside, the roof presents the appearance of a natural group of domes, or rather of a parent dome surrounded by its children. From the inside, the effect produced is that of a vast single vault, since the skilful transitions from the central to the lesser domes prevent the eye from distinguishing its separate members. The æsthetic significance of a roof so constructed is considerable, for this system of covering resembles the natural dome of the heavens more than any other. The furnishing of a Mohammedan house of prayer tends to strengthen the effect of spaciousness thus produced. If the spectator stands a foot or two within the entrance, his eye will range almost without interruption over the entire space which is enclosed by the walls of the quadrangle; for though the four columns which support the central dome are of necessity vast in themselves, in this wide space they scarcely seem to break the view. Moreover, being absolutely simple in construction, they offer nothing—not even a moulding or a cornice—to invite the eye, except the three necessary lines of the angle formed by the two surfaces they present. In the half light of the interior, the meanness of the decorations which embellish the surfaces of the roof are unperceived, and the effect of spaciousness produced by the wide stretch of floor, unbroken, save for the rich colouring of the ample carpets, by any furnishings, is heightened by the dim reds and blues, which give an atmosphere to the upward-heaving curves of the hierarchy of domes. Standing beneath these lofty and spreading surfaces the spectator can find a partial significance even for the chains of glass globes, and the chandeliers of tarnished crystals, which are the ungainly means by which the edifice is lighted when religious ceremonies are held at night.

On the south side of the mosque of Mohammed Ali there is a triangular space, which narrows westwards to a terrace running between the wall of the mosque and the battlements of the Citadel.

CAIRO FROM THE MOKATTAM HILLS.

Its southward base is closed by a nest of dilapidated buildings, once a palace of the Khedive, with offices for his ministers of state. From the end of this terrace the visitor commands an unbroken view southwards to the Pyramids of Dahshur, and westwards to the Delta. It was for this that we had come, and we sat down upon the rude stone seats that we might enjoy the prospect at our leisure. While we did so, other pilgrims came to worship at the same shrine of beauty. There were Germans, who exclaimed in guttural "achs," as they peered over the parapet with their field-glasses, and Americans, with a profane explanation for every marvel; and Tommy Atkins was there too, telling the friend he was showing round, what "we"—meaning Tommy and his gallant comrades—did and suffered while they made their home in Saladin's Citadel. In the intervals, when we were free from the gutturals, and the chatter, and Tommy's stolid sentences, we also gazed over the parapet, and this is what we saw.

Immediately beneath—for we seemed to be projected beyond the intervening roofs and towers—stretched a multitudinous sea of pink and white, brown and purple surfaces, with here and there a patch of green, broken by minarets and domes. Northwards it joined the green plain of the Delta, southwards it touched the yellow sands of the desert. Between the Lybian Hills on the western horizon and the city, a riband of emerald verdure, rent with shining spaces, marked the course of the Nile. Long after its waters were merged in the green plain of the Delta, the white-peaked sails that floated on its bosom revealed its unseen curves. Southwards the grey summits of the Pyramids of Gizeh showed above the bank of mist, which floated from the fields still rank with moisture from the autumn flood.

The "fortress of the mountain" was not the sole contribution which Saladin made to the embellishment of mediaeval Cairo. He caused fresh walls to be constructed round the south-western quarters, which had hitherto remained unprotected; and for the new works thus designed, as well as for the Citadel, he brought materials from the small pyramid at Gizeh. Moreover, being a *Sunnite*,[1] or orthodox Mussulman, and, in fact, the representative of the Abbaside Khalifs, he and the succeeding Sultans of the Eyyubite dynasty caused the erection of many colleges in which the four cardinal doctrines of the orthodox creed were taught.

Saladin's design for the enlargement of the city walls was only partially accomplished; and the three splendid gates which exist to-day are remains of the original line of fortifications constructed in the Fâtimite period.

Here it will be convenient for me to sketch the position of the chief streets and buildings in that quarter of the old town, to which I shall mainly refer. I have already remarked, that if a

[1] *i.e.*, following the "tradition" (*sunna*).

line is drawn from the railway station to the Citadel, the native quarters will be found for the most part in the eastern half of the area thus divided. But the most crowded and interesting district is the north-eastern section which is contained between the line of the sacred canal El-Khalig (which has recently been filled up at the instance of the sanitary authorities), on the west, and the desert on the east; while northwards it is terminated by the line of the city walls marked by the Gates of "Conquest" and of "Vic-

STREET OF BÁB EL-WEZÎR.

tory," and southwards, by the Muaiyad Mosque and the Gate ez-Zuwêleh. The dense network of streets thus indicated is entered from the European town by the Muski, which, with its continuation, the *Rue Neuve*, traverses the native town from the Ezbekiyeh Gardens on the west, to the Windmill Hill, behind which lie the Tombs of the Khâlifs, on the east. At right angles to this modern thoroughfare a line of streets, narrow in themselves, but broad in comparison with their neighbours, run from the Bâb ez-Zuwêleh on the south, to the Mosque el-Hâkim and the adjacent city walls on the north. On either side of this line of streets, which constituted in fact the main thoroughfare of mediaeval Cairo, are a series of mosques and other buildings of special interest. The bazaars are reached by narrow passages which strike right and left from this central thoroughfare; and the Mosque el-Azhar, the Mohammedan University, lies only a hundred yards or so southwards of the *Rue Neuve*.

The three gates, which still remain, are important as affording examples of the high degree of excellence which was attained during the Fâtimite period (972–1171) in the use of freestone as a building material. Nâssîri Khosrau, who travelled in Egypt and other Oriental countries, in speaking of the palace which was constructed for the first Fâtimite Khalif, El-Muizz, when Masr el-Kâhira was founded, says that the "separate stones were so admirably bound together that its walls seemed to consist of a single block."[1] This building dates from the year 970, and its construction marked the commencement of an epoch in which freestone came to be substituted for brick as the material in common use for public edifices. The three gates were constructed more than a hundred years later, in 1091, by three brothers, foreign architects, who were brought to Cairo by Bedr el-Jemâli, the Governor of Damascus, who was himself summoned to Egypt to exercise the office of Chief Vizier to the Khalif el-Mustansir. Of these the Bâb el-Futûh, or Gate of Conquest, is a remarkably complete example of the military architecture of the period of the Crusades, which was, of course, based upon the Roman models. Between the inner and the outer gates is a vaulted entrance; and the external approach is protected by two long flanking walls terminating in rounded towers. In addition to the fineness of the masonry, the mouldings of the archway, enclosing richly sculptured arabesques, and, in fact, every one of the many decorative details, are distinguished by the perfection of their workmanship. The Bâb en-Nasr, or Gate of Victory, which lies

[1] Translated by Charles Schefer, Paris, 1881, p. 129.

The Bâb en-Nasr

on the other side of the Mosque el-Hákim, is remarkable not so
much for its architecture as for the picture of Oriental life which
it affords. During the two or three hours that I sat sketching its
square towers, many characteristic incidents of Oriental life were
enacted before my eyes. There was a lively chaffering and gossip
around the booths which stood outside the gate; black-robed
women, balancing water-pots upon their heads, passed through
its portals to their homes within the walls; mules and camels
came laden with fruit or clover from the fields outside, and more
than once a funeral procession, with its weird chanting, swept
past me to the adjacent cemetery. The Báb ez-Zuwêleh—which
derives its name from the tribe so called which settled in Egypt
under the Fátimites—is at present being carefully restored by the
Arabian Monuments Committee. It amply justifies this expenditure, for it is not too much to say that it affords the most
beautiful "street scene" in mediæval Cairo. It is built at the
south-eastern corner of the mosque of El-Muaiyad, and above its
double portal—for it is built in two stories—it carries the two
exquisite minarets of this mosque. As I looked down the Suk-
kariey, which runs by the eastern side of the great mosque to the
Báb ez-Zuwêleh, I found before my eyes a scene the like of which
—for beauty of architectural forms, for richness of colouring, and
for fulness and variety of human interest—I have never seen in
any other city in the world.

The Báb ez-Zuwêleh closes the southern extremity of the
line of streets which runs, as we have seen, northwards to the
Báb el-Futûh. Two hundred yards northwards of the point
where it intersects with the Muski and *Rue Neuve*, there is a
group of mosques, including the Mûristân of Kaláûn, which is of
special importance. This group stands on the west side at the
commencement of the Shâria el-Nahhâsin, and opposite it there
is a short street leading eastwards to an open space in which is
the Bêt el-Kâdi, or residence of the religious judge. By the
entrance in the right-hand corner there stands a smart native
policeman on duty; none the less some part at least of this

ancient courthouse was built in the age of Saladin. As I sat opposite making my sketch, I could see a crowd of litigants sitting, or rather squatting, upon the floor of the wide open veranda, the roof of which is supported by ancient pillars, while others stood or sat in a row against the wall beside the entrance. Apart from the interest which attaches to the building itself, on account of its antiquity, the tribunal of which it is the seat deserves a word of comment. The religious courts, or

BÊT EL-KÂDI.

Mehkemeh Sheraieh, over which the Kâdi presides, are the last of the native tribunals to have been reformed.[1] Up to the present year they have preserved their mediæval flavour with singular success. The regulations which the Government framed for the direction of the Kâdi were ineffectual. "Unfortunately," Mr. M'Ilwraith writes, "these courts have displayed a marked disinclination to depart in any way from their traditional methods of procedure. As an instance of this pertinacious conservatism,

[1] See p. 66.

The Bâb ez-Zuwêleh

I may mention the circumstance that though the regulations provide that each case shall be conducted regularly, step by step, until its conclusion—statement of claim, defence, and judgment—in order that, so far as possible, each several case may be disposed of in rotation, the Kádis prefer to hear the statement of claims in five, ten, twenty cases, one after the other, and then adjourn till a future sitting for the hearing of a corresponding string of defences. It is difficult to imagine how, under such circumstances, justice can be done in any particular case, or, indeed, what security there is that the right defence will be attributed to its respective statement of claim."

In addition to deciding questions of marriage, divorce, and succession, these courts included offices where deeds were registered and deposited for safe keeping. Writing of the Somerset House of Cairo—this very Bêt el-Kádi—Mr. M'Ilwraith continues: " It would be impossible for any one who has not paid a visit to the repository of these archives to form any idea of the aspect they presented. Piles of crumbling mildewed documents are heaped up in every corner of the room, apparently without any attempt at arrangement or classification. Numbers of these sacks of paper, many of which fell to pieces on being touched, have lain undisturbed in the same corner for centuries. Yet they are all title-deeds of more or less value, Hodgets and Waktiehs, often of great importance to the parties interested. Such a thing as an index or a catalogue was inexistent, and it is difficult to understand how any one could ever obtain a copy of a particular document concerning him. Indeed, I believe, it is admitted that the functionary hitherto in charge was the only human being who could find his way about these archives."[1]

From the Bêt el-Kádi the traveller can make his way through some dark and evil-smelling, but withal charming, streets, to the Báb el-Nasr. In one of these, the Sháriá el-Gamáliyeh, there is an ancient *Okella* or caravanserai. The arch of the deep gateway is richly decorated, and the heavy chains which secured

[1] Quoted by Lord Cromer in his report (1899).

the merchandise of the caravan are still suspended across the doors; while above the entrance there is a fine *mushrebiyeh*. This term, which is used to denote the projecting wooden balconies, that form so characteristic a feature of the Arabian house, requires a word of explanation. The word itself appears to be derived from *el-Sharb*, the action of drinking: and it means literally "the place of drinking." The actual mushrebiyeh is the little round, or hexagonal, projection in which the *Kulleh*, or water-bottle, is placed to cool; but the name has been transferred to the whole balcony, the sides of which are constructed of turned wood like those of the original projections in which the water-bottles are placed. The use of the word has also been extended to denote any kind of turned woodwork of the same character as the sides, or windows, of the balcony; and it is also used in speaking of the small projecting balconies which are found on the first storey of the minarets. In the days of caravans the okella was a building of considerable importance. The chambers were grouped round an open courtyard, in the centre of which there was a simple place of prayer. The merchandise and beasts were bestowed in the vaulted chambers which opened on to the ground floor; the merchants and their servants were lodged in the rooms to which access was gained from the gallery above. In the smaller towns such buildings are still used to-day by traders, who bring their produce from the villages for the weekly markets. Such persons pay a small sum for the night's lodging, and cook the food which they provide for themselves at a common stove in the court.

The Bazaars of Cairo are too numerous and familiar to require any description in detail. But it is interesting to remember that they are survivals of institutions, which were established at a period when the wares, which the craftsmen of mediæval Cairo produced, were unrivalled alike for workmanship and for artistic grace. The word "bazaar" is Persian, and as such it supplies a further link in the interesting chain of evidence which goes to show how largely the craftsmen of mediæval Cairo

were indebted to Persian art for the motives and methods of some of their most important industries.

The Fâtimite Khalifs, under whose rule the mediæval Cairo was founded, were allied through their religious views with the people of this country; and apart from the direct evidence which is afforded by a study of the special arts of metal-work and pottery, this fact alone makes it at least probable that Persian artists should have contributed to the industrial development

THE KHÂN EL-KHALÎL BAZAAR.

fostered by the Shiite Khalifs of Egypt. But from whatever source the craftsmen of Cairo derived their first impulses, there is no question as to the extraordinary excellence to which they attained in these branches of the lesser arts which have been already enumerated. One or two sentences from the writings of the mediæval traveller from whom I have before quoted, will serve to give us a glimpse of the variety and perfection of the works which graced the bazaars of mediæval Cairo. This traveller, the Persian Nâssîri Khosrau, who traversed almost all the countries of the East, between the years 1035 and 1042, writes with enthusiasm of Cairo. Of its potteries he says: "Earthenware of all sorts is manufactured at Misr; it is so fine and so transparent that the hand which holds a vase is seen through the sides. The bowls, cups, plates, and other utensils which they produce are decorated with colours similar to those of the stuff called Bûgalemûn [a material woven in the neighbourhood of Thineh in Egypt]; that is to say, the shades change in accordance with the position in which the vase is placed." Of the manufacture of glass he writes, "A transparent glass of great beauty, having the effect of the emerald, is produced, which is sold by weight"; and again, in illustration of the abundance of the pottery and glass which he found in Cairo, he says: "In the bazaar the sellers of drugs and of metal wares themselves provide the glasses, the vases, and the paper in which the goods which they sell are to be placed or wrapped. The buyer, therefore, need not trouble himself to provide anything to hold the wares which he purchases." In Cairo at this period the difficult art of enamelling glass was perfectly understood; and it is probable that the Venetian industry, which maintains its monopoly to this day, was founded by craftsmen imported from the Arabian capital. Many exquisite lamps of enamelled glass have been gathered from the mosques, and are preserved to-day in the Arabian museum. Abundant evidence of the beauty and variety of the metal-work produced by the artists of mediæval Cairo is afforded by the doors and furniture of the mosques. Literature, however, alone tells us of the marvels which this industry produced in its earliest period, when the Cairene craftsmen were directly under the influence of the Persian models. At this time not only were the designs engraved upon metals drawn from animal life, but the forms of the animals themselves, cocks, peacocks, gazelles, and the like, were reproduced life-size in gold, inlaid with precious stones. None of these gorgeous and fantastic works have been preserved; but the Arabian chroniclers provide us with inventories, which enable us to form an idea of their splendour. But, while the modern traveller cannot see the throne of pure gold and silver, decorated with scenes from the chase, surrounded by borders which enclosed inscriptions, made for the young Sultan El-Mustansir, that filled Nässiri with admiration on the occasion of his visit to the palace of the Fätimites, he cannot go far among the mosques without stumbling upon some magnificent door, covered with plates of bronze exquisitely inlaid with gold and silver. He will also notice the pulpits and Kurân-stands of carved wood, decorated with designs formed by incrustations of ivory and ebony. But this last art, the art of wood-carving and decoration in all its branches, requires no comment: for it is the one art which has survived from the mediaeval city, and as such it can be studied in the workshops of the Cairo of to-day.

The Mosque el-Azhar, or "the Blooming," was the first building of its kind erected in the Fätimite period. Like the palace, it was built by Gohar, the general and vizier of the first Fätimite Khalif Muizz, in 973; that is to say, shortly after the foundation of the city itself. Fifteen years later it was made the seat of a university by the Khalif el-Aziz, the son of Muizz, who was distinguished by the impulse which he gave to the development of science and the arts in the new capital of Egypt. Since this time the building has been more than once restored and enlarged, but the central court still bears witness by its Persian arches[1] to the close connection which then existed between Persia and Egypt. But the antiquarian importance of the building is overshadowed by the wider interest which attaches to it as being the seat of the great Mohammedan university, that continued throughout the Middle Ages to be the centre of the scientific knowledge of the world. The Mosque el-Azhar is frequented to this day by thousands of Mohammedan students; but the attainments of its professors, and their methods of teaching, are absolutely puerile. The fact is that the Arabic literature, upon which

[1] As I was provided with a permission from the Wakfs Administration to sketch the interiors of the mosques, I was able to make a drawing of one side of this court, with the arches in question.

its studies are based, was arrested in its growth five hundred years ago; and it is impossible, therefore, to convey any knowledge of even the commonest facts of life, as we know them now, through the medium of literary Arabic. In the Government schools, geography, history, and mathematics are taught out of text-books written in French or English. In the meanwhile the

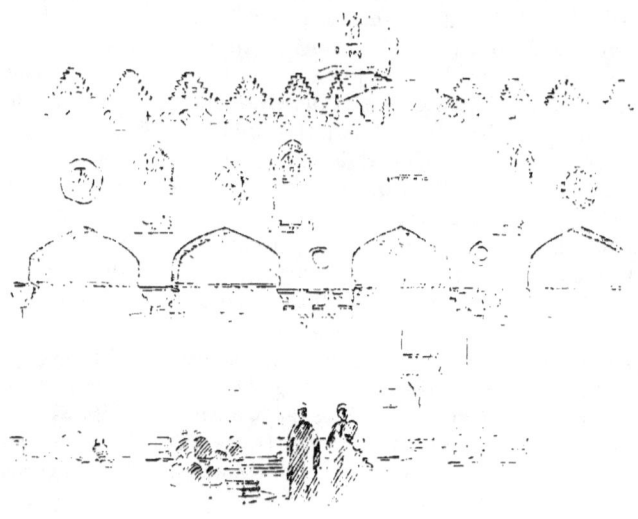

INTERIOR OF THE COURT OF EL-AZHAR.

El-Azhar mosque affords the curious spectacle of an ancient university, so crystallized by tradition that it employs to this day the literature and scholastic methods with which it was equipped in the Middle Ages.

At the present moment, the youth of Egypt are provided by the Government primary school with an education far in advance of any which their ancient and famous university can offer them.

To teach the Egyptians of the nineteenth century by the methods employed by the Shékhs of the University is as though one were to harness a camel to a train and expect it to do the work of the locomotive. Nevertheless, even in this stronghold of Mohammedan tradition the first signs of reform have appeared. In 1897 the authorities of the University of el-Azhar applied to the Education Department for the services of thirteen masters from the Government schools to give instruction in mathematics, geography, map-drawing, and history. Referring to the fact thus mentioned in the previous report, Lord Cromer now writes: " I am informed that this new departure has produced satisfactory results, but the university is in no way under the control of the Department of Public Instruction, and any outside interference with its administration is viewed with so much jealousy that it is difficult to express any trustworthy opinion on this subject. So far, however, as I am able to judge, there appears to be some slight movement in the direction of adapting the teaching at this ancient institution to modern requirements. This tendency should, of course, be encouraged by all reasonable and practicable means. I doubt whether it has so far acquired sufficient strength to be considered a very potent agency in the direction of reform."[1]

A brief description of Masr el-Atika, or Old Cairo, must conclude my account of mediæval Cairo. The little town thus distinguished lies about a mile south of modern Cairo (with which it is connected both by rail and tramway) on the east bank of the Nile, facing Gizeh. Beside the fact that it contains the little that remains of Fostât, the original Mohammedan capital, it is here that we find the ruins of the walls of the Roman station at Babylon which guarded the bridges across the Nile that led to Memphis. And, moreover, in the centre of the nest of antique dwellings which have been built under and over the Roman walls, the oldest of the Coptic churches of Egypt— styled Mâri Girgis, or St. George—is hidden away.

[1] Report, 1899.

These dwellings—to speak first of Babylon, or the *Kasr el-Shamâa*, as it is called to-day—are inhabited almost exclusively by Copts. The visitor might easily pass them by, for all that he sees, when he emerges from the narrow streets of the Mohammedan town to the open space beyond the station of St. George on the Helwân line, is the broken masonry of the Roman walls, mingled with the square fronts of some modern buildings which belong to the Greek Church. The church of Mâri Girgis lies directly at the back of this hospital, and it is in the very centre of the Coptic nest, which is entered by a low postern in the Roman wall to the north. Passing through this doorway, which is reached by a slightly descending path, we entered a dark passage that seemed not more than three or four feet in width, although it was in fact the main thoroughfare of the Coptic town. On either side we passed narrow entrances leading to the antique houses, among which the massive walls and rounded arches of the original Roman structures appeared. Taking one of the doors to the left, we went down into the church. This building, which is obviously of great antiquity, is said to have been constructed before the invasion of Egypt by the Saracens. Possibly this is true only of the crypt, into which we descended by a narrow flight of steps from the choir. The vaulted roof was supported by slender marble columns, which contrasted curiously with the rude masonry around them. Like the pillars of the church itself, they had obviously been appropriated from buildings of the Greek or Roman periods. At the east end was the circular niche which marks the spot where, according to tradition, the Virgin and Child rested on their way to Egypt: while a second niche in the south wall is said to have been the couch of St. Joseph. But whatever may be the precise antiquity of the building, it is valuable as affording unmistakable evidence of the close similarity which is to be observed between the details of the early mosques and those of the Coptic churches. Thus in the sanctuary of this church there is a rounded niche which is in all respects identical with the *Kibla*, or prayer niche, of the mosques. Moreover, it is impossible for one familiar with the mosques to visit the interior of this church without being struck by the manner in which its general features resemble the prevalent arrangements of the religious buildings raised by the Mohammedans in Egypt. It is not necessary to seek any additional proof of the extent to which the early Arabian sculptors were indebted to the Coptic or Egypto-Byzantine models already existing in Egypt for their decorative motives. Signal evidence of this—if the fact needed such evidence—is provided by the collection of Coptic sculptures, which is placed in the Museum of Egyptian Antiquities at Gizeh.

THE MOSQUE OF AMR.

The mosque of Amr lies about six hundred yards northwards of Old Cairo; and the path which leads to it passes through a region of rubbish heaps and sandy wastes. The sole interest which this dismal and unsavoury region could afford us arose from the ovens of the Kulleh potteries, with their rows of grey clay water-jars and basins set out to dry in front of them. The front of the mosque, with its ruined minaret and whitewashed façade, was as grotesque and desolate as its surroundings. But within, the great colonnaded courtyard seemed pleasant in spite of its broken columns and decaying walls; for it had been planted with trees, and the Hanafiyeh in the centre was shaded by the tall palm-tree, whose feathery head we had seen before we entered. There is, of course, no trace of the original building which Amr caused to be erected immediately after the conquest of Egypt had been effected, since, in fact, more than one mosque subsequently erected on the same site has been destroyed by fire, earthquake, or by the inundation of the Nile. The present building is therefore chiefly interesting as marking the site of the first Mohammedan capital of Egypt, but, at the same time, it presents an example of the earliest form of mosque, in which the chief feature was the colonnaded court open to the air, with its deep eastern Liwân or sanctuary.

After we had returned from the mosque of Amr to the ruins of Babylon, we climbed the dreary mound which lies behind them to the south to watch the sunset. In spite of the sordid masses of débris immediately around us, the view which we thus obtained was one of singular significance. At our feet were the three ruins which recalled three separate developments of life upon this bank of the Nile. The rounded towers were the sole survival of the Roman station of Babylon, the Coptic buildings were the memorials of the last manifestation of the corporate existence of the ancient inhabitants of Egypt, and the mosque of Amr, with its twisted walls and broken minaret, marked the place where the Mohammedan conqueror first pitched his tent in the valley of the Nile. To the left, the gardens and fields which edge both banks of the river showed green, and the river itself, seen from this height, spread an ample surface of shining waters. Beyond, in the distance, were the familiar forms of the Pyramids of Gizeh, with the Lybian Hills behind them. To the right, above the grey sands of the intervening desert and the white line of the roofs of Cairo, were the towers and walls of Saladin's fortress, crowned, as always, by the slender minarets and gracious domes of the alabaster mosque. The brown walls of the Fortress of the Mountain were coloured by distance to a delicate rose, and the arid crest of the Mokattam Hills behind them was touched to a marvellous crimson. As the sun fell lower, and the hollows of the hills and the recesses of the buildings grew shaded, an exquisite violet of the tint of heliotrope was mingled with the rosy surfaces of the Citadel walls and the crimson crest of the range: while the palms which fringed the Nile showed opalesque above the tawny walls and roofs at our feet.

CHAPTER VII

THE MOSQUES, AS ILLUSTRATING THE DEVELOPMENT OF ARABIAN ART IN EGYPT

Origin of Arabian art—Byzantine principles—Coptic models—Earliest period, 640-876—Origin and elements of the mosque—The mosque of Tulûn—Second period, 876-972—Fâtimite period, 972-1171—Mosques of El-Azhar, &c.—Development of "colonnaded" mosque—Persian influence—First example of Arabian portal at El-Akmar—Stucco decoration and wood-carving—Eyyubite period, 1171-1250—Introduction of (cruciform) college-mosque—Influence of Crusades—Development of "stalactite" pendentives—Period of Turkoman Mamelukes, 1250-1382—Use of Gothic forms in mosques of period—Development of lesser arts in Cairo—Introduction of dome—Creation of characteristic Arabian façade—Richness of internal decoration and furniture—Use of marble—Absence of distinctive Arabian column—Period of Circassian Mamelukes, 1382-1517—Completion of evolution of mosque—Kuttâb and Sebîl added—Perfection of exterior form-Mosques of period—Include "Tomb-Mosques"—Tombs of the Khalîfs—Sunset from Windmill Hill.

ALTHOUGH Egypt was conquered under the second of the successors of Mohammed, the Khalîf Omar, it remained for nearly 250 years practically outside the main stream of Mohammedan life. During this period, lasting from A.D. 689 to A.D. 870, it was governed by numerous representatives of the Omayyad and Abbaside Khalîfs, whose capital cities were respectively Damascus and Bagdad. Under the Abbasides the narrow traditions of the early Khalîfs were abandoned, and a policy of enlightened cosmopolitanism introduced an era of industrial and artistic development throughout the Mohammedan world. The nature and results of this policy are well described by Gibbon in the following passage. I quote it at length, because the facts which it embodies furnish a point of departure from which we can conveniently set out upon a brief survey of the growth of Saracenic art in Cairo:—

"Under the reign of the Ommiades, the studies of the Moslems were confined to the interpretation of the Koran, and the eloquence and poetry of their native tongue. A people continually exposed to the dangers of the field, must esteem the healing power of medicine, or rather of surgery; but the starving physicians of Arabia murmured a complaint, that exercise and temperance deprived them of the greatest part of their practice. After their civil and domestic wars, the subjects of the Abbasides, awakening (A.D. 754 and 813) from this mental lethargy, found leisure and felt curiosity for the acquisition of profane science. This spirit was first encouraged by the Caliph Almansor, who, besides his knowledge of the Mahometan law, had applied himself with success to the study of astronomy. But when the sceptre devolved to Almamon, the seventh of the Abbasides, he completed the designs of his grandfather, and invited the muses from their ancient seats. His ambassadors at Constantinople, his agents in Armenia, Syria, and Egypt, collected the volumes of Grecian science; at his command they were translated by the most skilful interpreters into the Arabic language; his subjects were exhorted assiduously to peruse these instructive writings: and the successor of Mahomet assisted with pleasure and modesty at the assemblies and deputations of the learned. 'He was not ignorant,' says Abulpharagius, 'that *they* are the elect of God, his best and most useful servants, whose lives are devoted to the improvement of their rational faculties. The mean ambition of the Chinese or the Turks may glory in the industry of their hands or the indulgence of their brutal appetites. Yet these dexterous artists must view, with hopeless emulation, the hexagons and pyramids of the cells of a beehive: these fortitudinous heroes are awed by the superior fierceness of the lions and tigers. The teachers of wisdom are the true luminaries and legislators of a world, which, without their aid, would again sink in ignorance and barbarism.' The zeal and curiosity of Almamon were imitated by succeeding princes of the line of Abbas; their rivals, the Fatimites of Africa and the Ommiades of Spain, were the patrons of the learned, as well as the commanders of the faithful: the same royal prerogative was claimed by their independent emirs of the provinces: and their emulation diffused the taste and the rewards of science from Samarcand and Bochara to Fez and Cordova. The visit of a Sultan consecrated a sum of 200,000 pieces of gold to the foundation of a college at Bagdad, which he endowed with an annual revenue of 15,000 dinars. The fruits of instruction were communicated, perhaps at different times, to 6000 disciples of every degree, from the son of the noble to that of the mechanic; a sufficient allowance was provided for the indigent scholars: and the merit or industry of the professors was repaid with adequate stipends. In every city the productions of Arabic literature were copied and collected by the curiosity of the studious and the vanity of the rich. A private doctor refused the invitation of the Sultan of Bochara, because the carriage of his books would have required 400 camels. The royal library of the Fatimites consisted of 100,000 manuscripts, elegantly transcribed and splendidly bound, which were lent, without jealousy or avarice, to the students of Cairo. Yet this collection must appear moderate, if we can believe that the Ommiades of Spain had formed a library of 600,000 volumes, forty-four of which were employed in the mere catalogue. Their capital, Cordova, with the adjacent towns of Malaga, Almeria, and Murcia, had given birth to more than 300 writers, and above 70 public libraries were opened in the cities of the Andalusian kingdom. The age of Arabian learning continued about 500 years, till the great eruption of the Moguls, and was coeval with the darkest and most slothful period of European annals; but since the sun of science has arisen in the West, it should seem that the Oriental studies have languished and declined."[1]

The remains which illustrate this early period are very scanty.

---

[1] Gibbon, vol. iii. chap. lii.

They consist of the inscriptions and designs which have been found on tombs and coffins, revealed by excavations conducted among the mounds of débris which lie to the south of Cairo; and these remains are identical with those afforded by the Coptic monuments. Possibly buildings were constructed whose ruins have only helped to swell the dust-heaps which cover the site of Fostât; but it is more probable that, with the exception of the mosque of Amr, no considerable edifices were erected by Arabian architects, until the time when, under the Sultan Ahmed ibn Tulûn, Egypt assumed the rôle of an independent Mohammedan state. Here then we have the two cardinal facts which determine the origin of the Saracenic art of Egypt. On the one hand, there is the fact that the Mohammedan world had become familiarized with Byzantine art and Byzantine culture; and on the other, the fact that the earliest examples of the work of Arabian artists show what are, to all intents and purposes, Coptic designs. As Coptic art was merely local Byzantine, we may conclude that a knowledge of Byzantine principles, aided by the practical experience which was afforded by a study of the Coptic buildings in which these principles had already been applied, was the source from which the Arabian architects drew their earliest inspirations.

With the Saracens architecture came to include both painting and sculpture as well as many of the lesser arts; and the mosque was the most typical and perfect of their buildings. In tracing, therefore, the evolution of this building, we can scarcely fail to make ourselves acquainted with most, if not all, of the more significant characteristics of Saracenic art in Egypt.

The germ of the mosque [1] is the *mosalla*, which is merely a space of ground preserved from pollution by an enclosure, and set in the direction of Mecca. The earliest form of mosque reproduces

[1] The word *mesgid*, from which "mosque" is derived through the French *mosquée*, means literally a place of "falling down" in prayer; and it is applied properly to the congregational mosque as opposed to the college mosque, or *medresêh*. Every religious edifice, however, is designated in colloquial Arabic by the word *gâmia*.

the mosalla on a large scale. It consists of a rectangular court, which is open to the air, surrounded on three sides by colonnades, and on the fourth—the side which faces the holy city—by a sanctuary, or principal Liwán. The earliest of the existing examples of this form is the mosque which the Sultan Tulún caused to be constructed in 876, when Fostát was extended north-

INTERIOR OF COURT OF MOSQUE OF TULÚN.

wards. It has been both enlarged and restored; but, nevertheless, it retains to-day, in its essential features, both the materials and form of construction employed by its original architect. A brief study of this mosque will not only put us in possession of the nature and purposes of certain main elements common to all mosques alike, but it will also serve to illustrate some special characteristics of the architecture of the period.

First to discuss these main elements.

They are :—

I. The great square court (*sahn*), which is open to the air. In the present instance the sides measure ninety-nine yards.

II. The chapels, or covered portions of the building intended to be places of prayer (*liwán*). Of these, the principal liwán, or sanctuary, occupies that side of the court which lies towards Mecca. In the mosque of Tulún the liwáns consist of covered arcades, the three lesser liwáns having two arcades, and the deep sanctuary five.

III. The external court or courts, which here surround the principal court on three sides—three, because the space which would have been occupied by the outer court on the fourth side is appropriated to the sanctuary.

IV. The fountain of ablution (hanefiyeh), placed in the centre of the court, and covered generally, as here, by a domed structure.

V. The arched prayer recess (mihráb or kibla), which is let into the centre of the wall of the sanctuary, and therefore points directly towards Mecca. Against the wall, to the left of the prayer recess, stands the pulpit (mimbar), which is constructed of carved stone, or wood inlaid with ivory and ebony. The pulpit of the mosque of Tulún is constructed of the latter materials, and when it was presented by Melik el-Mansúr in 1298, it was a piece of exquisite workmanship; but now its richest panels have been sold or stolen, and a skeleton framework is all that is left. The remainder of the ordinary furniture of the sanctuary consists of the *Kursi*, or desk, on which the Kurán is placed during service time, the *Dikkeh*, a low platform, from which the words of the Kurán are repeated by the assistants of the *Khatíb*, or chief minister, to the congregation at large, the numerous lamps, which are suspended by chains from above, and the carpets or mats with which the floor is wholly or in part covered. As the sanctuary of the mosque of Tulûn—and, indeed, the whole fabric—is in a very neglected condition, its furnishing is by no means complete.

VI. The minaret (*menáreh* or *madna*), a word which means "signal-post." It indicates the graceful towers of more than one storey and varying forms, which constitute alike the most characteristic feature of the mosque and the most original contribution of Saracenic art. The mosque of Tulûn had three minarets; of these the principal is placed outside that wall of the court which is opposite to the sanctuary, while the remaining two—of which only one is still in existence—were placed respectively at the west and east ends of the sanctuary wall. The chief minaret is remarkable as being the only construction of its kind which is furnished with an external staircase. This minaret, however, did not form part of the original fabric. The special purpose of the minaret is to signal the presence of the house of prayer to the distant worshipper, but it serves also to provide a lofty station from which the mueddin proclaims the hours of prayer five times a day. For this purpose it is provided with balconies, to which access is gained by the winding staircases which lead from storey to storey in the interior. From these balconies, or from the cupola, or dome, which crown the minaret, lamps are hung which signal the month of Ramadân—the annual period of fasting—to the faithful Moslem.

VII. The dome, of which there is no example—if we except the comparatively recent (1296) structure which covers the hanefiych—in the mosque of Tulûn. This form of roof, which is almost as characteristic a feature of Saracenic architecture as the minaret, appears to have been introduced from Babylon, in which country it was used as a covering for tombs; and it is properly used only in those mosques to which the tomb-chamber of the founder is attached. The dome is found, therefore, in its greatest variety and perfection in the collections of tomb-mosques which mark the burial-places of the Mameluke Sultans. The most recent and splendid of these

THE MOSQUES

are designated by the misleading title of the "Tombs of the Khalifs."

In the second place, we have to consider the special characteristics of the architecture of this early period, of which this mosque furnishes examples.

I. The material of construction is as yet not stone, but brick, with a surface-covering of plaster. The fact that the principal minaret is built of freestone and not of brick, is one among other evidences which show that it was an addition made at a considerably later epoch, and not a part of the original design.

II. The external walls are as yet comparatively plain, and serve only to enclose the interior. It is on the decoration of this latter that the entire resources of the artist have been concentrated. In other words, the building was to be looked at only from the inside.

III. The arches which support the roofs of the liwâns are almost identical in form with the pointed arch, which is familiar to us in Gothic buildings. Neither in them, nor in the arched niches which decorate the walls above, are there any traces of the "horseshoe," or of any other of the characteristic forms of the arch which have been subsequently identified with Saracenic architecture.

These are all characteristics which illustrate the fact that, so far as external form is concerned, the Saracenic art of Egypt was in its earliest stage when this building was planned.[1] But when we come to the processes and designs employed to ornament the building, the evidence is of an opposite character. Briefly it establishes the fact that at this early period, the characteristic principle of Arabian decoration, the interlacing of geometrical figures, either separately or in combination with foliage, was fully developed, and that the method of utilizing this principle by means of plaster for surface decoration was fully understood.

[1] If we accept the statement that the architect of the mosque was a Christian prisoner, this fact would account for the use of forms so closely allied to Gothic; but, on the other hand, it would show that there were as yet no Arabian architects in Egypt.

IV. The columns of the colonnades, which are constructed of brick, are ornamented by engaged pillars at each corner. The bases of these pillars are shaped in the traditional form, and their bell-shaped capitals are ornamented with acanthus designs. The arches are decorated externally by flat bands of stucco ornamentation, and on the inner side—for in some cases the original plaster has survived—this stucco ornamentation exhibits the characteristic network of geometrical figures engraved with arabesques. The niches between the arches are similarly surrounded with bands of stucco ornamentation, while above them an inscriptional frieze of the same material is carried round all four sides of the interior of the court.

V. The liwâns are covered by roofs of wood, which on the inside present compartments formed by the intersection of the joists and crossbars. These joists consist of trunks of date-palms, which have been sawn in two, and then encased on three sides by planks of sycamore. The shallow compartments thus formed were fitted with octagonal panels, and all of the surfaces presented by the ceiling thus constructed were painted or gilded, or decorated with inscriptions or designs carved upon the wood. In the course of the restoration which is now in progress, it has been found possible to preserve a small portion of the original roof of the mosque of Tulûn. Here again we find that the art of wood-carving and painting, both in respect of workmanship and characteristic motive, was as clearly established as the sister art of stucco decoration.

If we sum up the evidence thus afforded by a study of the mosque of Tulûn, we arrive at the following conclusion. A century before the birth of mediæval Cairo, Saracenic art in Egypt, while it was well established in respect of internal decoration, was possessed of no architectural forms by means of which it could express its special genius. In other words, it had followed thus far in the Coptic tradition, and had not yet set out upon a path of its own.

Nor did Arabian art definitely follow such a path until the

period of the Fâtimite dynasty, which lasted from 972 1171. It was a period which was marked, as we have already seen, by the foundation and development of mediæval Cairo. Four mosques remain of those which were erected under the heretic Khalifs of this dynasty. Taken together, they exhibit a transition both of form and of material. In the course of this transition the large colonnaded mosque, with its bare external walls, was replaced by a much smaller structure, in which the exterior is endowed with artistic form, and furnished with appropriate decoration. At the same time we find that the rough stone or brick coated with plaster, which served as the material of construction up to the end of the eleventh century, has come to be replaced in part by freestone at the beginning of the twelfth. We have already noticed that this material was used for the city gates, which were built in 1091. In the following century the use of freestone was adopted for the façades of the mosques, but from this date onwards until the beginning of the fourteenth century bricks or rough stone continued to be used for the construction of the interior, nor as yet had either dome or minaret been constructed of stone. The first stone minaret—that of the Mûristân of Kalâûn—was erected in 1330, that is to say, 150 years after the close of the Fâtimite period; and this material was not employed generally for these parts of the mosque, until it had become firmly established as the ordinary material for building at the end of the fourteenth century, when the dynasty of the Turkoman Mamelukes was coming to a close.

The four surviving mosques of the Fâtimite period are those of El-Azhar, El-Hâkim, El-Akmar, and El-Telayeh. Of these, three exhibit arches of Persian character, that is to say, the perpendicular lines of the pillars are continued above the capitals, and finally converge in a wide pointed arch, which resembles that of late perpendicular Gothic.[1] The exception is afforded by the mosque of El-Hâkim—built about fifteen years later than that of El-Azhar—where the arches return to the egg-shape form, which

[1] See illustration at p. 102.

is found in the mosque of Tulûn. The general use of this arch
illustrates the fact already noticed, that during this epoch Persian
art exercised an appreciable influence in Egypt.

With the exception of this use of the Persian form of arch,
the two earlier mosques, those of El-Azhar and El-Hâkim, which
were built respectively in 982 and 1003, reproduced the mosque
of Tulûn in its main characteristics. The two later mosques,

INTERIOR OF EL-HÂKIM, NORTH-WEST MINARET.

however, those of El-Akmar and of El-Telayeh, which were built
more than a century later, display those significant changes to
which I have already alluded.

The Mosque El-Akmar is in a ruinous condition, and is,
moreover, almost completely hidden behind the houses and shops
by which it is surrounded. Nevertheless, from a historical point
of view, it is one of the most important of the mosques of Cairo.
It is the earliest existing example of a mosque in which the

exterior is treated as being of the same importance as the interior; and its southward façade—for the construction of which, as we have already noticed, freestone is used for the first time—contains what is, I believe, the earliest example in Cairo of the

El-Akmar.

familiar and beautiful entrance, which, from constant employment in subsequent periods, has come to be recognized as the characteristic Arabian portal.

This portal forms so important and interesting a feature of

the mosque, and indeed of Saracenic art in general, that it is necessary to indicate its character with some precision. Its most marked characteristics are, first, the fact that it is set back from the level of the external wall without ceasing to belong to it structurally, and, second, its great height in relation to the façade

DOORWAY OF SULTAN HASAN MOSQUE.

of which it is a member. It consists in a niche, or recess, which is carried upwards for three-fourths or more of the height of the façade. The basis of the design is a union of a rectangular recess with a half dome; and of these two principal parts the rectangle occupies three-fourths, and the half dome one-fourth, or less, of the total height. The depth of the rectangular portion of the recess is determined by the necessity of providing sufficient space for the stone seats occupied by the door-keepers (*mastaba*), which are placed on either side of the doorway: but the transition from this deep interior to the level of the façade is gracefully effected by a variation of the concave surface of the half dome. For this purpose a system of flutings, or of shell forms, are employed in the upper and shallow part of the concave

MASTABA OF MOSQUE EL-MUAIYAD.

surface, while pendentives of polygonal brackets, or the characteristic stalactite, are used for the lower and deeper part. Engaged pillars are often placed at the corners of the rectangular portion of the recess, and the lines of these pillars are carried round, or over, the arch of the half dome by mouldings or bands. The intersection of these mouldings is, however, generally checked by a second and lesser half dome, which springs from them as they converge. Moreover, the mouldings or bands, which surround the arch, are sometimes rectangular, and sometimes, again, they are carried upwards in a series of curves. In some cases, moreover, the recess is covered by a sphere with a lesser central dome, and in this form also the transitions from the corners of the recess to the basis of the dome are effected by stalactites.

The doorway of the mosque of El-Akmar is furnished with certain special features. In the centre of the flutings which decorate the surface of the half dome, there is a rose-window closed by a decorated grating, and surrounded on the outside by a scroll pattern of Byzantine design. Again, the principal recess is accompanied by two lesser recesses, of which one is placed on either side; and all three are surmounted by an inscriptional frieze in which Cufic characters appear.

This mosque also affords us what is probably the earliest example of the stalactite cornice. The angle formed by the meeting of two of the façades is cut off, and the flat surface thus introduced is united to the proper lines of the angle so formed at the tops of the respective façades, by means of stalactites.

The mosque of El-Akmar was built by the Khalif Amir bi Ahkam Illah in 1125. The mosque of El-Telayeh—last of the four which belong to this period—was erected in 1160 by Telayeh ibn Rezik, the powerful vizier of the last Khalif of the Fátimite dynasty, and restored in 1302. It lies within a stone's throw of the Bâb ez-Zuwêleh, and is reached by a narrow passage which leads from the eastern side of the street Kasabet Radowân. The whole building is in process of restoration, but the repairs of the principal liwân have been already completed, and while I sat sketching, this was being used for the purposes of prayer and teaching. Like the mosque of El-Akmar it has been greatly

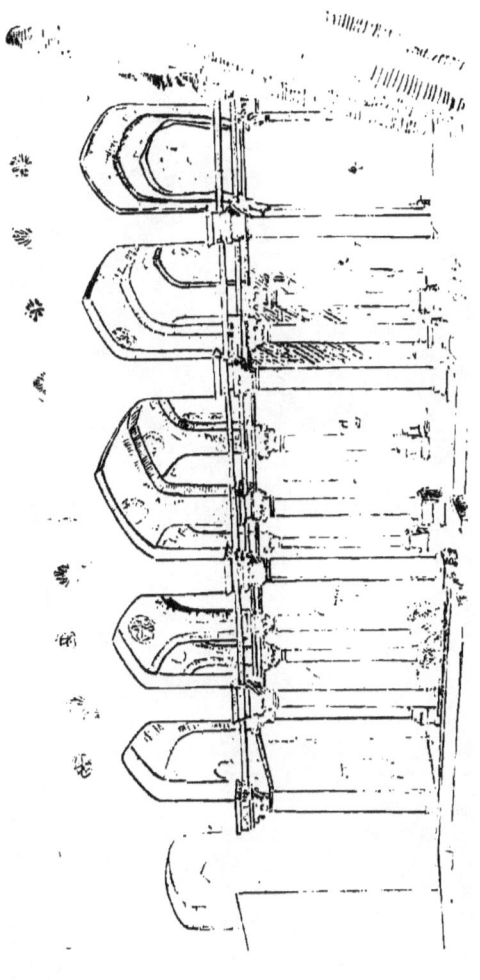

injured by the encroachments of the surrounding houses. It is built in the form of the colonnaded mosque, but its dimensions are on a greatly reduced scale in comparison with the earlier mosques of this type. The special significance which it possesses, as an example of the architecture of the period, is derived from the excellence of its decoration. Both the bands of stucco which border the arches, and the inscriptional friezes of the same material, exhibit arabesques which have never been surpassed in beauty of workmanship or design by the examples of any

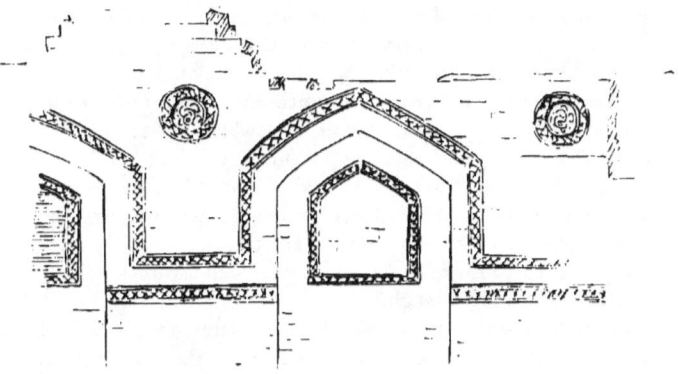

DECORATION FROM NORTH FAÇADE OF EL-TELAYEH.

subsequent period. At the same time, the abacus of every capital, and the horizontal beams which bind the pillars of the arcades, are covered with minute and beautiful designs carved in the wood. The art of stucco decoration, therefore, had been carried to its highest level of excellence before the close of the Fâtimite period, while that of wood-carving was fully, though not yet completely, developed.

During the short period, 1171 to 1250, Egypt was governed by Saladin and his descendants. The rulers of this dynasty, who were styled Sultans for the first time, are known collectively as the Eyyubites, or descendants of Eyyub (Job), the father of Saladin. This period is characterized by the introduction of the Medresch, or college mosque: and by the traces of western influence which reached Egypt, in common with other Mohammedan countries, through the medium of the Crusaders. When the Kurdish warrior, Saladin, wrested Jerusalem from the forces of Christendom in 1187, the missionary knights had been in possession of Palestine for more than 80 years. During this time they had erected churches wherever they went, and thus the towns and villages of Palestine presented the Mohammedan conquerors with architectural models which they did not fail to study. But beside the fact that the Mohammedan world had become familiarized with the cruciform church of Western Europe, there was another circumstance which led to the introduction of the cruciform mosque in Egypt. The Fátimite Khalifs had been Shiites, or heretics: and Saladin and his successors made it their object to recall their subjects to a knowledge of the orthodox faith. For this purpose they caused colleges to be constructed in which the four cardinal doctrines of that faith could be taught.

This college mosque consisted of a square court, called, like that of the congregational mosque, the *sahn*; and from the four sides of this central court, vaulted chambers projected, which were similarly known by the name of *liwân*. It was in these four chambers that instruction in the four doctrines of the orthodox creed was respectively given. This building, like the congregational mosque, was set in the direction of Mecca, and provided with a prayer niche in the wall of the principal liwân; and in course of time the distinction between the two disappeared. Ultimately the cruciform plan came to be preferred to that of the colonnaded mosque, as the population of the city grew and space became an important consideration.

The first of these colleges was established near the mosque of Amr, at Nasrich. Other examples of mosques built during this

THE MOSQUES

period are the mosque of the Sultan el-Kâmil, built in 1224, and the combined college and mosque which was erected by the Sultan Saleh Nigm el-Din in 1242. From a study of the remains of these two latter buildings, together with those of the tombs of this latter Sultan, and of the Imâm es-Shâfei, it appears that, in addition to the introduction of the new form of mosque, other advances were made. The domed mausoleum makes its appearance for the first time. The use of stalactites for masking

TOMBS OF THE MAMELUKES.

the transition from the dome to the rectangular body of the tomb chamber, and for similar purposes, was considerably extended. The art of wood-carving was further developed, for the designs on the doors of the tomb of Es-Shâfei, built in 1211, display a markedly higher degree of delicacy than the examples furnished by the buildings of the Fâtimite period.

During the three centuries that Egypt preserved its independence it was governed by the military Sultans, furnished by the Mameluke guards. The entire epoch is divided into two periods, lasting respectively from 1250 to 1382, and from 1382 to 1517. During the former, the Sultans were of Turkoman, and during the latter of Circassian origin. If we except the long and comparatively peaceful reign of En-Nâsir, which embraced a period of forty-four years (c. 1297 to 1341), the entire epoch was one continuous series of intrigues and revolutions. A striking indication of the bizarre character of this extraordinary military usurpation is afforded by the name of the Sultan Kalâûn. This Sultan, the father of En-Nâsir, added to his name El-Mansûr Kalâûn the further designation of El-Elfî, thereby commemorating the fact that he had been purchased for a thousand (*elf*) pieces of gold. Yet Kalâûn was himself distinguished as a ruler by the sagacious and enlightened policy which led him to enter into commercial relations with the Emperor Rudolph and Alfonso of Aragon. The architecture of the period of the Turkoman Mamelukes is marked in general by the introduction of features which must be referred to foreign influences; nevertheless, we find that at its close Arabian architecture has definitely assumed the forms to which its special character and significance is due.

The mosques of this period include, first the composite building known as the Mûristân Kalâûn, of which the greater part is now in ruins. This, the largest edifice of the period, consisted of a great hospital, to which was annexed the tomb-mosque of its founder. The building was commenced by the Sultan Kalâûn in 1285, and subsequently completed by his son, En-Nâsir. Second, the mosque of En-Nâsir, erected in 1300, which adjoins the Mûristân. Third, the mosque of Kalâûn, which was erected by En-Nâsir in 1317, within the walls of the citadel. And fourth, the monumental mosque of Sultan Hasân, which was raised between the years 1356 and 1359.

These buildings will afford illustrations of the two tendencies to which I have alluded—the use of foreign, often Gothic, forms, and the investment of the structure with an exterior which is definitely Arabian in character. Thus, to give a few of the more striking

Mûristân of Kalâûn

examples in detail, we find the corridors of the Mûristân are covered with Gothic vaulting, and the east façade of this building, while it is stamped unmistakably by the special characteristics of

ARCHES IN THE SANCTUARY OF THE MOSQUE OF KALÂÛN.

its Arabian builders, yet recalls in the square tower of the minaret, and in the disposition and style of the windows, the façade of a Gothic church. Again, in the sanctuary of the mosque of Kalâûn, in the citadel, and in the colonnaded court of the same building, we find alongside of the dome with its characteristic stalactite pendentives, and the no less characteristically Arabian ceilings, arcades of noble arches, which plainly reflect the spirit of Gothic. These arches and columns, I may remark, furnish the sole example

GOTHIC DOORWAY IN MOSQUE OF EN-NÂSIR.

of excellence in this class of work, which I was able to observe among the Arabian buildings of Cairo.[1] In these cases Gothic forms have been assimilated by the Arabian architects before

[1] For the explanation of this fact—the poverty of Arabian architecture in the column—see onwards, p. 134.

they were reproduced; but the mosque of En-Nâsir affords us the remarkable spectacle of a Gothic doorway thrust entire into an Arabian façade. This gateway was taken from the Church of Acre by the brother of the Sultan, and it stands immediately beneath a minaret, the surface of which is covered with decorations of the most characteristic Arabian style.

The second tendency—the creation of an exterior definitely Arabian in type—is illustrated by the great example afforded by the monumental mosque of Sultan Hasan. The use of the cruciform mosque had already become established during the previous period, and the only addition contributed by the present period is that of the founder's tomb, which now becomes a recognized part of the building. It is in the façades, therefore, that the significant development of which I have spoken is to be noticed. The process by which this distinctive character is produced is the accentuation and emphasizing of the various elements already developed in previous epochs. The height of the façade as a whole is raised, but a distinctive character is given to the surface thus extended by systems of shallow niches reaching almost to the full height of the building, in which the windows which light the successive storeys of the interior are set. The deep and lofty recess which encloses the portal unites with these shallow recesses to form a single system, which embraces the entire façade, while the unity of each separate façade, and of the façades which unitedly form the exterior, is further secured by the highly ornamented cornice by which the entire building is surrounded. The numerous transitions from the plane of the façade to the retiring planes in which the windows and the entrances are set give an opportunity for the free use of stalactites; and in the case of the mosque of Sultan Hasan these characteristic pendentives are employed for the massive cornice. The height of the walls of the interior chambers is raised in correspondence with this lofty exterior. This enlargement of the height of the interior was accompanied by the adoption of marble or mosaics for covering the walls of chambers, and we find that in the mosques of this and the subsequent period the walls of the liwâns, and in particular those of the principal liwân or sanctuary, are covered to a certain height by slabs of this material, which are generally arranged in horizontal layers of contrasting shades; and the same system of

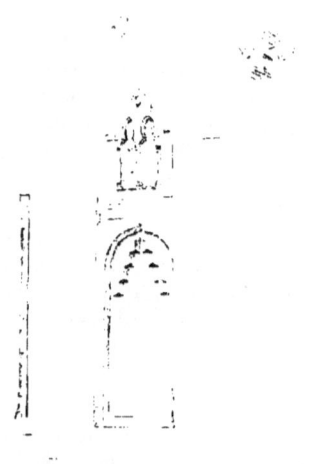

Corner of East Façade, Sultan Hasan Mosque.

decoration is also used for the entrance recess. Where arches are employed, the additional height required by the greater elevation of the interior, consequent upon the development of the façade, is gained in general not by lengthening the piers or columns,

THE MOSQUES 131

but by protracting the arch itself—a necessity which led to the adoption of the "horseshoe" form for the arches of the liwâns, especially for those of the sanctuary and of the corresponding and opposite liwân.

SANCTUARY OF SULTAN HASAN.

The industrial activity which marked the reigns of the Sultans Kalâûn and En-Nâsir, was accompanied by a remarkable development of the lesser arts in Cairo, and the effects of this development are apparent in the increased richness and perfection of the furniture and internal decorations of the mosques. In addition to the use of marble, with mosaics and incrustations for the walls, the sanctuaries were furnished with pulpits and Kurān-stands of exquisite marqueterie, while lamps of enamelled glass were suspended in lustres, in the manufacture of which the skill

PULPIT AT EL-MUAIYAD.

of the artificer was rivalled by the beauty and richness of the metals employed. Specimens of these works of art, rescued for the most part from the more ruinous of the mosques, are to be seen only in the museum of Arabian art; but the great doors, sheathed with bronze, inlaid with designs of the more precious metals, still remain in their places to bear witness to the perfection to which these artists in metals had attained.¹ At the same time the decorations in plaster were carried to perfection. Not only were the windows surrounded on the inside with bands of

PLASTER WORK ABOVE PRAYER NICHE AT EN-NÂSIR.

arabesques, but the lights were closed with delicate filigrees and enlacements cut out of plaster: and from these lights, fitted with brilliant glasses, rainbow hues were spread over the marvels of

¹ *e.g.*, that of the entrance of the El-Muaiyad mosque, removed thence from the mosque of Sultan Hasan.

the interior. Nor must all mention be omitted of the skill and beauty with which gilt and colour were blended in the decoration of the beams and panels of the ceilings, or of the lustrous porcelain which was employed for the adornment of mural surfaces. The Arabian buildings of Cairo afford so few examples of the use of faience of this character which is also of native manufacture, that it will be useful to mention one instance, which is at least authentic. This instance is the minaret of the mosque of Kaláûn, in the Citadel, where a few of the porcelain tiles employed in the decoration of the exterior are still left *in situ*.

In connection with the extended use of marble for internal decoration, it will be convenient for me to say here what has to be said sooner or later on the subject of the pillar—an architectural member of which, so far, no mention has been made. The explanation of this apparent omission lies in the fact that Arabian architecture developed no characteristic form of column, and only two distinctive forms of capital. The reason for this poverty in columns is very simple. In the early colonnaded mosques the walls and roofs were carried by square piers of brick or rough stone, which were in both cases plastered, or by pillars which were taken "ready made," so to speak, from the buildings of the Greek and Roman periods, or from the Christian churches. Not only did the Arabian builders draw supplies from the ruins in which Egypt was so rich, but they actually caused materials of the like nature to be brought from the deserted churches of Syria. Tulûn, we are told, had great difficulty in securing the erection of the mosque which he had planned, because he refused to despoil the Christian churches in the manner of the time. Nevertheless, even the mosque of Tulûn is embellished by the beautiful Byzantine columns, which are seen by every visitor, placed by either side of the prayer recess. In the other colonnaded mosques examples of capitals which exhibit evidence of the incongruity of their present employment are common enough. One of the capitals of the colonnaded court of the mosque of Kaláûn exhibits a Roman eagle; and there is a capital in the great mosque of El-Muaiyad—a building which belongs to the succeeding period—which is stamped with the Christian emblem of the united cross and crown. During the present period—the period of the Turkoman Mamelukes—only marble pillars were employed

PILLARS OF SOUTH LIWÁN OF MOSQUE OF KALÁÚN.

for such colonnaded mosques as were erected; and these, of course, were pilfered from the buildings of an earlier age. In the cruciform mosque, on the other hand, columns were rarely required to support any part of the structure. There is, therefore, no distinctive Arabian pillar. The two forms of capital are, first, that which is known as the "Kulleh" capital, from its resemblance to the water-jar so called; and, second, the "stalactite." As the first of these forms is used equally for both the base and capital of a shaft, the one genuine Arabian capital is the "stalactite"; and this capital only makes its appearance during the last period, when the Arabian architecture of Egypt is in its prime.

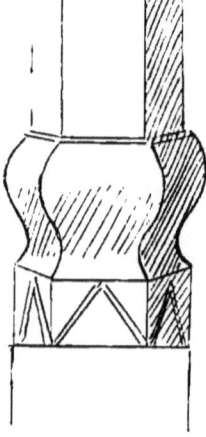

KULLEH BASE (AND CAPITAL).

During this succeeding and final period—the period of the Circassian Mamelukes (1382 to 1517)—the evolution of the mosque is rapidly completed. We have seen the original elements of the colonnaded mosque, the court, the four liwâns, and the minaret, blended with the cruciform Medreseh. To this has been added the tomb chamber of the founder with its dome — the characteristic covering of the grave. In the present period two new members are added: the *Kuttâb*, or elementary school, and the *Sebîl*, or public fountain. At the same time a final change is introduced in the interior. The reduction of size, consequent upon the changed conditions of environment, which have been already noted, allows the central court to be covered equally with the lateral chapels or colonnades. The mosque building, thus fully developed, embodies the place of prayer and assemblage, the college, the tomb of the founder, the school, and the fountain, while its exterior is characterized by the lofty minaret and the rounded dome. The basis of the design is still the cruciform Medreseh; but while this design is preserved almost unaltered in the interior, the façades and the general plan of the exterior conform to the requirements of the site and the relationship of

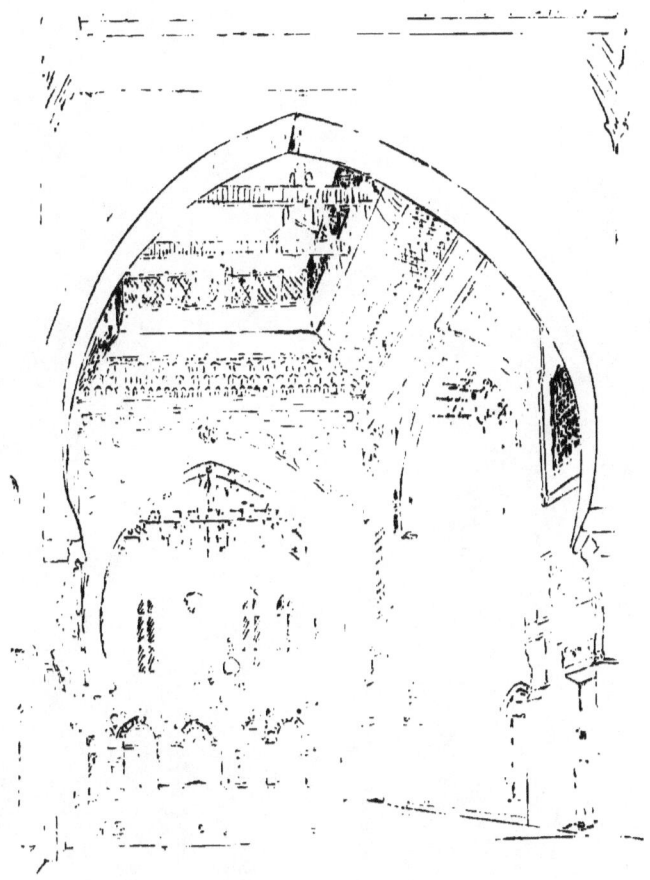

Interior of Mosque el-Ghûri

the structure to neighbouring buildings. These new elements, which became a regular and characteristic feature of the mosques of this period, were introduced into a prominent angle formed by the junction of two principal façades; the kuttâb being placed above and the sebil below. The wide arches or open sides of the kuttâb, and the handsome iron-work screens of the sebil, unite to form a characteristic and elegant feature of the exterior. The first example of the fully-developed mosque is that of the Emir Gâi el-Yusefi, which is to be found in the Sûk es-Sellâha, leading out of the open space below the mosque of Sultan Hasan.

The further processes by which the fabric of the mosque was perfected must be briefly indicated. The adoption of freestone as the common material to be employed in the construction of every part of the fabric, including the minaret and dome, permitted the artist to lavish his decoration at will upon the surfaces of the interior or exterior alike. But while the interior was covered indiscriminately with inscriptional friezes, arabesques, and inter-lacing geometrical figures, the decoration of the exterior came to be concentrated upon the entrances, the domes, and especially the minarets. It is due to this restraint that the Arabian mosque finally attained to the supreme beauty of a work of art. Only in the buildings of this last period do we find this characteristic beauty—the beauty of art; for the unity upon which it depends can only arise in a building where the parts are duly

STALACTITE CAPITAL.

subordinated to the whole, and this whole stands itself as the exponent and embodiment of the idea of its creator.

The mosques of this period which remain to-day are naturally numerous. They include the great mosque of El-Muaiyad, the minarets of which are built upon the Bâb ez-Zuwêleh: the mosque of the Sultan Barkûk, known as the Barkûkiyeh, in the street En-Nahhâsîn, and the mosque of El-Ghûri. All of these either have been restored, or are in process of restoration. The last, the mosque Ghûri, with the sister mosque of Ishmâs el-Ishâki, afford excellent examples of completely covered interiors. They also serve to furnish a striking example of the difference between the old method of restoration and that which is now pursued by the Committee for the Preservation of Arabian Monuments. For there is another mosque of almost identical form which has been restored under the old method. Of the results of this restoration it is sufficient to say that the present condition of this building—the mosque of El-Ashrâf—exhibits every defect and disfigurement which the ingenuity of a clumsy and ignorant restorer could produce.

CORNER OF EMIR GÂIEL-YUSEFI MOSQUE.

The development of the tomb-mosque is characteristic of the

THE MOSQUES 139

period; and the list includes, therefore, the beautiful monuments which are styled collectively the Tombs of the Khalifs. Among these the most significant are the mosque of Barkûk, which presents a unity of design attained by no other mosque of the

DOME OF EL-MUAIYAD, FROM SOUTH-WEST CORNER OF COURT.

"colonnaded" order, and the mosque of Kaït Bey, almost the last of the Mameluke Sultans. This latter has happily been restored, and although the repairs of the interior are not yet completed, the work of repairing the exterior is already accomplished. Thus the harmonious proportions of this most perfect of the mosques are presented to the eye of the spectator unmarred by any deficiency or decay.¹

Between the Tombs of the Khalifs and the eastern limit of Cairo there lies a huge mountain of débris, which is called the

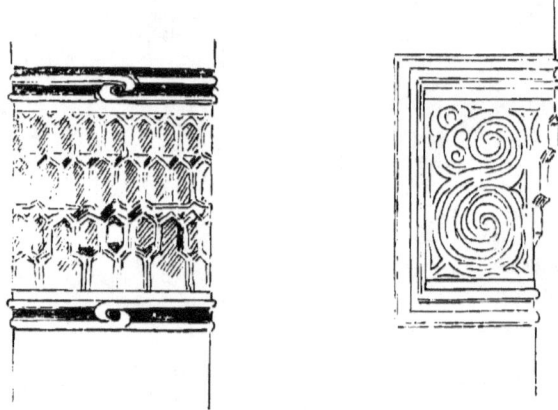

DECORATED CAPITAL FROM ISHMÁS EL-ISHÁKI.

Windmill Hill. The monumental rubbish heaps of which it is composed are pierced by a road—a pass between mountains of

---

¹ It will be useful for me to add a word on the work of the Arabian Monuments Committee. The manner in which the work of restoration is proceeding will appear from the following extracts, taken from Lord Cromer's Reports in 1898 and 1899. In the first of these he writes, *sub hac voce*, "A sum of about £12,000 was spent last year on the preservation and restoration of ancient Arab monuments. Attention was principally directed to the Mardâni, Kaït Bey, Fedawiyeh, and Barkuk mosques. A portion of the old city wall was repaired." And in the second : "Four mosques were taken in hand, the most important being El-Mardâni and Kaït Bey, on which £E2000 and £E1800 were respectively expended. A sum of £E500 was spent in buying out some of the small shops and buildings which surround and disfigure many of the monuments. £E800 was spent on restoring the old city walls."

Mosque of Kaït Bey

ashes, broken crockery, rubbish, and filth of every description. It is characteristic of Egypt, where the most splendid antiquities are surrounded by the vilest environment, that this unsavoury and unsightly eminence should command a scene of surpassing loveliness. On one of the many excursions which we made to the Tombs of the Khalifs, we, like other pilgrims, pushed our way from the mosque of Barkûk across the sanded space to the foot of the hill. At first sight, no conceivable spot could seem to be less promising; but when the traveller has once ascended by the unsavoury paths to the crown of the hill, he forgets the tainted air, and the uncouth pathway. Under the level rays of the setting sun the black masses of cinder, the yellow sand, and the brown hills beyond, are all transformed by hues of delicate beauty. Westward the white roofs and walls, broken by countless minarets and domes, lie at his feet. Just beneath him is the mouth of the New Street, which, together with the Muski, forms a black line that stretches right across the city. He is so near, that the murmur and the breath of Cairo rises around him. To the north-west a line of creamy white shows where the waters of the Nile are flowing. Beyond it, in emerald and opal stretches, are the fields watered by its overflow, melting into low blue hills, whose crests rise dark-blue against the opal sky.

Nor was the view eastward less significant. The dreary stretch of sand, through which we had waded rather than walked, had become a smooth surface of pure yellow. The domes and walls of the mosque tombs, dust-coloured and dim though they had seemed an hour ago, stood out in sharp relief against the yellow plain, themselves blood-red; and their background, no longer a scarcely distinguishable bank of mud, but a delicate accompaniment of their own rich hue, served to complete a contrast strangely simple, infinitely beautiful. Scattered among them the lesser structures, tombs, houses, and what not, took a tone of dead-white, and upon their surfaces the shaded recesses of the windows and doors showed squares of black.

But it was on the south-west horizon that the marvels gathered. Beyond the violet domes of Mohammed Ali's mosque, and the rising towers and bastions of Saladin's stronghold, two sharp angles showed above the low clouds that wreathed the horizon. They were yes, they could be nothing else than the Pyramids of Cheops and Chephren. As the sun fell—a crimson globe, the purple clouds gathered in ampler masses, and spread a veil over desert, hill, palm-trees, and city; but above the veil two blue triangles remained, beckoning us to Memphis as they had beckoned the Syrian merchant on his camel five thousand years ago.

CHAPTER VIII

THE EDUCATION SYSTEM

European Cairo—Absence of public buildings—Civilizing influences—System of education—Vernacular schools or kuttabs—Primary schools—Secondary—Special schools and colleges—School of Law—Engineering—Technical schools—Training colleges for teachers—Total attendance in Government schools, and cost of education—Policy of Government in respect of teaching of French and English—" Linguistic free-trade"—Results of this policy—Proportion of boys learning French or English—Relationship of the educational machine to population of Egypt—Reform of the kuttabs—Commencement of national education—Various attempts to improve the kuttabs—The results already obtained—Opinions of Artin Pasha—Prospects of education—Narrowing the interval between the educated official and the ignorant masses—The progress of women's education—Visit to the School of Agriculture—Practical work in the fields—Cost of students to the state—The Khedivieh school—Fasting and school work—Difficulty of maintaining social influence on boys after they have left school—A provincial school—Eton jackets.

THE regeneration of the Arab is being accomplished in more ways than one. Apart from the direct processes, of which the school and the prison are the instruments, other influences, less direct but still powerful, are ceaselessly at work to mould his character. These influences, which may be summed up as the environment of Western society, spread along the track of the railroad and the telegraph over the country at large, but they are strongest in the towns, and in Cairo they concentrate their forces. Alongside of the Arabian town, with its half a million of inhabitants, lies the European Cairo, an ever-present object-lesson in Western civilization. It is quite true that the great mass of the Arabian population regard this other Cairo as a neighbour whose encroachments should be repelled, yet there is nevertheless a minority which finds it advantageous to be on speaking terms at least with the intruder. The commercial instinct is strong in the Arab; and the same greed which led the Sultans to grant the capitulation teaches the donkey-boy and the itinerant vendor of Cairo to court the presence of the Frank.

European Cairo dates from the succession of Ismáil, in 1863, and the short-lived prosperity which came to Egypt from the failure of the American supplies of cotton during the Civil War. The new quarter, which was designated in honour of its founder Ismailiyeh, was laid out under French supervision. French capital raised the houses, and constructed the fine iron bridge which unites Cairo with the island of Gezireh. French architects built the palaces, and French gardeners laid out the pleasure-grounds. During the period of the English occupation, that is, since 1882, the general condition of the town has been materially improved. The drainage of the streets has been partially accomplished, and arrangements for lighting and watering them, and for the regulation of the traffic by police supervision, have been carried into effect. In all these ways the convenience of the European resident has been already secured; but a system of drainage, a vital necessity of European Cairo, has not as yet been provided. "The subject," Lord Cromer writes,[1] "has been under consideration since 1890, but owing to financial and other reasons" nothing has been done. He adds, however, that a scheme for draining Cairo at an approximate cost of £E750,000 is now being submitted to the Government by the Cairo Water Company; and that there is a prospect of this necessary work being commenced at no distant date. Nevertheless, private enterprise has in the meantime furnished Cairo with many comfortable, and even artistic, residences; and in the case of these new houses the authorities have rightly insisted, that only such structures shall be erected as will permit of adequate arrangements for drainage in view of the new system which is in prospect.

The feature of European Cairo, as thus developed, which

[1] Report (1899).

strikes the stranger is the absence of public buildings. The palaces of the Khedive, and those of the various members of his family, are sufficiently prominent; and as a matter of fact the ministries, and the great departments, with their numerous staffs of civil servants, are lodged in the discarded buildings of this class. Such buildings being of course designed for quite different purposes are both inadequate and inconvenient. At the same time the financial necessities of the Egyptian Government have hitherto prevented the erection of any new and suitably designed offices. The British advisers have acted with great restraint in this matter. Although they might justly have insisted upon the erection of such buildings as a necessity required for the due administration of the affairs of the country, the only public buildings which are at present in course of erection are buildings in which their personal convenience is in no way concerned. These buildings are the Museum of Egyptian Antiquities, to which the priceless collection now housed in Ismâil's flimsy palace at Gizeh is to be removed; the Arabian Museum, of which mention has already been made; the native Law Courts; and the new buildings for the School of Agriculture at Gizeh.

With this exception—an exception which is honourable to the English advisers and officials on whom the burden and responsibility of governing Egypt have rested—the machinery and methods of Western civilization are sufficiently in evidence in European Cairo. The primitive donkey has been replaced by cabs and electric tramways. The broad streets are lighted by gas or electricity, swept and cleansed by gangs of scavengers, and traversed by watering-carts, while at every corner a smart native policeman regulates the traffic. The Arabs who appear in these quarters reflect this Western environment in their dress and bearing; and the bi-lingual system which has now been introduced serves to familiarize them with the common terms and phrases of European life; for on the railway trucks and the tram-cars, on the cabs and the watering-carts, at the corners of the streets and about the doorways of every public building, they

K

see their familiar Arabic placed side by side with English or the official French.

But these and the like influences constitute a process of education which is independent of schools or teachers. What we are especially concerned with is the direct work of education, which is being accomplished by the Ministry of Public Instruction. In order to indicate the nature and scope of this work most clearly, I shall first sketch the outline of the system which is now in operation, and then lay before the reader the impressions which I have myself carried away from visiting certain characteristic schools of each grade.

The institutions which are at present controlled by the Department of Public Instruction are of four classes. First, there are a very small number of the Kuttabs, or Mosque Schools, which are styled officially the "Primary Vernacular"; second, the Primary Schools in Cairo and the provincial towns; third, the Secondary Schools, at present confined to Cairo and Alexandria; and fourth, the "Special" Schools and Professional Colleges which are established in or near Cairo.

This enumeration, I must point out, does not include the Military School now established at Abbasiyeh, which is under the direct control of the Ministry of War; nor the French School of Law—the *École Khédiviale de Droit*, an institution which is subventioned by the French Government. Still less does it take into account any of the numerous private schools which exist at Cairo and Alexandria, and in some of the larger provincial towns; or the Missionary Schools of the various denominations. The pupils of the former consist mainly of the children of European parents resident in Egypt, with a small percentage of Egyptian children of the highest or Pasha class: those of the latter are natives, but they are generally the children of Coptic parents.

Of the four classes of schools enumerated above, the first— the Kuttabs, or Mosque Schools—will be reserved for subsequent consideration. In the first place, the number of Kuttabs controlled by the Government is exceedingly small; for out of a total of 9000 throughout Egypt, only 55 are directly, and 110 indirectly, connected with the Education Department. In the second, having in view the fact that these village schools are practically the only instrument which exists for the education of the great mass of the native population of Egypt, the attempt to reform and utilize them constitutes a departure of the highest importance, and, as such, demands a more lengthy treatment.

Putting the Vernacular Schools on one side, then, we have three classes left to compose the educational machinery at the disposal of the Government. This machinery we will now examine a little more in detail.

The first class, the (higher) Primary Schools are 41 in number. In 1898 they had an average attendance of 140, and a total attendance of 5740 pupils. The goal at which they aim is the Primary Certificate. The examination by which this is obtained is in part oral and in part written; and it includes questions in the following subjects: the Arabian language, a European language, arithmetic and the elements of geometry, geography, and history. The possession of this certificate entitles the holder to be admitted to any Secondary School, the Technical School at Bûlâk, and the School of Agriculture, and to the lower grades of the Civil Service. In 1898, 1381 candidates were presented for examination from these schools; and of this number 427, i.e. 300 Mohammedans, and 127 Copts, were awarded the certificate.

The second class consists of three Secondary Schools, of which two—the Khedivieh and the Tewfikieh—are at Cairo, and the third, the Râs-el-Tin, is at Alexandria. The two schools at Cairo have respectively 273 and 170 pupils, whilst the Râs-el-Tin school has 72. These three Secondary Schools are directly under the management of the Department; one of them, the Khedivieh School, is actually under the same roof as the Department itself, and their goal is the Secondary Certificate. The subjects of the examination, which, like the Primary, consists partly of written, and partly of oral work, include: the Arabian language, a European language, which is either French, or English; translation; caligraphy, both Arabian and European; mathematics, including arithmetic, geometry, and algebra; geography and map-drawing; and science, which includes physics, natural history, and the laws of health. In 1898, 98 candidates, of whom 59 were Mohammedans, and the remainder chiefly Copts, were awarded the Certificate. The Secondary Certificate carries with it the right of admission to any of the Special Schools, or Professional Colleges, and to the higher grades of the Civil Service. I should add that the headmaster of the Khedivieh School is an Englishman, Mr. A. V. Houghton; while the headmaster of the Towfikieh School is a Frenchman, Mr. Théophile Peltier, and the headmaster of the Râs-el-Tin School is an Egyptian, who, however, was trained in France. The headmasters of the Primary Schools are not, of course, Europeans.

The third class, which consists of the institutions styled "Special Schools," includes the Schools of Law, Medicine, Agriculture, Engineering (the Polytechnic School), the Technical School at Bûlâk, and three training schools for teachers. In the first four of these institutions the course of instruction requires an attendance of four years. In the training colleges two years only is required, as in similar institutions in England. As regards the numbers of the students who attend these institutions, I have been unable to obtain any exact figures. In the School of Medicine, however, I find from Lord Cromer's last report that the attendance had risen from 2 in 1892 to 21 in 1898. The School of Agriculture had, at the time when I visited it, some 60 students; and I believe the attendance at the School of Law was about 50. The number of students attending the School of Engineering, which is said to be in an unsatisfactory state, would be small; while that of the Technical School—*École des Arts et Métiers*—at Bûlâk would be very considerable. The Training College which forms a department of the Khedivieh School had 15 students, and the corresponding institution at the Towfikieh School would have, I suppose, about as many.

THE EDUCATION SYSTEM

The third of these Training Colleges—the Dar el-Lûm (place of learning) which is attached to the Nasrieh Primary School, and has an Egyptian at its head, would, I suppose, have a larger attendance. The aims of these various institutions are in general sufficiently indicated by their respective titles; but a few words in explanation of some special features may be useful. The School of Law, which prepares, of course, for the legal profession, is the most popular, and attracts the most promising of the pupils of the Secondary Schools. Up to the present, however, French has been used as the sole medium of instruction, and that in spite of the fact that in all other Government schools the French and English languages have been placed on a footing of perfect equality. The reason for this preference is to be found in the circumstance that the English language is not recognized by the International Courts, in which the majority of the students would expect to plead. This circumstance, however, does not in itself constitute a sufficient reason for the exclusive use of French in the Law School, since Italian and Arabic are recognized by the Mixed Tribunals, no less than French; and on this and other grounds, which will be discussed more suitably in a subsequent chapter,[1] the Department has decided to establish an English section in this school in the course of the present year. The School of Engineering is intended to serve especially as a nursery for the officials of certain departments of the Ministry of Public Works; and so soon as the new buildings of the Agricultural College at Gizeh are completed, it is proposed to install this school in the premises thus vacated. As there is a considerable interchange of teaching between these two schools—the School of Engineering and the School of Agriculture—it will obviously be to the advantage of both that they should be placed side by side. The Technical School, or Schools, at Bûlâk, are interesting, because they serve as the nursery from which many of the lower grades of the Public Services are supplied. Boys who have obtained the Primary

[1] See pp. 173, 179.

Certificate are admitted from twelve years old and upwards; and it is here that the future engine-drivers, guards, and railway and tramway employés in general, the telegraph clerks and postmen, receive their training. The Dar el-Lûm Training College, again, possesses a special interest from the fact that it is in this institution that the native Arabic teachers or shèkhs qualify themselves for employment under the Department of Education. In the training colleges attached to the Khedivieh and Tewfikieh Schools, on the other hand, native Egyptian teachers are qualified respectively to give instruction in the English and French languages.

A few more facts must be added to complete this outline sketch of the educational machine. The total number of pupils receiving instruction in the Government schools, of all three classes, was at the end of last year 7735. In the previous year, 1897, the gross cost of this public instruction was returned at £E159,397, of which the Government supplied £E93,778. The difference is represented by the contribution made by the Egyptian parent, or the student himself; and as a matter of fact the proportion of paying pupils is stated by Lord Cromer in his last report to have risen from 5 per cent. in 1879 to 86 per cent. in 1898. It is scarcely necessary to point out that this increase of the parents' contribution constitutes satisfactory evidence of a growing appreciation of the educational advantages which are thus afforded, on the part of the persons most interested. There is another question of importance which must not be omitted. This question is the degree in which the English language is being taught. It will be remembered that owing to the deficiency of Arabic literature, all or most of the ordinary school subjects have to be taught by means of French or English text-books. It is necessary, therefore, for every pupil to acquire a knowledge of one or other of the two European languages in which these text-books are written. At the time of the English occupation, French was practically the sole language thus employed in the Egyptian schools; but as British influence increased

THE EDUCATION SYSTEM

a demand for instruction in the English language naturally arose. The policy which was adopted under these circumstances, and its results, are stated by Lord Cromer in his last report. Of the policy itself he writes, that it may be described as "linguistic free trade. No attempt has been made to discourage instruction in French. The number both of French teachers and of Egyptians employed to teach the French language in the Government schools has been more than doubled since 1881. For many years, although the proportion of pupils learning French, respectively to those learning English, was gradually undergoing a change, no diminution in the aggregate attendance at the French classes occurred. On the other hand, English has been placed on the same footing as French. Equal facilities have been provided in both cases. Every parent has been requested to state in writing whether he wished his son to learn French or English. He has been left entirely free to decide this question for himself. As time went on, and the demand for teaching in English grew, the facilities for instruction in that language were naturally increased."[1]

The result of this system, broadly expressed, is a rapid increase in the proportion of students learning English as compared with those who are learning French. Taking the years 1889 and 1898 as the basis of comparison, the percentage of boys learning English in the Primary Schools has risen from 24 to 72, while the percentage of boys learning French has fallen from 76 to 28. In the Secondary Schools the percentage of boys learning English has risen from 26 to 41, while the percentage of boys learning French has fallen from 74 to 59. In the Technical Schools and College of Agriculture, the English percentage has risen from 47 to 54, while the French has fallen from 53 to 46, and in the professional colleges the English percentage has risen from 22 to 49, and the French has fallen from 78 to 51. The present position may be summarized by saying that out of a total of 7735 pupils who are receiving

[1] Egypt, No. 3 (1899).

instruction in the Government schools of all grades, 5740 are being taught either French or English, and that of this latter number 3859 are learning English, and 1881 are learning French. Of the young men who are thus educated, probably two-thirds at least obtain employment in the various ranks of the Civil Service; the remaining third is made up mainly of those who have qualified for the professions of law and medicine, or have entered the offices of merchants.[1]

This, then, is the educational machine. In order to gauge its effectiveness and value we must ascertain the nature of the material upon which it works. The population of Egypt, as we have already seen, amounts in round numbers to 10,000,000. Of this population, according to the last census, 91.2 per cent. of the males, and 99.4 per cent. of the females were returned as illiterate, that is to say, they can neither read nor write. Excluding the Bedouin population and children under seven years of age, 88 per cent. of the total population is illiterate, or, to reverse the statement, 12 per cent. of the population thus limited are able to read and write.[2] It is perfectly obvious that a system of schools which provides instruction for 8000 pupils can in no sense be considered a national system of education for a population of 10,000,000; and, in fact, the scope of this system is practically confined to the preparation of candidates for Government employment. In concluding the review of the progress of education during the last ten years, which is embodied in the last report, Lord Cromer writes: "But the point which perhaps more than any other deserves notice is, that evidence is forthcoming of the capability of the Egyptian schools and colleges to turn out a number of young men who will be able to take an useful and honourable, albeit sometimes humble, part in the administration of their own country. It would be unduly optimistic to suppose that, for many years to come, the educational system can attain any higher ideal than this."

[1] Lord Cromer's report (1899), and *Considérations sur l'Instruction Publique en Égypte*. Par Yacoub Artin Pacha. Le Caire, 1894.
[2] Egypt, No. 1 (1898).

THE EDUCATION SYSTEM

Nevertheless, the Ministry of Education has already commenced the difficult task of educating the masses of the Egyptian population. The germ of a genuine system of national education is to be found in the reform of the Kuttab. The school so called may be described as the national school of Egypt. It is generally, though not exclusively, attached to the mosque, and it is to be found in almost every village and town throughout the country. The methods of teaching employed by the schoolmaster (Fikih). and his assistant (Arif), are of the most primitive description;[1] and the schoolroom in which the children are taught is as primitive and unsuitable as the method of instruction. It is estimated that there are 9000 of these schools, with a total attendance of 180,000 children. Small as these numbers are in comparison with the population of Egypt, it is obvious that if the Kuttabs could be reformed, they would afford at least an adequate basis upon which the fabric of a national system of education could be raised. Moreover, the value of the Kuttab as a vehicle of instruction is enhanced by the fact that girls, as well as boys, attend it. Having in view the general neglect of female education which has come to be a part of the social system of Mohammedan countries, this fact would in itself justify an earnest endeavour for the adoption of the Kuttab as the basis of the national education.

At the present time 55 Kuttabs, with an attendance of 2923 pupils, of whom 2481 are boys and 442 girls, are directly controlled by the Department; while 110 Kuttabs are indirectly controlled through a system of "grants-in-aid." The story of the reorganization of these Kuttabs reveals some interesting and significant facts.

At the end of 1890, the Ministry of Education assumed the control of 69 Kuttabs, which, together with their annual endowments, amounting to a sum of £E352, had been transferred to it from the administration of the Wakfs, i.e., religious and charitable foundations and trusts. Of these 69 schools, 4 were already

[1] See account of such a school in ch. iii. p. 54.

closed, and the first step of the Ministry was to inspect the buildings, and examine the teachers of the 65 schools which were still at work. As the result of this inspection, 19 school buildings were condemned on sanitary and other grounds, and thus the number of efficient Kuttabs was reduced to 46. The teachers of these Kuttabs were then subjected to an examination of the very simplest character in the subjects of writing and arithmetic. The result of this examination was very significant. Out of 57 Fikihs and Arifs, 18 failed to put in an appearance. Of the 39 who took the examination only 5 satisfied the examiners in arithmetic, while no single teacher passed in writing. Of the 34 who failed, 27 received no marks at all in arithmetic, and 29 received no marks in writing. In the face of these results the department decided to give the unsuccessful teachers a further opportunity of qualifying themselves. For this purpose it was decided to hold the same examination after a year's interval; while those who were still unsuccessful were to be allowed a second year, as the final period within which they must qualify themselves on pain of dismissal. At the same time it was arranged that the 5 teachers who had passed in arithmetic should receive an additional salary of 10 P.T. a month, while this subject should be taught by competent masters in the remaining schools; and that writing should be taught by these supplementary masters in all the schools. In 1892, the period of grace expired; but in the meantime none of the unsuccessful Fikihs or Arifs had presented themselves for a second examination.

In 1894 a second attempt was made to reorganize these Kuttabs. On this occasion a staff of separate inspectors was appointed, who were able, by periodic visits, to effect certain improvements in the school buildings, and to assist the teachers by their practical advice. At the same time black-boards and forms were provided, and the more competent and energetic of the Fikihs and Arifs were encouraged by extra remuneration. The slight improvement which was thus effected by means of these inspectors raised the attendance from 1839 pupils in 1894 to 2307 in 1895; and at the same time the impression on the part of the Fikihs and parents, that the admission of girls was forbidden, had been removed, and 139 children of this sex were received.

Encouraged by the results thus secured, the Ministry of Education made a third attempt to reform the Kuttabs. A modest scheme of work was drawn up by the inspectors, and in order to put it into effect, it was proposed to provide each school with a staff consisting of one Fikih, one Arif, and one servant. An application was then made to the Wakfs Administration for the increase of funds necessary to carry out these proposals. This application was, however, refused, on the ground that the funds at the disposal of the Administration were insufficient to meet the requirements of the religious foundations to which the Kuttabs in question were attached, and the proposed reform was therefore abandoned.

In the meantime the Ministry of Education continued to make such improvements in the Kuttabs as the limited funds at its disposal permitted. Twenty of the most incompetent teachers were dismissed, and their places were supplied by teachers who had at least satisfied the requirements of an elementary examination; books were supplied to the Arifs who were ready to improve themselves by study; and further efforts were made to protect the health of the pupils. In 1897 it was found possible to establish a regular examination of candidates for the posts of Fikih and Arif, and to place the Kuttabs under the inspection of the health officers, who visited the regular Government schools. In the same year, moreover, ten "new" Kuttabs were added. These were converted Government schools, formerly classed as "Lower Primary"; and although they had been unsuccessful and inefficient as schools of this category, yet they formed a valuable addition to the list of Kuttabs, for they were better equipped with school materials and provided with trained teachers. As a result of the change the attendance at these schools rose within the following year from 317 to 668; and while no girls had previously been admitted, in November 1898 there were 153 on the books.

Finally, in November of last year, 1898, the Ministry of Education decided to assimilate the original Kuttabs, in respect of teaching staff, to the ten new schools, and to distribute books and other necessary scholastic materials gratuitously to the scholars in attendance at all the fifty-five Kuttabs. For this purpose the annual sum assigned to the Kuttabs was raised from £E180 to £E2880.

At the same time an attempt has been made to improve the condition of the great mass of the Kuttabs throughout the country. At the close of 1897 the Department decided to offer grants-in-aid to those "private" Kuttabs which applied for such assistance, provided they reached a certain minimum standard of efficiency. Out of the 9404 Kuttabs in Egypt, 301 applied for this assistance. The composition of this total is interesting, as giving a rough idea of the prospects of educational reform afforded by the population of the three districts into which the whole of Egypt was divided. Out of 316 Kuttabs in Cairo, a large proportion—106, or one-third—applied. Out of the 6140 Kuttabs of Lower Egypt only 43 applied; while out of the 2948 Kuttabs of Upper Egypt 152 applied. These 301 Kuttabs were subjected to an inspection, in respect of their buildings and furniture and the capacity of their teachers. As the result of this inspection 110 Kuttabs were returned as deserving assistance, while 191 were rejected. Of the efficient Kuttabs, 24 were styled as first-class, and 86 as second-class. These Kuttabs have a total attendance of 3950 pupils, of which 319 are girls. Two or three points in the code of regulations which has been framed for the management of these assisted schools must be mentioned, as they are essential for the realization of the wider results which the Government have in view. In the first place, the teachers for the Kuttabs are to be chosen as much as possible from those qualified teachers who have received part of their education in the El-Azhar University, or some similar Mohammedan institution; and, at the same time, all tuition is to be given in the Arabic language, the teaching of any foreign language being expressly excluded. In the second place, a direct incentive to the encouragement of the attendance of girls by the Fikihs is provided, for the amount of the grant-in-aid is based on the average attendance of the school; but whereas 15 or 10 P.T. per head is respectively assigned to the schools of the first and second-class on account of each boy, this amount is doubled in the case of girls. It only remains to add that the smallness of the proportion of applications for assistance was attributed in part to a feeling of distrust and apprehension on the part of the Fikihs in general, and especially on the part of those of Lower Egypt. These apprehensions, it is hoped, will be removed in succeeding years, and in view of further accessions to the list of assisted Kuttabs, the Department, in preparing the budget for 1899, has raised the sum appropriated to grants-in-aid from £E700 to £E1000.

Before I proceed to give the reader a brief account of the impressions which I received from my own personal observations of the working of the Egyptian schools, it will be useful to sum up the results of this general review of the work of the Ministry of Public Instruction. We have, then, in Egypt at the present time, first, a very small but efficient system of schools and colleges, which is mainly, though not exclusively, employed in the training of young Egyptians for the various branches of the Civil Service; and second, the commencement of a tentative but skilfully designed scheme for the reform of the indigenous vernacular schools, and thereby for the foundation of a genuine system of national instruction.

In the course of a very interesting conversation, which was followed by a brief correspondence, Artin Pasha was kind enough to discuss with me some of the chief obstacles which, to my mind, appeared to stand in the way of educational progress in Egypt. Like the late Nubar Pasha, the present Under-Secretary of State for Education is an Armenian, and in addition to the unique practical knowledge which he has gained through his long and honourable service in the Ministry of Education, he has thought and written deeply on the subject. Anything that Artin Pasha said would, I know, be worth remembering, and I make no apology, therefore, in now acquainting the reader with the substance of the opinions which were expressed by so competent an authority.

The first difficulty upon which I sought information was the defect involved in the narrowness of the limits within which the action of the Government schools is confined. I ventured to express the opinion that so long as the machinery of education was employed almost entirely in the training of public servants, the very efficiency of this machinery would tend to widen the interval which separated the official class from the general mass of the Egyptian population; since, in fact, the officials were being well taught and the general mass not taught at all.

In reply to this the Pasha said that undoubtedly the fact was as I had stated it; but that nevertheless the education of a native class of officials, as it was conducted to-day, represented in itself an enormous improvement on the old state of things. The system of European education had been commenced by Mohammed Ali, with the establishment of a school of engineering, and that afterwards other schools had followed. These schools had not, however, produced satisfactory results, and in consequence young Egyptians were sent to Europe—mainly to France—to be educated there. France was chosen in preference to England, because higher education in that country was at once less expensive, and more accessible from a social point of view than in England. All of these young men were absorbed by the administration which Mohammed Ali established; and none of them were available to impart instruction to their fellow-countrymen. This policy of Mohammed Ali was absolutely selfish and narrow; but it produced two good results. In the first place, a Europeanized Egyptian was substituted for the Shékhs educated at the

El-Azhar University, or the Copts—the only two classes which had previously been available for such employment; and in the second, these educated officials served to spread among their relations and friends a certain desire for the acquisition of western knowledge. A system of schools for conveying European instruction was re-commenced by Ismáil in 1867, with results scarcely more promising, and it was not until the period of the English occupation, when properly trained teachers were brought from France and England, that anything like an effective system of schools had been established. That these schools were really appreciated by the class for whom they were intended was shown by the fact that, whereas in the days of Mohammed Ali and Ismáil pupils were obtained by compulsion, to-day the accommodation was insufficient to meet the demands for admission.

It was quite true, he added, that there was a wide interval between the educated official and the bigoted Mohammedan or the entirely uneducated masses; but there were significant signs that this interval was being lessened. In the first place, the students in the "special schools" were not exclusively candidates for employment in the Government service: a few students were already beginning to read law and medicine with a view of practising these professions: and in the second, boys of all ranks were seeking employment under Government, and through them—and their families—the desire for education, and the Government service itself, was being democratized. Moreover, these educated officials, together with the native professional men, would serve to constitute a sort of middle class, distinct alike from the Pashas and Shêkhs and the other privileged classes on the one hand, and from the uneducated masses on the other, which would throw the weight of its influence on the side of progress, and thus materially assist the Government in the execution of the reforms necessary to raise the social condition of the Egyptian people as a whole.

The second question on which I sought Artin Pasha's opinion was the neglect of female education. It seemed to me that very little provision was made under the present system for the education of girls; whereas any system of education which was intended to produce social or moral effects should pay almost equal regard to the children of both sexes. I had heard that the educated Egyptian, after he had left his school or college, was rapidly detached from the European influences, with which he had thus been brought into contact, by marriage, with its definitely Mohammedan ties and associations. That, in fact, until the girls were educated the effect of the European education on the men could only be transitory.

Here, again, the Pasha assured me that whatever might be the present position of female education in Egypt, the outlook was much more hopeful now than it had been in the past. It was true that Ismaïl had established the first girls' school in Egypt, but this was merely an ostentatious attempt to win approval from European sympathisers, since the institution in question was designed to furnish servants for the ladies of his harim. Practically there was no thought of education for girls before the English occupation had been effected. Now, however, there were good private schools for girls in Cairo and other large towns, and some of these—with a total attendance of 1382—were placed under the inspection of the Education Department. The prejudice against the education of women, moreover, was essentially Turkish, and not Arabian or Egyptian.[1] So long as the Education Department had been controlled by Turkish officials no one dared to speak of educating the girls. "In the Kuttabs," he continued, "the Ministry are making a definite effort, as you know, to provide education for the girls of the lower classes. When we took over the forty-five Kuttabs from the Wakfs Administration there was not a single girl in attendance. I inquired into the matter, and I found that the teachers were under the

[1] In his book *L'Instruction Publique en Égypte*, Paris, 1889, the Pasha quotes a Mohammedan authority, Rifaï-Bey, a pupil and doctor of the El-Azhar University, in support of his opinion. "The girls," says Rifaï-Bey, "must be educated as much as the boys, in order that, when they are subsequently united in marriage, the husbands and wives may be able to live in good accord."

impression that the Ministry would be offended by their taking girls, and that they would be dismissed. I disabused them on this point, and the result is that out of 2500 children now attending these schools we have 400 girls—a wonderful result, considering the long period of previous neglect."

On the general question of the prospect of educational progress in Egypt, Artin Pasha expressed himself in sanguine terms. The Department was moving slowly but steadily. It was hampered, of course, by want of funds, but at the same time no rapid extension of the machinery of education would be desirable under any circumstances, since to provide an entirely free education would be a mistake. It was necessary that the parents should themselves be willing to contribute in part to the cost of their children's training, and to create such a feeling would be a work of time. The most immediate requirement was the supply of sufficient funds to pay an efficient staff of competent inspectors, and so to place the 9000 Kuttabs, with their 200,000 children, under Government supervision. At the present, of course, these additional funds were not forthcoming. But there was no reason to despair that they would not be supplied at some future date, since the aim of the Egyptian Government under its British advisers was not merely to make money out of the country, but to improve the social and physical condition of the mass of its inhabitants.

Among the introductions with which Sir Rennell Rodd had furnished me was one to Dr. Mackenzie, the Director of the School of Agriculture, at Gizeh. Pending the erection of the new buildings, for which a grant of £E15,000 has just been made by the Caisse de la Dette, this institution is housed in the servants' quarters and stables of Ismaïl's palace. The Egyptian antiquities are placed in the palace itself, which is known generally as the Gizeh Museum; while the beautiful pleasure-grounds, laid out, it is said, for the ladies of his harim, are appropriated to the wild animals of the Zoological Gardens.

It was a morning in the second week of January, and the sky

L

was leaden-hued—such a sky we had found by no means remarkable at this season of the year in Cairo—and we were met by a wind as cold as a March wind in England, when we struck across the unsheltered fields which lie in front of the college. From the entrance-gates we were conducted by an Arab servant across two courtyards, surrounded by class-rooms, and through a long passage to Dr. Mackenzie's room. Here he joined us after a brief delay, and courteously offered to take us over the school. But before we set out, Dr. Mackenzie was good enough to tell us something of the past history and the present circumstances of the institution which had been placed under his charge.

The School of Agriculture, he said, was originally established in 1867, during the reign of Ismail. In November 1896 it had been reorganized, and a new scheme of work had been adopted. The changes which had then been introduced consisted in the introduction of a large element of practical work in the fields which were attached to the school, and in the substitution of the Primary for the Secondary Education Certificate as the qualification for admission. As a matter of fact the majority of the pupils before the standard of admission was lowered had not obtained the Secondary Certificate, but had been drafted into the School of Agriculture from the Secondary Schools, where they had been educational failures. Under the present regulations every student was required to devote eight hours out of the thirty-three of which the week's work consisted to actual work in the fields. The course of instruction occupied four years, but a pupil was allowed one year's grace in passing from one class to another, and thus the maximum period allowed for gaining the diploma was five years. The examinations at the end of the first and second years were conducted by the staff; but those at the end of the third and fourth years were conducted by a board of examiners appointed by the Ministry of Education, in conjunction with certain members of the staff. The subjects upon which the students were examined included agriculture, agricultural chemistry, natural science, chemistry, farm book-keeping, land surveying, hydraulics, veterinary, physics, mathematics, Arabic, and English: and the students who were successful in passing the final examination of the fourth year received a diploma of proficiency in Agriculture from the Ministry of Education.

I think it was just then, as Dr. Mackenzie was turning over the leaves of the college register to show us the various nationalities of the students, that an Arab servant came in carrying a tray with three minute cups of coffee à l'Égyptienne. After this pleasant and characteristic interruption, Dr. Mackenzie continued to tell us that there were at present sixty students on the roll, but that next year this number would be increased to seventy, the normal attendance in the future. About 25 per cent. of these students were Europeans, principally Greeks, also French, Italians, Germans, and Russians; but no English at present. The lowest age for admission was fourteen, and the average students ran from this age to twenty-four or twenty-five. As regards fees, there were fifteen day-pupils paying £E15 a year, and forty-five boarders paying £E25. These fees did not of course cover the cost of the education and maintenance which they received. The £E15 of the day-pupils paid for one midday meal, and for books and materials; while the additional £E10 paid by the resident students met the extra cost of the extra food and the lodging with which they were provided. Each paying student cost the Government £E45 a year; but as a matter of fact only twenty-nine out of the present pupils did pay fees. As a general rule only those students who could bring reliable evidence to show that they, or their parents, were unable to pay for their education were admitted without payment of fees; but in exceptional circumstances a pupil was put on the free list, as a reward for good work in the examinations. By these means it was expected that the School of Agriculture would be able to produce ten diplomaed students every year, and the sum appropriated to the institution in the Education Budget for 1899 was £E4797.

After this, Dr. Mackenzie led us from his room to one of the class-rooms, where a number of students were at work under the direction of an assistant professor, a Greek gentleman and an old student of the school; and afterwards to the chemical laboratory. From the college buildings we proceeded to the fields, consisting of some fifty acres of land, where the practical work was done. Here, among the plots of the different students, Dr. Mackenzie explained to us how this the most interesting and useful work of the institution, was arranged. The college, he said, provided the student with land, with tools, and, in general, with seeds and plants. A first year's student was assigned a quarter of an acre of land, which was increased to half an acre in the second, and three-quarters of an acre in the third and fourth years. The students often joined their plots, and worked in companies of three or four. This practice was encouraged, because it simplified the irrigation of the land and the rotation of crops. The students were not allowed any hired assistance except in the case of the cotton crop, which was cultivated as part of the third year course; but they were permitted to sell the proceeds of their plots with the approval of the Director. In this way a student might obtain £E4 in his first year, £E8 in his second, and £E12 in his third and fourth years if he worked his plot successfully. In the case of sugar, Dr. Mackenzie said that no individual planting was possible, since three annual crops were taken from the canes before they were exhausted. Sugar, therefore, could not be conveniently included in the rotation of crops arranged for the students; but it was proposed to assign a portion of the college land to the exclusive cultivation of sugar, so that the students might be properly instructed in the best methods of cultivating this important product.

From the fields we passed over to the farm buildings attached to the college. Here we came upon a group of cattle, several of which, we were told, had won prizes at the agricultural show— the first held in Egypt—which we had ourselves visited a fortnight ago at Gezireh. After we had properly admired these handsome animals, we said good-bye to our courteous host.

In a country like Egypt, where the national income is

THE EDUCATION SYSTEM 165

derived not from minerals but from the produce of the fields, the importance of such an institution can scarcely be overrated. Nevertheless, owing to the fact that its diploma leads to no direct employment under Government, the college has not hitherto attracted so many pupils as the Ministry of Education had a right to expect. Since the date of my visit, however, I see that Lord Kitchener has applied for five students from this school for ser-

PRIZE CATTLE, SCHOOL OF AGRICULTURE.

vice in the Sudân, and this circumstance will no doubt help the young Egyptian to believe that a useful and remunerative career should be opened up to him by a course of training at the School of Agriculture.

In the course of my interview with Artin Pasha, I had made the acquaintance of Mr. A. V. Houghton, the Headmaster of the Khedivieh School, and Principal of the Training College attached to it. On this occasion Mr. Houghton had kindly invited me to visit this school, which is the largest of the three secondary schools in Egypt, and I had gladly promised to avail myself of his permission. In subsequently arranging a convenient day and hour for my visit, I was incidentally made acquainted with one of the special difficulties with which a schoolmaster is confronted in Egypt. Friday, I knew, would not do, because it was the Mohammedan Sunday, but it was also the month of Ramadân—the fasting month, when all orthodox Mohammedans abstain from food from sunrise to sunset. During this month football was "knocked off," and the rigour of the school routine had to be considerably modified, for even the staying powers of an English schoolboy would fail to carry him through his ordinary school duties, if he had to take his breakfast before sunrise and wait for his next meal until the evening. It was necessary, therefore, that I should come early in the morning, otherwise I should find the pupils in a state of partial collapse.

Under these circumstances it was arranged that I should call about half-past ten in the morning; and when I presented myself accordingly at the Khedivieh School, which occupies part of the buildings appropriated to the Ministry of Education, I had a little talk first of all with Mr. Houghton in his private room. The Khedivieh School, he told me, was a sister institution to the Tewfekich. It included (1) a Normal School, in which native schoolmasters were trained in English, and which had an attendance of 15; (2) the Secondary School, with an attendance of about 300; and (3) a Primary School of about 60 pupils. The total staff consisted of 14 English, 10 French, and 18 native masters. The arrangements at the Tewfekich were identical in all respects, with the exception that French was the European language chiefly taught, and therefore the proportion of French and English masters was reversed. Speaking of the wider aspects of his work, Mr. Houghton said that it was very difficult to keep in touch with the boys after they had left the school. As a rule the Egyptian boys fell back more or less completely into their native habits a year after they had been removed. Last year an

Old Boys' Club had been started, with the object of keeping these young men within reach of the school influences. That was a step in the right direction, but much more was needed. The education of the girls was the key to the position; for marriage at present completely severed the educated Egyptian from European influences. Two boys were sent from the Khedivieh School every year to finish their education in England; but even in the case of these young men the marriage tie obliterated the effect of their European training. One source of this weakness, Mr. Houghton added, was the fact that the English masters, and the English officials generally, did not speak Arabic. In order to maintain the influence which was established by the training of the schools, it was necessary that social relations should be preserved with the young men after their education had been completed.

After this conversation, I was taken round the school by the headmaster's secretary. We went into several class-rooms, in which both English and French masters were engaged in teaching pupils of the various "years." Where all was excellent it would seem almost invidious to particularize; but I remember that I was especially struck by a charming lesson in literature, which was being given by a French gentleman to one of the higher forms. The subject was taken, I think, from La Fontaine, and the oral explanations of the master were supplemented by written work. Some of the note-books in which the master's comments had been reproduced in the pupils' language were shown to me, and the effect of what I read was to make me think that these Egyptian boys were very fortunate in their teacher. But apart from the appearance of the class-rooms, there was a business-like and orderly air about the place which was sufficiently significant. The silent and empty corridors, the murmur of subdued voices broken only by the clear tones of the master's voice, revealed the characteristic discipline of an English Public School.

Almost two months after this visit to the Khedivieh School, I had an opportunity of visiting one of the Primary Schools. It was in the town of Medinet el-Fayûm (the City of the Fayûm), which is the centre of the interesting district known as the Fayûm. I had met the headmaster, M. Abd-el-Rahman Yassine, at the Mudiriyeh, and gladly accepted his invitation to pay a visit to the school.

Over the entrance we found the words "The Fayûm Government School," so we had no excuse for going astray. The school had been established eleven years ago, the headmaster told us, and there were now about 120 pupils, of whom 96 were learning English, and only 20 French. We went through all the classes, from the fourth year class to the first. The buildings were good, and the class-rooms were well equipped with the ordinary furniture for teaching, while the walls were provided with picture-cards and maps. The boys of the fourth year we found reading English under the (Egyptian) English master. For our benefit he put them through a searching examination on the shifting meanings which certain puzzling words assumed in different contexts, and extracted from them all manner of irregular plurals, perfects, and past participles. In the third-year class the boys were doing arithmetic out of an English school-book; and in the second year, where the pupils had only just begun to learn a European language, they were repeating passages of easy poetry and prose which they had committed to memory. It was a good example of the manner in which the one European language, French or English, which the pupils were required to learn, was made the basis of instruction in useful knowledge of all kinds—geography, arithmetic, Euclid—everything, in fact, except Arabic, was taught out of the familiar "Nelson" or "Macmillan" text-books. Not that the native language was neglected; on the contrary, we were moved to envy when we saw the ease with which a small Egyptian boy wrote our names in Arabic on the blackboard. In the playground outside the boys were taught drill and gymnastics, and played football and cricket. Only a few pupils, the sons of poor parents, were admitted to the school without payment of fees, but these fees, the headmaster told us, amounting to about

£2, 10s. a year, only covered the actual cost of the books and writing materials which were supplied to them; that is to say, this primary education is practically provided by the State.

Still, making all allowance for this fact, there was enough, and more than enough, in this school to justify the existence of the present system. We had scarcely expected to find a school, to all appearance perfect in equipment and discipline, in a small provincial town in Egypt; but we experienced something like a genuine shock of astonishment when we saw its boys in Eton jackets and turn-down collars.

CHAPTER IX

LAW AND ORDER

Inherent defect of the Mixed Tribunals—Reasons for retaining them—Commercial community favourably disposed to them—Amendment of Bankruptcy Law required—English language should be recognized—Compromises—System of Native Tribunals—Personnel of judges must be raised—Improvement of administration—Committee of judicial control—Extension of summary jurisdiction—Amendments of criminal law—The Prosecutor-General's department—The Parquet—Improved relations between the Mudirs and the police—Results of these reforms shown by criminal returns—Improvement of the prisons—New buildings required—Defects of the old system—Reform introduced by Coles Pasha—Visit to the prison at Gizeh—Organization of prison labour—Classification of prisoners—Food—General impressions.

It is not my intention to attempt to present the reader with anything approaching a complete account of the various judicial systems which are at present established in Egypt. The international judicial authority, as represented by the Mixed Tribunals and the Consular Courts, has already been discussed in Chapter IV., in its relation to the general system of government. In the same chapter it has also been stated that the reform of the Native Religious Courts—so long sheltered, in spite of their absolute incompetency, by an impassable barrier of Mohammedan prejudice—has been at length undertaken; and in a subsequent chapter some indication of the need and character of this reform has been given.[1] Moreover, any fuller account of these institutions would be of doubtful value; since whatever may be the precise changes, it is at least certain that their present condition, and their relationship to the Native Courts, properly so called, will be very materially altered in the near future. I shall therefore

[1] See Chapter vi. p. 96.

content myself with a brief statement of the requirements of the situation, so far as I could ascertain them from hearing the opinions of representative and competent authorities; and I shall then proceed to sketch the main lines of progress, which are to be observed in what must be considered the permanent judicial system of Egypt, that is, the Native Courts directly controlled by the Egyptian Government.

The inherent defect of the Mixed Tribunals is the extreme difficulty which attends the introduction of any reform, whether it relates to the Code administered or the procedure of the Courts; since the assent of all the fourteen Powers, by which they were established, must be obtained before any change can be effected. Another obvious disadvantage is the fact that both the Code and the procedure of those Courts is exclusively French. Apart, therefore, from any question of intrinsic merit, the use of this Code and procedure serves to perpetuate French influence, when French influence is still synonymous, in spite of recent events, with obstruction. Both these circumstances constitute strong *prima facie* reasons for the abolition of the Mixed Tribunals. On the other hand, there are many reasons which make it desirable that these Courts should be maintained for some time to come at all events. In the first place, the hands of the Egyptian Government are full, and they would find it both difficult and inconvenient to replace the Mixed Tribunals by any adequate substitute. The commercial community would object very strongly to bring their disputes before the Native Tribunals, as at present constituted; but to suddenly raise the personnel of these Native Courts to the necessary standard would require both funds and men, to say nothing of the administrative effort involved in constructing a homogeneous judicial system, and in readjusting the business at present transacted by the Native Courts. Moreover, however anomalous the use of a French system of law in Egypt may be under the now existing circumstances, there are two reasons why this system should be allowed to remain. In the first place, the commercial classes have become accustomed to the body of law thus administered, and are generally satisfied with it; and in the second, the mere fact that the Code is in French is not in itself a sufficient ground for rejecting it, since both the provisions of the Code and the rules of procedure could be translated into English, if the predominance of English trade should in the future make such a step desirable. I gathered that, with one exception to be noted subsequently, the English merchants were rather favourably disposed than otherwise to the law as administered by the Mixed Tribunals. In the course of an interview with a representative member of this class, I was reminded that business men had grave faults to find with the commercial law of all countries, not excluding England. What they wished in Egypt, my informant said, was not so much an alteration of the existing law, but the improvement of the personnel of the judges, and of the manner in which the business of the Courts was conducted. He mentioned the fact that a system of summary jurisdiction, equivalent to the County Court system in England, was in existence, and that small sums could be recovered within a few days. He regarded the system of Registration of Titles under the Mixed Tribunals as good and convenient. I said that I had heard that the practice of endorsing debts, secured upon property, over to a third party—treating them practically as negotiable instruments—was used as a means of harassing the Fellâhîn. He replied that it might be so in some cases, but that it was generally convenient for such debts to be assignable, since a creditor who had advanced money on the security of land or crops might wish to acquire his capital for his own purposes, before the date at which the debtor had promised to pay. His experience of the Fellâh, he added, went to show that he was quite sufficiently wide-awake nowadays to look after his own interests. There was, however, one reform which the commercial community urgently required—the alteration of the Bankruptcy Law. It was necessary that the Mixed Tribunals should be empowered to punish fraudulent bankrupts penally. Under the Code, as it stood at present, the judge was only empowered to order a fraudulent bankrupt to be imprisoned at the cost of his creditors; and even this punishment, which involved the creditors in heavy expenses, could only be enforced by slow and difficult proceedings. That, he said, constituted an evil which affected all commercial classes; for out of one hundred failures in Egypt, ninety-five were fraudulent, but so far as his knowledge went no bankrupt had ever yet been punished.

Under these circumstances it is obviously to the interest of the Egyptian Government to preserve the Mixed Tribunals for the present; but they are endeavouring to introduce such modifications of law and procedure as the peculiar constitution of these Courts permits. The steps which are being taken to remedy the gravest of the evils connected with the Mixed Tribunals—the encroachment of the international authority upon the administrative freedom of the executive, and upon the sphere of the Native Tribunals—have already been noticed.[1] In addition to the amendment of the Bankruptcy Law—proposals for which have already been submitted to a sub-commission composed almost entirely of judges of the Mixed Tribunals—some progress has been made in the direction of securing the recognition of the English language in these Courts. In view of the predominance of English commerce, and of the relative numbers of British and American litigants, common sense and justice alike require that English should be placed on an equality with French, Italian, and Arabic, the three languages in which proceedings can be at present conducted. Nevertheless, says Lord Cromer, the adoption of such a course is "for the present impossible. It would require the unanimous assent of the Powers, and the difficulty of obtaining that assent, which is in all cases considerable, would in this instance be materially enhanced from the fact that some at least of the Powers concerned are unable to give their assent without previous reference to their respective parliamentary bodies."[2] Accordingly, Lord Cromer continues, it was necessary to find

[1] Chap. iv. p. 64.   [2] Egypt, No. 3 (1899).

some means of lessening the most serious of the practical inconveniences due to this exclusion of English, which consisted in the " necessity of obtaining legalized translations of documents in the English language" at considerable expense and delay. For this purpose he communicated with M. Bellet, the President of the Court of Appeal, with the result that a circular has been addressed to the presidents of the various tribunals, requesting them to dispense with translations whenever possible. At the same time an endeavour is to be made to appoint English-speaking registrars to those Courts which are most frequented by English-speaking litigants.

Such compromises are not, as Lord Cromer says, "altogether satisfactory"; but the balance of convenience makes it unlikely that the Egyptian Government will adopt any drastic measures, unless the international judicial authority, of which these Courts are the chief instrument, should become actively obstructive. Then, however, they would not hesitate in the general interests of Egypt to sweep them away; and, in this case, the judges of the Mixed Tribunals would be partly pensioned off, and in part retained to form a *Cour de Cassation*. In the face of this contingency the strengthening of the personnel of the Native Courts and the improvement of their procedure have become more desirable than ever.

The Native Courts were established in pursuance of a decree of June 14, 1883, but they did not attain any degree of efficiency until the recommendations of Sir John Scott—a judge of the High Court of Bombay, who was summoned in 1890 to Egypt to advise on this subject—had been put into effect. They consist of a Court of Appeal, which sits at Cairo, and of five Courts of First Instance for Lower Egypt, sitting at Cairo, Alexandria, Benha, Mansûra, and Tanta; with three for Upper Egypt, sitting at Benisuêf, Assiût, and Kench. The law which they administer, both civil and criminal, and their procedure, are based upon the French Codes and procedure. The reforms introduced by Sir John Scott effected, on the one hand, a large increase of the machinery for the summary administration of justice throughout the country at large; while, on the other hand, the efficiency of the judges was improved by the creation of a Committee of Judicial Control, which, with the assistance of a body of inspectors, is able at once to check any flagrant miscarriage of justice, and to educate the native bench by its advice and assistance. The native bench, thus constituted in 1884, was at first ludicrously incompetent. Of the judges originally appointed it was estimated that only one in four possessed any degree, or other evidence of legal training. If these numerous judges—for the Courts at first were absurdly large, ranging from fourteen judges in the Appeal Court to seven in the Courts of First Instance—had been subjected to the same process of examination as the teachers of the Kuttabs, they would probably have given no better account of themselves. As it was, it was not until 1892 that it was found possible to introduce the principle that the possession of a law degree from a European university, or of a diploma from the School of Law at Cairo, was a necessary qualification for the judicial office. And even to-day a glance at the long list of these judges reveals an ominous majority of native names; and it is only in the Appeal Court, where, out of twenty-two judges, seven are Englishmen, that a tolerable standard of efficiency has been attained. It has been said that the first European judges were little more than witnesses to the incompetency of their native colleagues. A circumstance that occurred during my stay in Cairo caused me to surmise that this state of things had not yet been entirely remedied. On one occasion I asked one of the English judges of the Appeal Court, if he would have any objection to take me with him to one of its sittings. In place of the immediate assent which I expected from a member of my own profession, my friend's face lengthened, and he replied, with some hesitation, that he could not say either "yes" or "no," but that he would do his best to see if it could be arranged, and in that case that he would let me know. I remained in Cairo many weeks after I had made this request, but my friend never did "let me know." And apart from any inference which may be drawn from the reluctance manifested in this case, it is only too obvious that the association of men possessing the double qualifications of a graduate of Oxford or Cambridge, and a member of the English Bar—the class from which the English judges are now appointed—with the native Egyptian, or the miscellaneous European judge, must be, to say the least, somewhat incongruous.

Nevertheless, in spite of the multifarious difficulties, the double task of raising the personnel and improving the administration of the Native Courts is being steadily accomplished. The first of these objects is being attained by a gradual process of "weeding out" the most incompetent occupants of the native bench, and introducing in their place capable native or European judges, with a good stiffening of Englishmen. And this process is accompanied by the supervision which is exercised by the Committee of Judicial Control over the occupants of the existing bench. In evidence of the utility of this latter institution, Lord Cromer quotes some words of Mr. M'Ilwraith, Sir John Scott's successor in the office of adviser to the Ministry of Justice. "The system," Mr. M'Ilwraith reports, "has been the subject of much hostile criticism in some quarters, but it is found to work well in practice and has a markedly educational influence on the native judiciary in stimulating their efforts generally, and preventing the recurrence of particular errors of law."[1] The second object—the improvement of the administration—is being secured by a further extension of the machinery for summary jurisdiction, and by a reduction of the cost of legal proceedings. Not only has the work of the Court of Appeal and of the regular Courts of First Instance been simplified by the creation of Summary Courts, in which a single judge has power to try all misdemeanours and to decide all disputes in which the value of the property (of whatever class) concerned does not exceed £E100 in value, but these Summary Tribunals have been themselves relieved by conferring a limited

[1] Egypt, No. 3 (1899).

jurisdiction among a certain number of the village headmen or Omdehs. This jurisdiction is limited to cases in which personalty of the value of not more than £E1 is involved; but small as this sum is, it is believed that the new arrangement will relieve the judges of the Summary Courts of a great mass of trifling business. The reduction of costs was effected by a new judicial tariff which was introduced at the end of 1897; and the fact that the receipts from the Native Tribunals have risen from £E110,000 in 1897 to £E115,000 in 1898 is evidence that the step was appreciated by the Egyptian public.[1]

At the same time improvements have been effected in the criminal law administered by the Native Tribunals. The most important of the amendments thus introduced was the repeal of Article 32 of the Code, under which the punishment of death for the crime of murder could only be inflicted, if (1) the accused confessed the crime, or (2) the evidence of two eye-witnesses could be produced. "The objections to this provision of the law," Lord Cromer writes, "are obvious. In the first place, the use of torture to insure confession was encouraged. In the second place, circumstantial evidence, which is of special importance in Egypt by reason of the prevalence of perjury, had to be set aside in considering whether, in a case of murder, the death penalty should be inflicted."[2] While this Article was in force it was very difficult to obtain a conviction for murder; but since its repeal the crime of murder in Egypt has been made subject to the general rules of evidence which apply to all other crimes. And in addition to this and some lesser amendments, a complete revision of the Penal and Criminal Procedure Codes has been undertaken during the present year.[3]

In any mention of the Native Tribunals, however brief, some mention must be made of the system in force for the investigation of crime and the conviction of criminals. The Egyptian system, like the codes and procedure, is based upon the French

[1] Egypt, No. 3 (1899). [2] Ib., No. 1 (1898). [3] Ib., No. 3 (1899).

At the head of what is practically a criminal department in the Ministry of Justice is the Prosecutor-General (Procureur-Général), who is himself represented by a number of prosecuting counsel, called collectively the Parquet, who are attached to the various Courts. The duty of the members of the Parquet is to review the evidence collected by the mudirs and the police, and then to conduct the prosecution before the Court. Even if the native police force were a great deal more intelligent and reliable than they are said to be, and the capacity of the mudirs or provincial governors was far greater than it is now—or can be expected to be for some time to come—a heavy responsibility would still rest upon the Parquet. But when to these conditions we add the further fact that the members of the Parquet were often unqualified, and generally inexperienced, native lawyers, it is easy to understand that convictions for crime were not as frequent as they should have been, and that sometimes the innocent was punished in place of the real offender. Moreover, about six years ago, the experiment was made of entrusting the post of Prosecutor-General to a native lawyer—possibly with a view of preventing friction between the mudirs and the Parquet. Under these circumstances it is not surprising that the duties of this important office "were not carried on to the satisfaction of the Ministry of Justice," nor that "frequent reports of an unfavourable character regarding the conduct of prosecutions were received." In order to put a stop to this unsatisfactory condition of affairs, an Englishman, Mr. E. K. Corbet, was appointed public prosecutor, and at the same time the important amendment of the law of evidence in relation to the crime of murder, already mentioned, was effected. Since Mr. Corbet's appointment a "marked improvement" is reported[1] to have taken place in the business of detecting and punishing crime. At the same time the material out of which the members of the Parquet have to be selected is still very unsatisfactory. The applicants for these posts are young

[1] Egypt, No. 1 (1898).

men possessed of doubtful qualifications, which often take the shape of a cheap degree from some Continental university. In order to check this latter practice, Mr. Corbet is rightly requiring an examination in Arabic and Egyptian (sacred) law from the holders of these Continental law degrees; while, at the same time, he is encouraging the young Egyptians, who are preparing for the profession of law, to qualify at the Law School at Cairo. This institution, under its present head, M. Testoud, has become perfectly efficient, and the diploma which it offers, if less attractive at first sight, is in reality a more solid guarantee of proficiency than any law degree that is ordinarily within the reach of the Egyptian student.

The various reforms thus in progress have all tended to a better administration of the criminal law; and the good effect produced by them has been seconded by an endeavour to improve the relations between the mudirs and the police. Under the old system the provincial police were placed under the direction of resident English police officers, who were responsible, not to the mudirs, but to the English Inspector-General at Cairo. There were, therefore, two independent authorities in each province or district, both of which were charged with the duty of preserving public order; and it was not unnatural that a considerable amount of friction resulted from this arrangement. In order to remove this evil, a change was introduced in 1895, under the direction of the late Nubar Pasha, then Minister of the Interior. Under the new system, the mudir is wholly responsible for the maintenance of order, and the police are placed under his control; while the resident English police officers have been replaced by English inspectors, who visit the various districts from time to time. At the same time, the proceedings of both the mudirs and the inspectors are subjected to a general supervision exercised by the English adviser to the Ministry of the Interior. As the net result of all these various reforms, the Egyptian Government were able to announce that the total number of felonies annually committed had fallen from 1866 in 1896, to 1342 in 1898; and that 10 capital sentences for murder had been executed in 1898, as compared to 5 in 1897, and 4 in 1896, owing to the repeal of Article 32 of the Criminal Code.[1]

It remains for me to speak of the long-delayed but necessary reform of the prisons, which is now in a fair way of being accomplished. A suitable penal code, and an efficient administration of its provisions are useless unless the sentences thus pronounced can be carried into effect. The Egyptian prisons have hitherto suffered from two cardinal defects. In the first place, the accommodation has been altogether insufficient; and in the second, as the Government had no funds at its disposal to pay for the prisoners' food, frequent communication between them and their friends was allowed, when the food was brought. Both of these evils are now in course of removal. A sum of £E33,000 was granted by the Caisse de la Dette for the construction of prisons in 1898; a further sum of £E26,000 was granted for 1899; and it is hoped that an additional grant of £E30,000 may be secured for expenditure in 1900; and that thus the Egyptian Government will at length be provided with adequate prison accommodation by the end of the year last named. In the meantime, the Director-General of Prisons, Coles Pasha, has found a means of supplying the prisoners with food, which involves no relaxation of prison discipline, while at the same time it relieves the State of any fresh expenditure on this account. Under his direction the labour of the prisoners has been carefully organized, and the proceeds of this labour have been found sufficient to defray the cost of food; and so, although in some prisons the old system still prevails, in the rest food is now supplied by the authorities.

As I was permitted, through the courtesy of Coles Pasha, to visit the prison at Gizeh, I was able to see the new system in operation. Here, in a room not far from the entrance, we found specimens of various articles manufactured in the prison. There

[1] Egypt, No. 3 (1899).

were boots and shoes, and brushes for cleaning floors, carpets, and horses; there were mats and baskets of various kinds and sizes; there were rugs, and cloths, both plain and coloured, and rolls of canvas cloth, kharki, and matting of date fibre. But what we saw, our guide told us, was far from representing the entire results of the prisoners' labour. From this room we were conducted to various workshops, of which some were fitted with spinning machines worked by hand and foot; while others were furnished with the accessories required by carpenters, cabinet-makers, and smiths. In fact, so far, the establishment bore rather the appearance of a manufactory than a prison. But the empty, whitewashed cells, which we next visited, served effectually to dispel the illusion. They were used, our guide said, for "probationers," as the prisoners were termed during the first six months after their arrival, and for insubordinate prisoners. In passing from the cells to the dormitories, our guide explained the method of classification: a prisoner remained for six months unclassed; at the end of this time he ceased to be a "probationer," and if he had earned a sufficient number of good marks he was ranked in the third class, wearing a canvas jacket with three blue stripes down the back, and a close-fitting black cap of felt. From the third class he could pass successively into the second and first; and in each of these latter he would enjoy extended privileges. That is to say, the hours of work were successively shortened, and the privilege of corresponding with relatives was more frequently permitted. Prisoners who behaved well were discharged after they had served three-fourths of the periods for which they were sentenced; and these discharged prisoners were then placed under police supervision until the end of the periods of their sentences. Before, however, any prisoner was thus discharged, a communication was made to the mudir of the district to which he belonged, and an assurance was obtained from this official that the presence of the prisoner would not be dangerous to the public order. The dormitories of the third class were bare whitewashed chambers, with unglazed windows, and the sole furniture provided for each prisoner was a pair of blankets. The dormitories of the first and second classes were supplied, however, with plank-beds and small canvas pillows filled with straw. As for food, the prisoners were allowed three meals a day, at each of which every man received a cake of brown wheaten bread, about half a pound in weight. In addition to these cakes, they were provided with stews of rice, beans, lentils, cabbages, &c., once

PRISONERS MAKING MATS.

every day; and twice a week they had a meal of some kind of meat.

In passing from the dormitories to the prison garden, we crossed a courtyard where a number of prisoners were engaged in picking date fibre and in weaving it into mats. One group to which our guide directed our attention were making a mat for the Savoy Hôtel at Cairo. All the clothing of the prisoners, as well as that of the warders and the rest of the staff, was made

by the prisoners themselves; and an appreciable sum was also
earned by the sale of the articles which they produced. The
men whom we found at work in the garden, under the supervision of a warder, were prisoners who had been sentenced to
short terms of imprisonment for trifling offences. The comparative docility which this class of prisoners display may be understood from the following fact, which is mentioned by Lord
Cromer in his last Report. " In the course of last year," he says,
" a law was passed allowing prisoners sentenced to imprisonment,
in default of fine or costs, the privilege of substituting labour in
the place of imprisonment. Up to the close of last year 40,070
persons had claimed to work rather than be imprisoned. The
operation of the new system has enabled the Department to close
the prisons for 'contraventions' (petty offences), both in Cairo
and Alexandria." [1]

There were about 600 prisoners at Gizeh, we were told, and
the buildings, which were partly new, had been taken over in
1890. The most striking impression which this institution left
in our minds was the comparative simplicity and ease which
marked its arrangements. The warders were scarcely apparent,
the only officers in arms were the two sentries at the main
entrance, and one who was on duty in the garden; and the
prisoners themselves, so far from appearing desperate or blood-
thirsty, seemed to be attending to their various duties with the
usual nonchalance of the Arab. They all looked clean and
healthy, and nearly all happy. One prisoner whom we saw in
the smith's shop had committed murder, we were told; but a
glance at the man's face was sufficient to show that his crime
was to be attributed to mental weakness rather than vice. He
had been sentenced to imprisonment for life; and although his
want of intelligence prevented him from attaining any considerable degree of proficiency, he had been trained to do useful work
under the direction of others. Nevertheless, corporal punishment

[1] Egypt, No. 3 (1899).

and relegation for hard labour had sometimes to be inflicted upon the more insubordinate offenders. At the same time it was quite possible to believe, as our guide said, that some of the prisoners, who had been released after short terms of imprisonment, deliberately committed a second offence, in order that they might return to a place where they could obtain good food and ample shelter at the cost of only so much labour as would keep them sufficiently employed.

CHAPTER X

SOCIAL CAIRO

Gezireh—The Anglo-Saxon playground—Unobtrusiveness of English in Cairo—Army of Occupation forms an exception—The Khedive—Chief figure in social life—The Khedivia—Mother of Khedive takes precedence of wife—Life of English residents—Race meetings—Gymkhanas—Opera House—Position of native women—Presentation to *Vice-Reine Mère*—Description of ceremony—Participation of Egyptian men in social life of the English—Of Egyptian women—Calls upon European ladies—Native servants—Difficulty of language.

THE visitor who has crossed the iron bridge which leads from Cairo to the island of Gezireh[1] finds himself at the junction of three roads. Of these, two, namely that which runs directly in front of him across the island, and that which turns immediately to the right and runs down stream, are arched over by the thick foliage of avenues of lebbek trees. Taking this latter, we will suppose on a morning in January, he will not proceed far before he encounters twos and threes of men and women on horseback, or pairs of bicycle riders. When he has walked two or three hundred yards, noticing thankfully the solid roof of foliage above his head, he is confronted by the red flag which marks the holes of the golf links waving in a sunlit stretch of level grassland. This is the Anglo-Saxon playground of Cairo. The circle of white palings mark the race-course, with its grand stand showing far away to the north-west, against the opposite side of the lebbek avenue. A quarter of a mile further he finds a sanded road which divides the race-course and golf links from the football, cricket, and polo grounds. If he were to follow it, this road

[1] The word *Gezireh* means "island," but the term has become identified with this one island in the Nile.

would lead him to the "Sports" Club-house,[1] a comfortable building, with a deep veranda, where idle men and women can catch the sun, while they hear the shouts from the racket and tennis courts, or the sharp crack of the croquet mallet.

In the afternoon the great majority of resident and fashionable Cairo—that is, English Cairo—are to be found in these sunny fields. They are seated in their carriages or on the grand stand; they are on horseback, or they lean upon their cycles; they are playing cricket, tennis, or croquet; they are going round the links, or they are looking on at their more energetic neighbours who are engaged in one or other of these forms of sport.

It is due to the existence of this playground that the English children laugh as they gallop their ponies, that the women keep the pink in their cheeks, and the men who sit all through the morning—and sometimes up to six o'clock in the evening—in the quiet rooms of dilapidated palaces, drive the creaking machinery of the *Gouvernement Egyptien* with the comparative ease and success which has extorted the admiration of a captious Europe.

Of course there is nothing extraordinary in the Gezireh racecourse, or the Sports Club. The same institutions, giving the same opportunities for out-of-door exercise, exist in every Anglo-Indian centre, at Singapore, at Hong-Kong, and on a larger and more democratic scale in South Africa, Australia, and New Zealand. But what is noticeable at Cairo is the comparative display of Anglo-Saxon characteristics which is made at Gezireh, when we notice, as we cannot fail to do, the unobtrusive manner in which the Englishman otherwise lives. You may wander through the European quarter of Cairo, that is to say, the handsome streets and open spaces, sown with walled-in palaces, without detecting any external sign of the Anglo-Saxon domination. Even the Agency shows only a monogram of the Queen upon its outer gates, with a sentry-box without a sentry, to mark the residence of the real ruler of Egypt. The great houses, the numberless palaces, many of them imposing enough with their high outer

[1] The full name of the club is "The Khedivial Sporting Club."

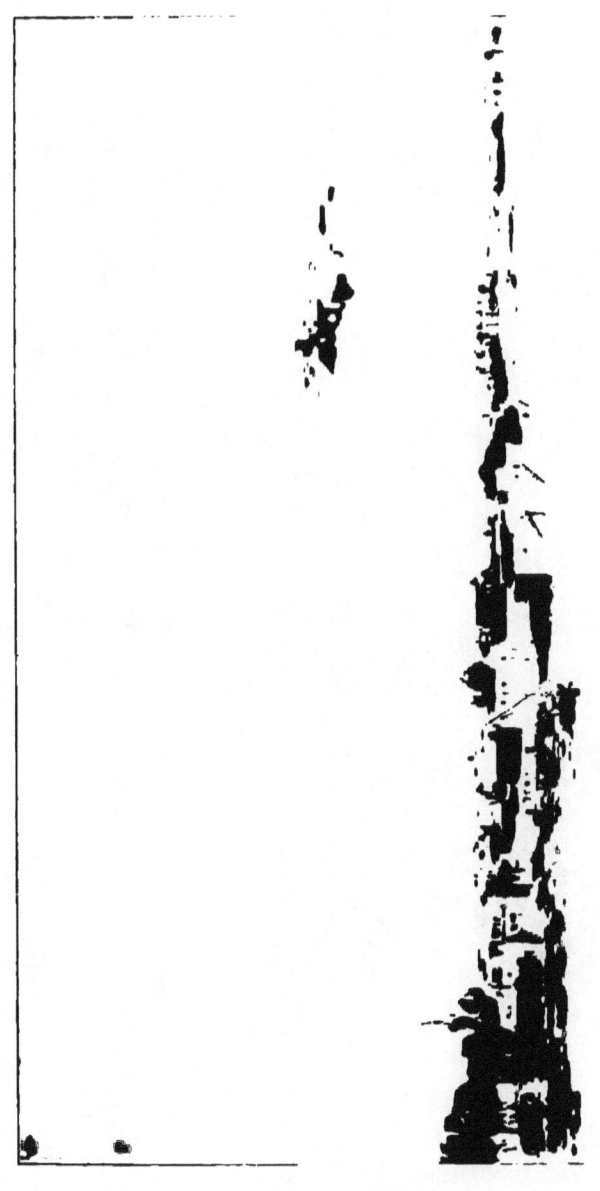

walls and arched gateways, round which groups of servants lounge in picturesque Turkish costume, belong to the Pashas, or to the Khedive's brother, uncles, or cousins. The largest and the smartest of the new houses which are springing up, especially on the Kasr-ed-Dubbara estate, are being built for the native landowners and grandees. The English officials are hidden away among the crowd of comfortable detached houses of moderate dimensions, in which the bulk of European Cairo resides. Among these houses, the residences of the twenty or thirty Consuls or Consuls-General, who so pertinaciously safeguard the interests of their respective nationalities, are alone distinguished by the coat of arms and the sentry-box. If the visitor penetrates into the recesses of any of the great Government departments, which are lodged for the most part in the discarded palaces of former Khedives, he will find himself in a busy hive which to all appearance is Egyptian or French, but certainly not English; and yet he knows that the real work of each Ministry is done almost without exception by an English adviser, who is hidden away somewhere in a corner of the building.

There is, however, one exception to this unobtrusiveness. In a quiet street in the European quarter the visitor will some day stumble upon a modest building, which bears over its entrance the uncompromising legend: HEADQUARTER OFFICES—ARMY OF OCCUPATION; and not far from this he will probably notice a comfortably sized house which has a sentry-box, where a smart sentry in a pipeclayed helmet and gorgeous kilt paces up and down. This is the General's house. Moreover, when he climbs the rock which Saladin crowned with solid battlements constructed of the stones from the outer layers of the Pyramids of Gizeh, he will find that the gates of Saladin's fortress are guarded by Highlanders. By the Nile Bridge, too, in the great square of the Kasr-en-Nil Palace—once the Ministry of War, and the chief scene of Arabi's intrigues—English soldiers are to be seen drilling in squads, or practising bugle notes under the shade of the isolated lebbek trees, or playing football, or riding bicycles. And not many days pass without the stately tramp of the Camerons being heard through the streets of Cairo, or the great drum and bagpipes of the Seaforths echoing round the rocks and battlemented walls of the Citadel. Once a day, too, the twelve o'clock gun booms from the Citadel, and reminds the docile Arabs of the presence of the English.

With this exception, no opportunity is lost of presenting the hereditary ruler of the Egyptian people to the public of the capital as the head of the State. By far the most imposing building—that is, of course, of the modern buildings—in Cairo, is the Abdin Palace. Its long façades look directly over the largest open space, the Abdin Square, which the capital possesses; and the entrances of this building are provided with their due complement of military sentries on the scale of any European palace. As a matter of fact, Abbás II., following the custom of Egyptian grandees, does not reside at this, his father's palace. He uses it solely for the transaction of the business of the Government, and for such official and court entertainments as he feels called upon to give. His favourite place of residence is the suburban palace of Kubbeh. For an Egyptian of position, when he succeeds to his inheritance, never occupies his father's palace, but at once sells it, or gets rid of it, or merely leaves it, in the manner of the country, to fall to pieces by decay. His Highness the Khedive is also brought forward as the head of the social life at Cairo. At every public function, whether it be the distribution of prizes at an agricultural show, or the opening of a library, His Highness, supported by one or other of his Ministers and of the Consuls-General, is the chief figure. On such occasions he is attended by a body of his household troops. At the chief of the numerous race meetings held on the Gezireh course, the most crowded moment is marked by the arrival of the Khedive's carriage, with its smart mounted escort. The Khedive is not, of course, accompanied by his wife or by any of the ladies of the harim on these occasions. The very limited portion of the social duties, which would in a European country be discharged by the wife, are in Egypt undertaken by the mother of the sovereign, who takes precedence of her son's consort. These duties are, of course, very restricted. For in accordance with Moslem manners the wife of the Khedive, or ex-Khedive, like any other woman of the upper classes, is absolutely precluded from all intercourse with any member of the male sex except her own husband and her nearest relatives.

The English residents have no more to do with the picturesque ruins and mud-heaps of mediæval Cairo than the average West-end Londoner has to do with the Mile-End Road and Tower Hamlets. He passes through the Muski, or follows one or other of the narrow streets which strike right and left from that familiar thoroughfare, when he wishes to show a visitor the tombs of the Khalifs, a mosque, or a bazaar. At other times his movements are entirely confined to the broad streets of the European quarter, to the island of Gezireh, or the drive to Gizeh and the Pyramids. The barracks at the Citadel and at Abbasiyeh form social centres which occasionally attract him in these directions; but for the most part he walks or drives from his house to his office or his club without passing beyond the broad and shaded streets of the European quarter, and leaves that quarter only for the open spaces and avenues of Gezireh. During the hot months, that is, the months of May, June, and July, when the Nile is rising, and the ground is broken into fissures and all vegetation is parched and withered, and in the three following months, August to October, when the Nile is in flood, and the arid soil has been changed into drenched fields with a moist and steamy atmosphere, the English women live at home. At this time all who are not tied by domestic duties or other considerations fly from Cairo. Of those who are prevented from returning to England, many betake themselves to Ramleh, the seaside suburb of Alexandria, where, at any rate, the heat of the Egyptian summer is tempered by sea breezes. The men, too, as a general rule, take a holiday of considerable length in England at least every second year. It is only, therefore, during the cool months that there can be said to be an English society in the Egyptian capital. The normal numbers of this society are swollen by the many visitors who reside for a longer or shorter time in Egypt for the winter. When I speak, then, of the life of the English residents, it must be understood that what I am describing exists for only six or seven months out of the twelve, that is to say, from November to May.

Apart from the engagements of the Sports Club, already described as constituting part of the routine life of the English residents in Cairo, there are additional events which give variety to social intercourse during the winter months. In December, January, and February race meetings are held at intervals of a fortnight or three weeks at Gezireh, under the auspices of the Khedivial Sporting Club. At the same period gymkhanas and other regimental gatherings, public and private, frequently take place at the barracks at Abbasiyeh and at Gezireh. During this period, which constitutes the season of the Egyptian capital, a certain number of official receptions are given at the Agency, and by the General-in-Command, and by the chief English officials. There is also a full allowance of private dinner-parties and dances, and the hotels, with their respective contingents of visitors, also contribute to the evening gaieties. At many of these latter, concerts and other evening entertainments are given beside the hôtel dances. Moreover, there is a handsome Opera House where French and Italian companies frequently appear during the season, and where sometimes both actors and singers of the first rank are to be heard. At Cairo, too, as elsewhere, the talent of the amateur actor and playwright is encouraged. In addition to these English, or mainly English, gatherings, occasional festivities on a larger scale are held at the Abdin Palace. The receptions and balls which the Khedive gives are of course attended by what a Frenchman would call *tout Caire*. Not only are the leading European residents of the foreign nationalities —French, German, Italian, Greek, and English—fully represented, but the Pashas, the Beys, and the Effendi, or official classes in general, together with the judges, the mudirs, and other notables from the country, assemble to pay their respects to the Khedive, or to enjoy his hospitality. On these occasions the Egyptians are not, of course, accompanied by their wives or daughters—or to use the appropriate native term, their harim. The nearest approach to allowing the women to share in social intercourse, is the permission accorded to the ladies of the Khedive's household to watch the dancing in the ballroom from behind a mushrebiyeh screen, much in the same way as English ladies watch the debates of the House of Commons. In order to participate in these State receptions, it is necessary for an Englishwoman, or any other European lady, to be presented to the *Vice-Reine Mère*, styled, like the Khedive's wife, the Khedivia;[1] while the Englishman is similarly presented to the Khedive. The Khedivia generally resides in her palace at Kubbeh, which is three or four miles from Cairo; and the presentation sometimes takes place here, and sometimes at the Abdin Palace. As the ceremony, in spite of its simplicity, is interesting, I will describe it. After a formal *visite de cérémonie* at the Abdin Palace, Mrs. X.—as we will call the lady who wishes to be presented—sends in her name to the wife of the Consul-General who represents the country to which she belongs, and it is submitted in due course to the Khedivia. Mrs. X. is then informed of the date of the next presentation, and is requested to meet the lady upon whom the duty of presenting her and the other European ladies falls, at the palace where the reception is to be held, or elsewhere as may be found convenient. Assuming that the reception is to be held at the Khedivia's palace at Kubbeh, Mrs. X. —who wears morning dress—will first have a pleasant drive of half-an-hour or so over roads for the most part shaded by lebbek and sycamore trees, with glimpses of the golden sands of the desert to her right, until she reaches the palace gardens. Here she will drive through groves of orange trees to the stone

[1] Strictly speaking the title "Khedivia" is used only of the Khedive's wife, and the title when applied to the Khedive's mother is qualified by the addition of the word *mère* (or mother). For the sake of brevity the term "Khedivia" is used in this passage in place of the more correct "Khedivia *mère*."

staircase which leads to the entrance-hall. After her wraps have been taken by attendants, she will wait in this hall, in the company of other ladies, until her turn has come for passing into the reception-room. As she does so, she will notice that in lieu of the regulation black dress and white cap these attendants wear coloured dresses, while their caps are adorned with artificial flowers to match the colour of their costumes. The presentees are introduced in groups of eight or ten. During the actual ceremony of introduction the Khedivia stands in the centre of the room, with the wife of the senior Consul-General—upon whom the duty of presenting falls—by her side. When Mrs. X.'s turn has come, her name is given by the latter to the Khedivia: Mrs. X. thereupon shakes hands and curtsies, and then passes towards one or other of the two lines of chairs, which are placed round the walls of the room. When all the presentations have been made, the Khedivia, accompanied by the Consul-General's wife, walks to a divan, where they both take seats, and Mrs. X. and the other ladies also find seats around them. The most trying part of the ceremony now begins. A conversation, conducted in French, is commenced by the Khedivia with the Consul's wife. The topics of this conversation are naturally confined to the commonest commonplace. Happily the conversation is limited to the two chief actors in the scene; for the Khedivia occasionally puts a question which would be difficult for any one unversed in such conversational exercises to answer without offending against the canons of Egyptian etiquette or the rules of French grammar. Fortunately, too, the conversation is soon closed. Then the Consul-General's wife rises (with the Khedivia), and the ceremony is brought to an end by a little speech, in which she expresses the thanks of all the ladies who have been presented for the trouble which *Son Altesse* has permitted herself to take in receiving them. When this has been done, Mrs. X. and the other ladies rise, and once more curtsey and shake hands with the Khedivia before leaving the room. The Khedivia, it may be remarked, is short, with black hair, and an olive complexion. Her manner is pleasing, and she bears evident traces of her former good looks. She was born in the purple, being a Turkish princess; she is said to be wealthy, moreover, and she possesses a large number of magnificent diamonds. These she sometimes displays at her receptions, which are held at three o'clock in the afternoon. It remains to add that the Khedive's wife is generally present, and in this case, of course, Mrs. X. has to make two curtseys.

Except at these state receptions, French society, which consists mainly of the chief of the numerous French officials, holds itself rigorously aloof from the English. Any Frenchman whose sympathies are enlisted by the unmistakable progress which Egypt has made under English direction, and who would naturally desire to live on friendly terms with the English officials, is regarded with some suspicion by his fellow-countrymen. In 1894, when the Khedive exhibited an open hostility to the English, and there was some talk of England withdrawing, one of these enlightened French officials gave an expression of his opinion at once emphatic and witty: "Si les Anglais partiront demain, moi, je quitterai hier." With the Italians and Germans there is no such feeling of jealousy, but the residents of these nationalities are mainly of the classes who would not be suited for such social intercourse, even if they desired it.

As regards the participation of the Egyptians themselves in this society, it may be said at once that the high officials, and the men of the Pasha class, meet the English on equal terms, and form an appreciable and characteristic element of Cairo society. In one point, indeed, the Egyptian politician has a distinct advantage over a man of the same class in England. According to Egyptian etiquette a Minister takes precedence of all other guests with the exception of royalties, although his social rank may be inferior to that of one or more of his fellow-guests. Intercourse with the Egyptian ladies is more difficult. The Moslem custom, which excludes a woman of the upper classes from all association with persons of the opposite sex, with the exception of their near relatives and respective husbands, makes it of course impossible for them to take part in any of the ordinary social gatherings of Europeans. The only opportunity, therefore, which European ladies have of exchanging ideas with Egyptian ladies is to visit them in their own houses—or rather in that part of their husbands' houses which is assigned exclusively to them and their female attendants. These visits are sometimes returned, but in this case notice is first sent to the European hostess, in order that all male servants may be removed—a necessity which causes some little inconvenience, as the native servants in European households are exclusively men. The European husband, too, must disappear; as his presence would, of course, be contrary to Moslem etiquette.

In conclusion, a word or two may be added on the important domestic topic of servants. With the exception of a few upper servants, natives are employed for all domestic duties—that is, of course, native men.[1] In the first place they are very easily fed, and in the second, they have a very picturesque appearance. It cannot be said that the native servants in Cairo, or generally in Egypt, are very successful in performing the duties which are entrusted to them, or that the relationship which exists between these servants and their English masters and mistresses is very satisfactory. The natives are undoubtedly careless and indolent. To avoid going indoors to make an inquiry, a native dragoman will state as a fact information which he either knows to be untrue, or about which he is quite uncertain. And the indoor servant grows remiss in his work unless he is constantly supervised. The general verdict, representing the experience of the majority of English residents, is that they are "very bad." But this inefficiency must be referred, in part at least, to the fact that the means of communication which exists between them and their masters is in most cases singularly defective. If the

---

[1] *Arab* servants are rarely employed. Nearly all the native servants are Berbers or Nubians. The former are said to be easily trained, intelligent, and sometimes devoted; but they are in general given to petty thieving.

English master (or mistress) speaks Arabic—a circumstance much less frequent than one would expect—his knowledge of the language is only just sufficient to enable him to give the commonest orders. On the other hand, if it is the native servant who speaks the foreign language, his knowledge of French or English, as the case may be, is elementary; and his anxiety to appear to possess the important qualification of speaking a European language often causes him to pretend to understand an order when he really knows nothing of its purport. In either case the result is the same. With few exceptions anything like a proper relationship between master and servant is practically impossible; and owing to this difficulty of language the European master (or mistress) fails to acquire any influence over the servant, or to feel any interest in him; while, on the other hand, the native servant often appears careless or stupid when he is really doing his best to carry out orders, the meaning of which he can only guess. There is, however, one redeeming feature in the situation. With a rapidly increasing native population, it is easy to get rid of a native servant and engage another, who cannot be worse and may be better. Moreover, since the "stricken field" of Omdurman, the English language has become very popular in the primary schools of the towns, while within the last few years a commencement of a genuine system of national education has been made by the endeavour of the Education Ministry to utilize and regenerate the mosque schools—the Kuttabs—which form the sole resource of the small towns and villages. If the regeneration of the Kuttab brings with it the education of the hitherto almost entirely neglected girls, a new era of moral and intellectual development will ensue, and one of the results of this development will be to provide a new and more reliable class of servants.

CHAPTER XI

THE BARRAGE AND THE IRRIGATION SERVICE

Story of the Barrage—System of irrigation different in Upper and Lower Egypt—Importance of the Barrage—Designed by Mongel Bey in 1843—Rosetta branch completed in 1863—The whole structure abandoned in 1867—Moncrieff organizes irrigation service in 1883—Anglo-Indian engineers—Temporary repair of Barrage—Effect of this—Permanent repair undertaken—Source of its insecurity—The remedy—The design put into execution by Colonel Western and Mr. Reid—Method and difficulties of work—Accomplished in 1890—Effect upon cotton crop of Delta—Completion of irrigation system of Lower Egypt—Perfect organization of irrigation service—Attempt to employ Egyptians as inspectors—Present appearance of Barrage—Consolidation of the piers and foundations now effected—Construction of subsidiary weirs—Efficiency and stability of Barrage secured - Drainage of cultivable area of Egypt now in progress.

If I were desired to mention the two most interesting objects in the immediate neighbourhood of Cairo, I should add to the inevitable Pyramids the great weir which bars the Nile, and is known by its French title—the Barrage. Of these two dissimilar objects, the first has probably occupied a larger space in the thoughts of men than any other existing group of structures in the world; the attraction of the latter dates from yesterday, and the interest which centres around it is of an entirely different order. A philosopher might find an effective contrast in the character and purposes of the two structures, and see in them each the type of two vastly divergent epochs in the history of Egypt. But apart from these wider considerations, the story of the Barrage has an intrinsic interest sufficient to arrest the attention of the most matter-of-fact observer. It is the story of a brilliant conception converted by dishonest workmanship into a costly failure; of a costly failure raised against all expectation to fulfil the purposes of the original design; of five provinces saved from starvation, and a country from financial ruin, by Anglo-Saxon skill and Anglo-Saxon determination.

But before I tell the story of the repair of the Barrage[1]—or rather repeat it, as Sir Colin Scott-Moncrieff has himself told it with no unnecessary word in the official records—it is necessary to say something of that system of irrigation in which this work is an all-important factor. Throughout Egypt, as the reader knows, the fields are watered not by the clouds, but by the Nile. In Upper Egypt, with the exception of the fields under cane and cotton, the water is brought to the fields during the season of high Nile only, that is to say, once a year during the months of August, September, and October, when the river is in flood. When the flood has passed away, the fields, thus fertilized by water and rich deposits of red mud, are sown with seed, from which the crops are gathered in the early spring. Then the fields lie fallow until the season of flood returns. This natural system of irrigation—natural, because it involves no artificial interference with the seaward flow of the Nile—has served to fertilize the fields of Egypt from the time of the Pharaohs, and it is still practised in Upper Egypt, where the sole channels of irrigation are the *nili*, or "flood" canals. In Lower Egypt, however, the artificial and more effective system, in which the nili canals are supplemented by *séfi*, or "summer" canals, was introduced early in the century by Mohammed Ali. Here the fields are no longer flooded for a brief period, and then left fallow when the winter crops have been gathered; but they are furnished with a moderate and regular supply of water throughout the year. For the purpose of furnishing these perennial supplies, the Nile flood is no longer sufficient; but the seaward flow of the great river must be checked, and a sufficient head of water maintained at all times to fill the summer canals. The immediate object of the change was to introduce the cultivation of cotton and sugar, since for these more valuable crops it was necessary that the land should not be submerged, but

---

[1] More correctly *Barrages*, as the work consists of two weirs.

irrigated—and irrigated during the dry season, when the flood canals would be empty and useless.

To-day the necessary works—the Nile reservoir at Assuân and the subsidiary dam at Assiût—for the storage of water in Upper Egypt, are already under construction, and in a few years the system of perennial irrigation will be applied to the whole of the Nile Valley. In the meantime the cultivated area of Upper Egypt, as a whole, receives its supplies of water once a year only, when the river is in flood; and where in these districts perennial irrigation has been already introduced, the necessary supply of water is raised from the Nile, either by the primitive sakíyeh or shadûf of the felláhin, or by the steam pump of the European planter. But in the Delta the system of perennial irrigation has long been in active operation, the network of canals and drains has been fully developed, and the subsidiary works necessary to secure the permanence of the Barrage, which regulates and maintains the flow of the river, are on the verge of completion. The essential element in this system is the Barrage; and if any untoward incident destroyed this work, and thereby prevented the storage of the necessary supply of water, the whole of this intricate and perfect system of canals would be rendered worthless, the cotton crop of the Delta, which affords three-fourths of the income of Egypt, would fail, and the financial resources of the Government would be seriously impaired. In short, for the present at least, the prosperity of Egypt depends upon the efficiency of this single work.

When the cultivation of cotton was first introduced by Mohammed Ali, and a perennial system of irrigation was established in the Delta with this end in view, it was at once recognized that the natural method of securing the necessary supply of water was to hold up the Nile at the point where its stream divides into the two main branches which flow respectively to Rosetta and Damietta. The design of the Barrage was furnished by a French engineer, Mougel Bey, and the work was commenced about the year 1843. Eighteen years later, in 1861, the structure was completed at a cost of £1,800,000, "besides the unpaid labour of uncounted annual corvées, and of whole battalions of soldiers." Across the whole width of the river—from the east bank to the isthmus which forms the apex of the Delta; from the isthmus to the west bank—there stretched two long lines of arches, crowned at intervals with graceful towers and gateways. Of the two bridges thus formed, the first was carried by seventy-one arches across the Damietta branch of the Nile, and measured 535 metres in length; the second, which crossed the Rosetta branch, had sixty-one arches, and was 465 metres in length. The united length of the roadway carried by both bridges was 1095 yards. Each arch was to be fitted with gates, and by means of these gates the flow of the river was to be regulated or entirely checked. When the river was in flood the gates were to be open; when the river was low the gates were to be dropped and the up-stream level raised $4\frac{1}{2}$ metres, or 14 feet 9 inches, while the head of water thus secured was to be distributed by three main canals throughout the Delta. At the same time the navigation of the Nile was maintained by two locks, placed respectively at the eastern and western extremities of the dam. In due course the eastern or Rosetta Barrage was fitted with its gates, and in 1863 this part of the structure was put in operation. The immediate result of closing the gates was to show that the Barrage was wholly incapable of bearing the strain to which it was subjected. Although the maximum head of water held up—and that only for a short period—was 5 feet 9 inches, the masonry commenced to crack, and in 1867 a "serious settlement" was reported. The arches of the Damietta branch were never even furnished with gates; and from the time of the settlement in the Rosetta branch the entire structure was practically abandoned as being useless for the purpose for which it was intended. The whole magnificent structure had been ruined by the worthlessness of the foundations upon which it had been built, and a meagre supply of water for the summer irrigation of the Delta had to be henceforth provided by steam pumps and other costly expedients. It is true that in the time of Ismâil, Sir John Fowler reported that the Barrage could be rendered efficient at a cost of £1,200,000, but no attempt was made to realize a scheme at once so doubtful and expensive.

Nor did the mischief end here. While the Barrage remained condemned as a "costly failure," the condition of the cultivated area of the Delta was slowly deteriorating. The canals were becoming choked and useless, the old land had been impoverished by the neglect of any proper rotation of crops, and there was no water-supply to bring fresh lands under cultivation. In short, the very existence of the cotton industry—the chief resource of Egypt—was endangered.

This was the position of affairs when Sir Colin Scott-Moncrieff was summoned from India, in 1883, to organize an irrigation service for Egypt. In this and the following year he was joined by a small group of Anglo-Indian engineers. How these men, by dint of strenuous exertion and a skilful application of their Indian experience to the conditions of Egypt, succeeded in the course of the next ten years in providing the whole cultivable area of both the Delta and the Nile Valley with a reliable supply of water, forms one of the most brilliant episodes in the record of the Occupation. Of this episode only a few words can be said here. For the purposes of irrigation the whole country was divided into five "circles" or districts, of which three were in Lower and two in Upper Egypt. The whole of the irrigation works within each circle were placed under the absolute control of one capable official, styled the "inspector." Under the direction of these inspectors the canals were cleared and improved, new canals were constructed, the Nile banks were repaired, and an effective system of drainage was commenced. But the immediate and pressing task which awaited the new Inspector-General was to supply the cotton plantations of the Delta with water. It was a task which admitted of no delay, and with it the question of repairing the Barrage was immediately involved.

"When I came to Egypt in May 1883," writes Sir Colin Scott-Moncrieff in his official Note,[1] "I was warned by all,

[1] Egypt, No. 2 (1890).

English as well as foreign engineers, to have nothing to say to so unsound a work.

"I found the Public Works Ministry had then just concluded a contract to last until 1915, with a private company, to supply irrigation to the Western Delta (Behera Province), at a cost of £50,000 per annum; and the first thing that I had to do on arrival at Cairo was to pronounce on a proposal to continue this system of irrigation by means of pumps to the whole of Lower Egypt, at an initial cost of £700,000 and an annual outlay of £248,550."

But before he accepted "so extravagant a programme," Sir Colin determined to "see what the Barrage was really worth." Externally its appearance was not promising. "The work had been so long neglected," he says, "that timbers were rotten, iron was rusted, there were no appliances or tools, and attached to it there was a large establishment of superannuated and incompetent men, who for years had done little besides drawing their pay." Nevertheless Sir Colin and his Anglo-Indian colleague, Mr. Willcocks, proceeded to test it. In the spring of 1884 a sum of £25,611 was spent in "patching up and working" the Barrage. That year, during the period of low Nile, the water was held up 7 feet 2 inches. "This flushed the canals, and gave an unwonted impulse to the irrigation. Fortune so far attended us that the cotton crop of 1884 was the best on record, and the General Produce Association of Alexandria did us the honour of publicly thanking us for our efforts." In 1885 the process was repeated, and in this year the water was held up 9 feet 10 inches, at a cost of only £18,246.

In this same year the Egyptian Government was permitted by the Powers to borrow £1,000,000 for irrigation works; and with the "irrigation million" came the opportunity of converting these temporary expedients into a permanent restoration—in other words, of rendering "this Barrage, on which hung the irrigation of Lower Egypt," at once efficient and secure.

The source of its insecurity is clearly described in the Note.

"The Barrage," Sir Colin writes, "is built on nothing more solid than alternate beds of fine river sand and alluvial mud. This is not a very favourable foundation for an ordinary bridge, and during the flood-season the Barrage is not only exposed to the risks of an ordinary bridge, but during low Nile it is exposed to much more. The water on one side in June 1885 was 15.74 feet deep, on the other side only 5.90 feet, a difference of nearly 10 feet; hence a constant tendency of the water to percolate under the foundations and establish a uniform level. Had the Barrage been built in a bed of loose boulders this percolation would have deprived us of all the water intended to fill the canals, but it would not have hurt the work itself. Not so with a foundation of mud and sand. The water passing through these is likely to carry the particles along with it, and by degrees undermine the whole. Evidently some such action had caused the alarming cracks in 1867." The remedy was to place an "impermeable bar" across the river, through which the water either could not travel at all, or, if it did travel, would travel with a velocity so checked that instead of washing out the sand and mud beneath the arches of the dam, it would leave the sand or mud, which it brought with it, behind; and so the substratum, instead of being loosened, would become firmer every year, "like an old filter." "It was not a new idea," Sir Colin adds, but "only the system pursued by Sir Arthur Cotton with the great river dams of Southern India. In no Indian river that I know, however, is the sand and mud so fine as in the Nile." In applying this remedy, it was decided, in view of the danger of making deep excavations in so treacherous a surface, to "spread the foundations out so as to form a broad water-tight platform." And in order to give increased solidity to the whole work, "a solid bed of Portland cement concrete four feet thick," covered where necessary with masonry of stone, was placed over the old flooring; while at the same time a "line of sheet piling 16 feet deep was to be carried across the whole river 85 feet above the bridge," to hold the loose sand and mud of the river bed.

In putting this design into execution the engineers, Lieut.-Colonel Western, R.E., and Mr. A. G. W. Reid, who had been summoned from India by Sir Colin Scott-Moncrieff, were confronted by two special difficulties. In the first place, interference with the ordinary service of the Barrage would have caused enormous loss to the Delta; in Sir Colin's words, "it was like mending a watch and never stopping the works." And in the second, the "working season" was a very short one, lasting only from 1st March to the end of June. It was necessary, therefore, to repair the foundations of the whole structure in sections. The method pursued was "to inclose the portion to be operated upon by great earthen banks forming a coffer-dam all round," and then to pump out the water and expose the masonry. After a successful experiment in the spring of 1886, when six bad floorings were in part repaired, the work was commenced in earnest during the following December; and in the course of this and three succeeding seasons the foundations of the whole series of arches from shore to shore had been rendered stable.[1]

The precise conditions under which the successive repairs were executed differed in each season; but the general character of the operations, and the special difficulties under which they were conducted, are sufficiently indicated by the account which Sir Colin Scott-Moncrieff gives of the repair of the western half of the Rosetta branch of the Barrage in 1886-87.

"On the 2nd December 1886, the coffer-dams were begun. It was not until the 24th March 1887 that the first stone of the new work was laid. From that day work continued day and night, the night-work being done by the light of electric lamps. Nine powerful steam-pumps kept the water down all this time. On the afternoon of the 1st July the last piece of machinery

[1] The west half of the Rosetta branch was finished in the season of 1886-87, the east half of the Damietta branch in 1887-88, the east half of the Rosetta branch in 1888-89, and the west half of the Damietta branch in 1889-90. In executing this last operation, the number of the arches of the Damietta branch of the Barrage was reduced from seventy-one to sixty-one—the ten westernmost arches, with the adjacent lock, being cut off. Hence the Barrage to-day consists of two branches, each of which has an equal number of arches, that is, sixty-one.

was removed from the completed floor. Before the next morning the rising flood had covered all that had been done. Every day fresh and unlooked-for difficulties arose. It was found that the massive outer wall of the western lock rested on foundations, the bottom of which was eight feet higher than the bridge flooring. To dry the latter, then, we had to work below the lock foundations, and it was with difficulty prevented from falling over bodily. The flooring, as well as the arch of one opening, was cracked across diagonally, showing a complete fracture of the work, the fissure being four inches wide. Strong springs burst out daily in fresh places, and had to be staunched at an immense expense of material. Daily Mr. Reid had to face some new trouble, and to invent some new expedient, and he never failed."

In 1890 the repair of the Barrage had been practically accomplished; it only remained to "spread a broad apron of large, heavy stones across the down-stream edge of the work." The entire cost of the improvements effected was estimated to be £420,000. Regarded merely as an outlay of capital, this expenditure was amply justified. The results which followed directly from the increase of the water-supply of the Delta were startling in themselves. Writing under date June 24, 1890, Sir Colin says, " Next year and in future, if the Nile supply is sufficient, we shall not hesitate to hold up 4 metres, or 13 feet, at the Barrage. Hitherto, we have limited ourselves to 3 metres, or 9 feet 10 inches. During the five years previous to 1885 the market price of cotton was considerably higher than it has been since. The ravages of the cotton worm have been chiefly in the latter five years. Nevertheless, the mean cotton exports for the five years, 1880–1884, amounted to 2,750.171 kantars per annum, while for the five years ending 1889 they amounted to 3,084,064 kantars. Here is a mean annual difference of 333.893 kantars, which, at the moderate price of P.E. 250 per kantar, comes to £E834,732 annual benefit to the country, which I think we may fairly claim to the credit of the Barrage while as yet incomplete. I say nothing of the increase in cotton-seed, rice, or bersim."

BARRAGE AND IRRIGATION SERVICE 205

Since this date, as we have already seen,[1] the amount of the Egyptian cotton crop has been doubled. But, putting on one side the value of this increase, and any estimate we may form of the increase in the subsidiary crops grown in the Delta, the successful completion of this difficult task afforded a significant example of the financial advantages which could be obtained from a judicious expenditure on public works. As such it was of the greatest service to the Egyptian Government, for it enabled them to obtain from the Caisse de la Dette, as the representative of the European creditor, a more generous recognition of the fact that Egypt was a country in which capital could be safely invested. As the result of this improvement of Egyptian credit, a second million[2] was secured for further reproductive works, and by this means the irrigation system of Upper Egypt was set in order. In the meantime, that is to say while the restoration of the Barrage was in progress, the system of main canals, which formed part of the original scheme for supplying the Delta with water, was completed. Of the three main canals which were destined to distribute the head of water held up by the Barrage, one only—the Menûfiyeh—had been constructed, and even this otherwise fine work required the addition of a lock to make it navigable—for it fulfils the double purpose of a channel of irrigation and navigation. The Menûfiyeh canal passes southwards through the isthmus which divides the two branches of the Barrage and carries water to the central provinces of the Delta, Menûfiyeh, and Ghabiyeh. The Behêrah, or western canal, destined to serve the province so called, had also been constructed, but it had become useless by continued neglect. This canal was accordingly dredged, and its banks repaired. The eastern canal, by which the two provinces of Dakaliyeh and Sharkieh are supplied, had not even been commenced. It was constructed at a cost of £320,000 during the years 1887-89, and was opened in February 1890 by the

[1] Chap. iii. p. 44.
[2] Actually £E910,000, obtained through the conversion of the Privileged Debt from 5 per cent. to 3½ per cent.

Khedive Tewfik, in honour of whom it was called by its present name, the Tûfikieh canal.

Since the date of the restoration of the Barrage, continued improvements have been made in the system of canals and channels of which it is the centre and source of supply. At the same time, the irrigation service, both in Lower and Upper Egypt, has been gradually raised to its present condition of perfect efficiency. Some idea of the completeness of the organization of this all-important branch of the Public Works Department, and of the perfect order to which the entire irrigation system of the country has been reduced, may be gathered from the following fact. Last year (1898), the Nile rose to an exceptional height, and the flood was long continued, but in spite of this circumstance, which involved an additional strain both upon the banks of the river—always carefully watched at the season of flood—and upon the regulating sluices and banks of the main channels of irrigation, no single officer had to be recalled from leave. Moreover, although the inspectors still keep their steamers in readiness on the river during the period of flood, in case they should be summoned to some distant point, the occasions on which their presence is thus hurriedly required are becoming more and more rare. The attempt to employ natives in positions of responsibility in this service appears to have been attended with the same unsatisfactory results, as those which followed the attempt to promote native officers to independent commands in the army. The experiment of promoting native engineers to inspectorships, I was told, had failed; for not only were the men themselves incapable of assuming any responsibility, but the native subordinate officials would not work cheerfully under their direction. Some engineers from Cooper's Hill, I was informed, had willingly accepted positions under Egyptian inspectors; but in spite of the invidiousness of the proceeding, the Public Works Department had been compelled, in the interests of the country, to place these young Englishmen over the heads of Egyptians who had grown old in the service. Again: the native cultivator is entitled to make a complaint at the irrigation offices if his land is insufficiently supplied with water; but he objects to make this complaint before a native official, and often in an office full of Egyptian clerks, he will loudly demand to be brought into the presence of an Englishman.

To one who knows the history of the Barrage, the most powerful impression which the first sight of the great weir brings is a feeling of surprise—surprise at the apparently perfect condition of its masonry and mechanism. We had left Cairo by the ten o'clock train. As there were no first-class carriages attached to it, we had travelled as far as Kaliûb, where the branch line to the Barrage joins the main line from Cairo to Alexandria, in a dilapidated second-class carriage, which afforded one more excellent example of the condition to which the rolling stock of the Egyptian Government railways had been reduced by the neglect of which Mr. Robertson, the late President of the Railway Board, complained so bitterly. A native passenger attracted our attention by his characteristic attitude. He sat cross-legged in the corner of a seat, leaving his large red shoes on the floor entirely divorced from his large stockinged feet. Both at Cairo and at the intermediate stations Arab boys entered the carriages with French and English newspapers and books, or with baskets of fruit and native cakes. After waiting half-an-hour at Kaliûb, we eventually reached the Barrage station at 11.20—a rather tedious but otherwise agreeable and interesting journey. Before we had arrived we noticed the chimneys and roofs of the engineering works in the eastern village, and when we left the station we were invited to traverse the three-quarters of a mile, roughly measured by the two weirs and the isthmus between them, in the conventional manner, that is, by trolley. As, however, we desired a more intimate acquaintance with the great weir than any which we should obtain by this rapid method of transit, we rejected the overtures of the Arabs, and proceeded on foot to the entrance of the Damietta branch. On our way we crossed the Tûfikich Canal, a broad channel which ran southwards in a perfectly straight course. We were now confronted by a graceful gateway designed in the style of military Gothic; and as we passed under its arches we crossed the swing bridge of the eastern lock, which permits the passage of the Nile boats. After we had passed through this gateway, we found the roadway carried by the arches of the weir stretching out before us. Down the centre of this roadway, which was paved by blocks of wood, ran the narrow line of rails over which the Arabs made the trolleys spin; and its surface was

TRAVELLING WINCH.

traversed by groups of camels and donkeys amid the crowds of foot passengers, for the Barrage serves the double purpose of bridge and weir. On our left, that is, up-stream, were the sluices, which are raised or lowered, as occasion may require, by a travelling winch, which runs on rails, and thus serves all the sluices between the eastern and the central gateway. Beyond this central gateway a second travelling winch performs the same office in respect of the remaining sluices of the Damietta branch. On

BARRAGE AND IRRIGATION SERVICE

the right of the roadway was the parapet, relieved by the semi-circular projections which mark the centre of each of the sixty-one arches which formed the down-stream front. The Damietta Barrage led us to the isthmus which separates the two branches of the Nile. The broad roadway was pleasantly shaded with trees, and on the left of it some pretty gardens had been laid out. These gardens, we were told, were thronged by holiday parties, both native and European, who came from Cairo on Friday—the Mohammedan day of rest—and on Sunday. In the centre of the isthmus we found the system of sluices and locks which marked

MENÛFIYEH CANAL AND LOCK.

the head of the Menûfiyeh Canal, and east and west of these works were the offices of the Barrage and the residence of the Director, Mr. Allan Joseph. Both of these buildings, and the public gardens—although these latter had not yet been completed—appeared to be in perfect order. From the Director's house a fine avenue leads to the gateway of the Rosetta Barrage. By this branch, which resembles the Damietta branch in all respects, we passed to the west bank of the Nile. Here we found an untidy Arab village, and amused ourselves by watching the passage of several boats through the western lock. From this bank the down-stream front of the Rosetta Barrage spread its arches in a long and imposing line across the brown water of the Nile.

At the time of my visit the piers and foundations of the Barrage had just been strengthened by an ingenious device. It was found by experiments, made in January 1897, upon the Rosetta Barrage, that cavities existed in the masonry of some of the piers. As the result of this discovery, the Public Works Department determined to take all possible measures for securing a work of such vital importance against the imminent risk of accident thus revealed. In order to consolidate the existing masonry, four holes were drilled in each pier. They were driven through the piers, through the successive layers of the masonry of the foundations to the sand beneath. Then "pure cement grout, of the consistency of thick cream, was poured until both cavity and tube could take no more." In this way it was hoped that the cavities in the interior of the piers would be filled up by sound material, and that the foundation, as a whole, would be "tightened up" by the cement thus introduced under pressure of the weight of its own column. This pressure was estimated to vary from 19 to 26 tons per square metre. The probable effect of this operation—and the necessity for it—may be understood from the fact that five holes of one pier alone in the Rosetta Barrage took 439 barrels of cement; this, however, was an exceptional case, for the average amount taken by each pier was 25 barrels. The consolidation of the Rosetta Barrage was accomplished in 1897, and the Damietta Barrage was treated in the same way during the following year.[1]

But a second and more extensive work, undertaken with the same object in view, was in progress. This work consists in the construction of two subsidiary weirs—one on each branch of the Nile—a few hundred yards below the Barrage. These weirs, which

---

[1] Egypt, No. 1 (1898), and No. 3 (1899). This important work was completed under the direction of Major Brown, the Inspector-General of Irrigation for Lower Egypt, and Mr. Alien Joseph, the Director of the Barrage.

BARRAGE AND IRRIGATION SERVICE 211

are to be constructed of "rough rubble masonry laid in cement," will be submerged during the period of flood; but when the Barrage is holding up the stream of the Nile, they will lessen the strain by raising the down-stream level of the water. In this way it is expected that the difference between the water level on either side of the Barrage will be reduced from 4 to 2½ metres. And, in addition to this reduction of the strain

WEST END OF ROSETTA BARRAGE.

upon the parent weir, the subsidiary weirs will also increase its efficiency; since it is intended to raise the gates of the Barrage so that the depth of the water held up will be increased from 14½ to 15½ metres (about 50 feet), although, at the same time, the difference between the two levels will not exceed 2½ metres. A sum of £E530,000 has been granted by the Caisse de la Dette for the construction of these weirs, and it is expected that the works will be completed by the end of 1901.[1] As we crossed the Damietta Barrage we noticed the barges filled with building material and other signs of the progress of the first of the two weirs which is being constructed in this branch of the Nile. We were told, however, that although the engineers could complete the work before the Nile rose, they did not intend to do so; because they wished to see what effect would be actually produced by the weir before they determined the height to which it was to be finally raised.

In addition to the construction of these subsidiary weirs, which are intended at once to assure and increase the water-supply of Lower Egypt, and in addition to those great works in Upper Egypt, which will subsequently come under our notice, the irrigation service is at the present time engaged in improving the drainage of the whole cultivable area of the country. In 1897 a sum of £E296,000 was devoted to this purpose, with the result that 325 kilometres of new drains were made, and 163 kilometres of previously existing drains were improved. In 1898 £E281,000 was spent upon drainage works in Lower Egypt, producing 308 kilometres of new, and 267 kilometres of improved, drains. The greater part of the money thus expended was furnished by the Caisse de la Dette, and a further sum of £E200,000 has been granted by the same authority from the General Reserve Fund for drainage in the present year. Of the benefits to be derived from such expenditure Lord Cromer writes: "Every landowner in the country understands the advantage of a drain, and every one appreciates the work which is now being done. In a few years' time the country will possess a complete system of drains; the projects for the future are all well in hand, and fairly mapped out. Five years of annually decreasing expenditure should see them all finished, so that by the time that the increased water-supply resulting from the Nile reservoir is available, the country will be able to make use of it without risk of water-logging and deterioration of the soil."[2]

[1] Egypt, No. 1 (1898), and No. 3 (1899).   [2] Egypt, No. 3 (1899).

CHAPTER XII

THE PYRAMIDS

The museum at Gizeh—Egyptian statues—Conventional attitudes—Type of face revealed—Coptic sculptures—Egyptian art "barbaric"—Visit to the Pyramids of Gizeh—Absence of romance—The Sphinx—Enormous bulk of Pyramids of Cheops and Chephren—Origin of the Pyramids—Immortality of the soul—Herodotus's account—View from the plain—Merits and defects of Pyramids as essays in architecture—Esthetic significance—Due to size—Power of association—Remains of Memphis—Sakkâra—Apis tombs—Mastaba of Thy—Heliopolis—Plato's residence there—Strabo's account—Revision of the calendar due to priests.

In the last week of January we visited the Pyramids. The old Cairo had proved so absorbing, and the new Cairo so full of the palpitating interests of the present, that our second month in Egypt had almost run out, when we began to think of Memphis, the great predecessor of the Arabian town. The ancient capital of the Pharaohs has indeed passed almost utterly from the face of the earth, but its necropolis still stretches from Gizeh to Dahshûr; and from the heights of the Mokattam Hills, from the Citadel, from the minaret of Tulûn, from the Windmill Hill, from the mounds of Babylon—from every elevated place where we had been, the grey triangles of the Pyramids had risen in the distance, and seemed to reproach us for our long neglect.

But the Egypt of the monuments was a novel study, and we felt that we must furnish our minds with new ideas before we dared embark upon so strange a subject. The book of its history is "writ large" in pyramid, tomb, and temple; but before the traveller can read the meaning of these forms his eye must be familiarized with the atmosphere, thought, and circumstances of that far-off age in which these monuments took shape. Happily the materials for this process were near at hand. In their temporary home in the "matchboard palace" of Ismáîl at Gîzeh, were the representations of the men and women of the age of the Pharaohs, carved in stone and wood. Here, too, were the furniture of their houses, the implements of their husbandry, the cotton cloth they wore, the ornaments of gold and silver with which their women adorned themselves, the books of their priests, the drawings of their artists, the chariots on which they rode, and most wonderful of all, the actual bodies of their kings and priests, brought once more into the light of day from the deep recesses of their tombs. Here, surely, if anywhere, in the presence of these grim relics, we could think the thoughts which found expression in broad pylon, giant column, in colossus, pyramid, and Sphinx.

To the museum of Gîzeh, therefore, we went first; taking a modest luncheon-basket, that we might spend the whole unbroken day among its chambers and corridors. Of the statues and sculptured stones here collected, the greater part belong to ancient Egypt; and these examples of its art range from the third of Manetho's "dynasties" to the last and thirty-first, when Egyptian civilization was merged by Alexander in the more splendid civilization of Greece. That is to say, the periods in which they were produced were separated not by centuries but by millenniums— such intervals as serve to divide the England of Boadicea from the England of Victoria. It would seem as though in those remote ages the hand of time had as yet gathered no strength: for these works showed no sign of its "might"—of the silent and resistless action of "years unnumbered" that moved the Hellenic poet to a noble outburst of lyric song; of the power which, in our age, changes by its swift strokes the novelty of to-day into the commonplace of to-morrow. All these statues in stone, or in wood, were identical in form, and conventional in treatment; the painful limitations of the artist were apparent in the execution of all alike. Again and again we saw the same face, staring directly in front, and set in the same conventional representation of hair, beard, and head-dress; the same rounded shoulders and flat breasts, the same line falling from the armpits to the waist, the

same stiff arms and legs, the same flat feet always extended
directly in front at a right angle with the legs above them, and
the same loin-cloth with its conventional lines for folds. When
the figure—for it could not be called a man—stood, its arms fell
stiffly to its loins; when it sat, its arms and legs were bent at
right angles and its hands rested stiffly on the knees, the right
hand clenched, the left hand spread flat. In the faces alone
could any signs be discerned to show that any part of the block
had been chiselled in the presence of a living subject. Nor did
the figures which we saw carved on stone, or traced on pottery
and limestone tablets, or drawn on papyri, exhibit any higher
motives. Judged by the standard of Greece and Italy, Egyptian

PYRAMID OF MEDÛM.

sculpture was the sculpture of the barber's block and the wax
model; while Egyptian painting and drawing had the colouring
and lines which we observe to-day in the work of young children,
and admire as such for its piquant defects and shrewd imitations.

Nevertheless, childish in conception and crude in execution
as were these figures, they had revealed to us certain significant
facts. In the first room, where the oldest monuments had been
placed, we found two figures which had been discovered in 1870,
in a mastaba near the Pyramid of Medûm. This Pyramid, which
yields in antiquity only to the step Pyramid of Sakkâra, is
identified as the tomb of Snofru, the immediate predecessor of
Cheops; and it was constructed in the form of seven square

towers, of which three only are now standing. If, therefore, we take the Pyramid of Cheops as exhibiting the most fully developed form of the structure so called, the Pyramid of Medûm represents a stage of evolution even earlier than that of the step Pyramid of Sakkâra. The figures, which are those of Prince Rahotep and his wife Nofret, are carved in limestone, and the manner in which they are executed is in general the manner of the barber's block. Yet the expressions of the faces are intelligent, vivacious, with no trace either of the effeminacy of Asia, or of the animality of Africa. These faces, which must have been faithfully copied from the originals—since there is no trace of idealization in the art of ancient Egypt—were just such faces as we might see to-day in France, Italy, or even in England. In the second room, too, there was a statue of Ra-nofer, a priest of the fifth dynasty, discovered at Sakkâra, the face of which exhibited the same expression, although the rest of the figure, and indeed the face itself, was clumsy in execution. The face, arms, and legs, which had been stained flesh colour, and the hair and eyebrows, originally jet black, had preserved their colour in part. This face, which, as in the preceding case, could only have been produced by the faithful imitation of a living original, was in the highest degree refined and intelligent: it bore, in fact, all the traces of those character-forming influences which we identify with Græco-Roman, or modern civilization.

In an adjacent room were the mummies of Sethos I. and Ramses II. The shrivelled faces of these kings, marvellously preserved by skilful embalmment, bore unmistakable traces of the same refinement. Neither the faithful imitations of the living, nor the actual faces of the dead—representing epochs separated by a thousand years—showed any trace of the conventional Egyptian type perpetuated by the sculptures and the paintings, and thus rendered familiar to the whole civilized world; in short, they appeared to be absolutely free from any of the characteristic defects associated with Asiatic or African races.

In the room where we had found the statue of Ra-nofer we

saw the wooden statue from Sakkára; the so-called Shêkh el-Beled, or village chief. Here again the face had been obviously carved whilst the artist's eye rested on the original. The other parts of the figure, which is about three feet in height, were executed in the style of the toy shop. But the crowning example of the conventionality which characterized the whole collection of sculptures was afforded by the group of nine statues of Usertesen I., which we found in the twenty-first room. They had been brought from the South Pyramid of Lisht, and were of limestone. The king was represented as seated on his throne, in the conventional form adopted for this attitude; and each of the nine statues was identical with its fellows in all respects. In the changeless atmosphere of ancient Egypt the sculptor was converted into a machine for carving blocks of stone, and it was not until we had reached the forty-fourth room, where the collection of Græco-Roman remains began, that we found what our eyes had hitherto sought in vain—one human figure carved in stone which bore the stamp of art.

The collection of Coptic sculptures and other objects, which follows the antiquities of the Græco-Roman period, was interesting; for it showed at a glance how largely the Arabian architects were indebted for their decorative motives to the indigenous inhabitants of Egypt. The remaining collections took us back to ancient Egypt. These examples of the lesser arts were full of interest, nor was the standard of excellence revealed by them separated any longer by so wide an interval from the corresponding standard of Græco-Roman civilization. Here we found the common objects of the Egyptian household, the beds and chairs and stools, the pottery, the cooking utensils, the tools, and the linen clothes and shoes; the images and emblems, and all the sacred objects they used in the worship of their gods, and ornaments for the decoration of temple, shrine, and tomb. Elsewhere—in room seven—we had seen the exquisite work wrought by Egyptian goldsmiths four thousand years ago for the adornment of the women of the royal house; here we found the like objects of simpler make for women of humbler rank—mirrors, fans, and pin-cushions. Further on were specimens of drawing in line and colour, and the papyri, with their hieroglyphic texts and grotesque illustrations; and further still numberless mummies in part uncovered and in part enclosed in painted coffins.

There can be no question, of course, as to the antiquarian value of the contents of the museum at Gizeh. From this point of view they must be regarded as priceless possessions gleaned from the remote past. But if we regard them from the point of view of art, an entirely different estimate must be given. All of the objects which had met our eyes, with the exception of the Græco-Roman and Coptic antiquities, were barbaric; "barbaric," in the simple and etymological sense of the word, that is to say, they were beneath or outside of the standards of art and taste, set once for all by Greece and Rome, and maintained with appropriate developments ever since by the western nations. In short, while this collection at the Gizeh Museum had shown us that the civilization of ancient Egypt was the highest to which any people had attained before the development of Greece and Rome, it had also served to emphasize and define the enormous interval which separate these two stages in the evolution of society. One thought was uppermost, how *small* must the mind of man have been at this remote epoch; how limited his outlook upon the world.

We had determined that nothing less than a perfect day would serve for an excursion to the Pyramids, and at this time of year, when a hot mid-day sun was accompanied by a cold and boisterous wind, such days in Cairo were few and far between. A cold wind would make the long drive tedious; a hot sun would rob us of the pleasure of wandering all day on foot among the giant tombs. Several days passed before this perfect day came, and we were able to pack our luncheon-basket and sketching umbrella into the carriage, and bid the Arab coachman drive us to the Pyramids.

There is no romance about a visit to the Pyramids to-day. You hail a carriage from the stand, as we did, or you ride out on your bicycle, or a "tram" or coach will take you there with as little fuss as an omnibus takes you to St. Paul's. When Kinglake went to see them—not so very long ago—in the days of Mohammed Ali, he tells us that an Arab, disappointed of bakshísh, had proposed to the Shékh to rob and murder him in the interior of the Great Pyramid. No such opportunities await the traveller of to-day. When in due course we left the lebbek avenue, and turned up the slight incline which leads past Mena House to the plateau of the Pyramids, we were confronted by a ticket-office and a photographer's shop, with policemen to direct the traffic. It was a little discouraging, and we hurried away from the throng of cabs and tourists along the sandy path, between the east side of the Pyramid of Cheops and the three lesser Pyramids to the south. From the south-east corner of the Great Pyramid the path curved eastwards, and led us by a slight descent to a hollow, in the centre of which a tawny mass arose and bid us know the Sphinx. We climbed down from the embanked sand to the excavated space in front. Here, in a shaded corner, we sat and watched her rise to her full stature against the giant triangle behind her.

As we sat, groups of tourists, English, American, German, French, and Italian, passed around the bank above us, or climbed over her giant back and limbs. Some of them came mounted on camels, others were on donkeys, and a few had walked; but in each case they were accompanied by an Arab guide, with whom they conversed volubly. Every-day phrases and remarks, borne faithfully by the clear air, reached us in many languages, and the incongruity of this polyglot chatter served to separate us from our fellows, and made us feel as though we were alone with the Sphinx. As we gazed on her face she seemed to challenge us to read its broken lines, and under the spell of this challenge we gazed the longer, till at length a message came. "I am neither man nor woman," she seemed to say, "beast nor man. My face is not the face of one but of many, and in my countenance is gathered the meaning of them all. Of all ancient things in Egypt, I alone have kinship with the present. Therefore I speak now, and shall speak to-morrow, even as I spoke to Pharaoh yesterday. I am Egypt."

From the Sphinx we passed on to the Granite Temple, which is in process of excavation, and from this point we retraced our steps to the north-eastern corner of the Pyramid of Cheops. Here, from the edge of the ridge along which the lesser Pyramids lie, we looked out over the plain to Cairo. Across the emerald stretches of irrigated corn-lands at our feet the lebbek avenue, through which we had driven in the morning, ran in a line of darker green. The fields were broken here and there by brown patches of fallow land, by lines of date palms, and by pink and white villages. The plain was terminated by a dark-green fringe, which marked the more luxuriant foliage of the trees that grew on either side of the unseen Nile; and beyond this fringe was Cairo, a red and white mass, edged by a riband of bluish-green, where its gardens and groves touched the violet slopes of the Mokattam range behind it. From this point we again made our way southwards, reconnoitering the giant flank of Cheops' Pyramid as we passed; and then we struck across the sandy plain to the Pyramid of Chephren, and thence to the third, and lesser, Pyramid of Mycerinus. Here, resting under the shelter of the ruined walls of the Temple, which lies beneath the eastern flank of the third Pyramid, we looked backwards across the level stretch of white sand upon the Pyramid of Chephren, which spread the whole extent of its southern side before our eyes, upon the Pyramid of Cheops, the three lesser Pyramids, and the emerald plains beyond.

After we had gazed awhile, I unpacked my portfolio and began to sketch. As I proceeded with my task, the enormous bulk of the yellow mass in front of me grew upon my senses. It has been calculated that the Pyramid of Chephren contains more than two million cubic yards of solid masonry, being some five million tons in weight; while the Pyramid of Cheops, rising from a base little less than thirteen acres in extent, contains over

three million cubic yards of stone. But these figures told me less than the black-robed Arabs that, moving across the plain of sand, dwindled to ants as they approached the mighty triangle of stone. It was no business of mine to probe the secrets of the past, but, with this enormous flank before my eyes, it was impossible to avoid the questions, when, and how, and wherefore, had these gigantic masses been erected?

The account of Herodotus, the first traveller who carried a note-book, has not yet been superseded. He visited Egypt at the time of the Persian domination, a century or so before Alexander's conquest introduced the era of the Ptolemies, and he has, therefore, the advantage of Strabo by some four hundred years. Before he tells us the story of the building of the Pyramids, as he heard it on the spot, he records a pregnant statement which in itself explains the third of these questions—Why did the Egyptian kings cause their bodies to be buried in the heart of these mountains of masonry? "The Egyptians," he writes, "are the first to declare this saying also: that the soul of man is immortal; and when the body has perished, it passes into a series of living things that are not men, and when it has completed a cycle of migration through all the beasts of the earth, and the fishes of the sea, and the fowls of the air, it returns to the body and enters into it again, accomplishing the cycle in three thousand years." Under five million tons of masonry, the body of the king, skilfully embalmed and hidden in a secret chamber, would lie secure and undisturbed, until the soul came back after its long wanderings.

Having thus told us "Wherefore," Herodotus tells us "When" and "How." "Now up to the time of King Rhampsinitus," he writes, "they said that justice prevailed in Egypt, and that the land flourished mightily; but that after him Cheops became their king, and vexed them with all manner of evil. For he closed all the Temples, and prevented them from offering sacrifice; and then he bade all the Egyptians do tasks for him: some he made cut stones from the quarries on the Arabian hills, and drag them even to the Nile; and when the stones had been conveyed across the river in boats, he gave command to others to receive them, and drag them to the hills that are called Lybian. Now the companies of men numbered one hundred thousand, and each company worked for the space of three months. For ten years did the people labour at the building of the road along which they dragged the stones—a task scarce lighter than the Pyramid in my judgment; for five furlongs is the length thereof, and the breadth ten fathoms; and the height, even where the road is highest, eight fathoms; and it is made of polished stone, with figures of living things engraved thereon. Even so the ten years were consumed in the making of the road, and in the building of the chambers under ground, upon the ridge whereon stand the Pyramids, even the vaults that the king builded for himself on an island made by the conduit, which he brought from the Nile. And the time of the making of the Pyramid itself was twenty years. It is square, and each face thereof is eight hundred feet in length and the same in height,[1] and it is built of polished stone, fitted exceeding close, whereof no stone is less than thirty feet. This Pyramid was builded thus: even in the manner of the stairs, that some call courses and others steps. And when they had builded it at the first in this manner, they proceeded to raise the remaining stones by machines that were made of short staves of wood. From the ground they raised them on to the first tier of the stairs, and when the stone was let down upon this tier, it was placed upon another machine that stood even on the first tier, and from this tier the stone was dragged upon another machine to the second tier. For there were even as many machines as there were tiers of the stairs. Or it may be that, in raising the stone, they shifted one and the same machine,

---

[1] *i.e.*, eight plethra of 101 English feet. The actual measurements of the Great Pyramid are as follows: perpendicular height, 451 feet; length of each side along the base, 750 feet; length of each side from base to original apex, 610 feet; original perpendicular height, 482 feet; original extent of sides, 768 feet. It must be remembered that the apex of the Great Pyramid has gone, and that the outer coverings of both Pyramids were stripped off, and used for the buildings of mediæval Cairo.

being easy of management, from tier to tier. For the story was told me in both ways, even as I have said. The upper parts, therefore, of the Pyramid were finished first, and afterwards they finished the parts that followed, and at the last did they finish the lowest parts that were upon the ground. And it is recorded in Egyptian writing on the Pyramid, how many both of radishes and onions, and roots of garlic, were served out to the workmen. If I remember rightly, my interpreter, in reading the writing, said that one thousand six hundred talents of silver had been spent thereon. If this be so, how much must have been spent beside upon the tools of iron wherewith they wrought, and upon the victuals, and the clothing of the workmen, during all the time that these works were thus in the building. To say nothing of the time that was spent in the cutting of the stones, and in the carriage of them, and while they wrought the passage underground—in my judgment no short period. . . . And the Egyptians said that this Cheops reigned for fifty years, and that after his death his brother Chephren received the kingdom, and dealt with them in the same manner, both in other respects and in this, that he built a Pyramid. This Pyramid of Chephren came not to the greatness of Cheops' Pyramid. This I know, for I took the measurement thereof. Neither hath it chambers beneath the earth, nor doth a conduit from the Nile flow into it as into the other, for this conduit flows through a channel that was builded, and encircles an island within the Pyramid, and in this island they say Cheops himself was placed. An underground chamber of mottled Ethiopian stone he built for a foundation, and then built his Pyramid next to the Great Pyramid, making it forty feet less in height. They stand both upon the same ridge, which is about a hundred feet in height; and the Egyptians said that Chephren reigned for six-and-fifty years. Thus is the tale of one hundred and six years reckoned, in which the Egyptians suffered all manner of evil ; and throughout this time the Temples that had been closed were not opened. The Egyptians are loath to name these kings from hatred of them: and the

Pyramids they call after the name of Philition, a shepherd that pastured his flocks at this time round about these places.

"And after him they said that Mycerinus, the son of Cheops, became king of Egypt. He abhorred the works of his father; he both opened the Temples, and let the people that had been afflicted to the uttermost return to their works, and to their sacrifices. Moreover, of all their kings he judged them the most righteously. . . . He, too, left a Pyramid, smaller by far than that of his father, in that each side is but two hundred and eighty feet in length; it is square, and the half of it is built of Ethiopian stone."[1]

When I had finished my sketch it was time to think of returning. We walked leisurely, skirting the western side of the Great Pyramid, to the northern front where we had left our carriage. When we had driven half a mile or so down the lebbek avenue, in the direction of Cairo, we stopped to look back. As we did so the Pyramids began to assume a certain dignity and beauty. The three triangles, rising one after the other in a natural succession—for they are all built four square to the points of the compass—grouped themselves in a mighty system. They had added the hundred feet of the ridge upon which they are built to their proper stature, and the strong light of the setting sun behind them threw their surfaces into an even tone of purple shade, which served to unite them in a single mass. When we had driven further on, we looked back again. The sun had now sunk behind the Lybian hills, and the sky was flooded with crimson light. A small village, with its flat-roofed houses and tall palm trees, glowed in the evening light, and its brightness served to emphasize the low tones and broad masses of the Pyramids behind it. Nor had the sun fallen long enough to let the colour die out of the fields of young corn which spread across the plain.

Our perfect day had not altogether fulfilled our expectations, but in spite of a cold wind we had ranged at will among the

[1] II., 123-134.

giant tombs, and we came away with our minds enriched with
a fresh experience of no little significance. During the six or
seven hours that I had been in the presence of these brown
masses of masonry, and among the yellow sands out of which
they spring, I had become familiar with their external forms and
scenic values. My mind had been unconsciously at work, and
now as I drove back in the quiet evening the impressions of
the day began to shape themselves in thought. The antiquity
of the Pyramids and their historic interest is alone sufficient to
give them an incontestable claim to the consideration of mankind.
But is this antiquarian interest, I asked myself, in itself sufficient to account for the fascination which they undoubtedly
exert over the mind of the spectator? I felt that I could not
limit myself to the antiquarian standpoint, but that I must try
to form some wider estimate of their qualities in which their
æsthetic significance would be included. From this point of
view they are not merely tombs of almost superhuman size, not
merely structures admirably designed to fulfil the purposes for
which they were created, not merely the oldest of the world-
famed monuments, but the greatest examples of the first known
effort of man to create structures which should not only fulfil
some useful purpose, but also produce an impression upon the
senses sufficient to affect the mind of the beholder.

Considered thus as man's first essay in architecture, it is
comparatively easy to distinguish alike the merits and defects
of the Pyramids. In the first place, they have the merit of
utility. They are perfectly designed for the purpose which they
were intended to perform—that is, to preserve the body of the
dead king until, after the lapse of ages, his soul should return to
it again. Not only so, but the manner in which this design
was executed, shows that skilful workmen were employed under
the direction of men who were conversant with certain principles
of architecture. For in addition to the admirable workmanship displayed in the setting of the stones, the whole plan of the
interior chambers, with their passages, air-vents, false passages, and

P

super-chambers relieving the tomb-chamber from the super-incumbent mass, show technical skill of the highest degree. In short, they offered an asylum to the body more secret, more safe, and more durable, than that of any other form of tomb.

But though this was the first it was not the only purpose of the Pyramid. Besides affording an inviolable asylum to the dead king's body, it was also intended to present a symbol of his

GROUP OF ARABS, WITH PYRAMIDS IN DISTANCE.
(*Photo. by Mrs. Kay.*)

greatness, which should serve to preserve his memory in future ages. Here again, the form of the structure employed was determined, in part at least, by the conditions under which it was erected. In the Nile valley the area of cultivable land was too small to permit of any part of it being used as a burial ground; and the tombs were therefore erected in desert places at a distance from the town. The tombs which were erected here must, if they were to serve also the purpose of monuments, be great objects, vast enough to be seen from a long distance. In these circumstances the Pyramid was the most fitting of monumental erections: for its solid mass and simple outline caused it not only to be seen from a distance, but to lose as little as possible of its original effect when thus seen.

The Pyramids, therefore, were perfectly adapted to fulfil the purposes which were required of them. But utility is not alone sufficient to invest a work of architecture with æsthetic significance. Such significance is generally attributed to the arrangement of the members of a given structure in such a manner that a sense of unity is produced without sacrificing the sense of variety caused by the presence of the separate members. Out of this mingling of unity and variety arises the characteristic quality which makes the Parthenon and the Coliseum, St. Peter's and Westminster Abbey, alike beautiful. These are examples of the art of architecture in its highest development, and the Pyramids have as little claim to produce the gracious effects which such works of art do produce, as the rock painting of the Bushmen or the rude circle of Stonehenge. Judged from this absolute standard the Pyramids are wholly deficient, for they have no trace of architectural beauty as thus understood. Of the elements which unite to produce the proper effect of a work of architecture, they have one, and one only—the element of greatness. But this element, while it is in itself powerless to produce those more subtle and delightful effects which together constitute the quality of beauty, is none the less capable of affecting the imagination in the highest degree. So fully is this element developed in the vast proportions of the Pyramids, so perfectly are the giant triangles relieved by the level of the desert, so strong is the force of associations that have gathered since the very dawn of history, that this one quality of greatness is in itself sufficient to produce an impression upon the mind of the spectator, which rivals, though it does not resemble,

228   THE REDEMPTION OF EGYPT

the sense of beauty which is produced by any masterpiece of architecture.

A few days later we visited the remains which mark the site of the southern quarters of Memphis, and saw the pyramids and tombs of Sakkâra. Starting from Bedrashên we traversed the palm groves, and crossed the irrigated plain between the Nile

THE STEP PYRAMID OF SAKKÂRA.

and the low range of sandy hills on which the Pyramids of Dakshûr, Sakkâra, and Abusîr are built. From the plain we ascended through the desert sands to the crown of the ridge where stands the famous Step Pyramid of Sakkâra; then turning to the right, we dipped into the hollow which shelters the brown mud walls of Mariette's house. Over the veranda the flag of the *Directeur-Général du Service des Antiquités Égyptiennes* was

flying, and under its welcome roof a crowd of tourists were taking
luncheon. The Apis Tombs and the Mastaba of Thy, the chief
fruit of the famous antiquarian's labours, lay a few paces beyond
the house.

We went first to the Apis Tombs; and here, in the deep
shadow of the descending passage which led to the entrance, we
rested and ate our lunch. The hungry Arab guardian of the
place looked on, and helped us to dispose of the broken remnants,
some of which he ate and some he carried away. Then we lit
the candles which we had purchased at the Greek shop at
Bedrashên, and burrowed through the darkness and the stifling
heat within. In the massive sarcophagi, placed for the most part

MARIETTE'S HOUSE.

each in a separate niche, were laid the embalmed bodies of the
Sacred Bulls, whose form the god Apis, or Ptah, assumed as the
medium of his incarnation. "This Apis, or Ptah (Epaphos),"
Herodotus writes, "is the calf of a cow which is no longer able to
bear other offspring. The Egyptians say that lightning descends
upon her from heaven, and that the Apis is thus conceived.
Now this calf that is called Apis hath the following signs. It is
black, and bears a white square upon its brow, and upon its back
a mark like an eagle; the hair of its tail is twofold, and on its
tongue it hath a beetle." And in the passage in which this
description occurs, he relates how Cambyses, with his own hand,
stabbed one of these sacred bulls in the thigh, so that the animal
died of the wound; adding that the Egyptians attributed the

subsequent madness of the Persian conqueror to the wrath of the
god whom he had thus outraged at Memphis.[1]

From the Apis Tombs we returned to Mariette's house, where
we sat awhile under its shadow, looking on to the white sands
which a pitiless sun bleached from sunrise to sunset. Then,
turning once more from the pleasant shade to face the glittering
light, we pushed through the sands to the Mastaba of Thy.[2] This
Thy, they say, was an architect and steward of the kings of the
fifth dynasty, and the house which was built to be his habitation
in the long years that follow man's brief span of life on earth, is
therefore now some 4500 years old. The masonry of which the
walls of the various chambers are formed, we found so finely set
that the cemented blocks presented the appearance of a single
unbroken surface. On the walls of the chambers scenes from
the life of Thy were sculptured in relief, and these sculptures are
said to be amongst the finest examples of the kind which have
as yet been discovered upon the broad surfaces of the Egyptian
monuments. Here, as in the statues of the Museum of Gizeh,
the human figures were represented in the conventional attitudes
which rob these efforts of the Egyptian artist of any claim to
æsthetic value: but the figures of animals were generally graceful
and natural, and in some cases their lines were inspired by that
intimate knowledge of the subject which characterizes the work
of the true artist.

From the Tomb of Thy we returned to the Step Pyramid,
and descending thence to the foot of the ridge, crossed the plain
to the station at Bedrashên. The lights that played over the
distance in the early morning and late evening, the quaint masses

---

[1] iii., 28 30.
[2] The so-called Mastaba (Arabic, door-seat) was originally the recess outside the *stele*, or door-shaped stone, placed outside a tomb as a symbol of the passing of the dead to the under-world. In this original recess the relatives of the dead placed gifts of food, &c., and it was subsequently developed into a group of chambers, reproducing the main features of the ancient Egyptian house. The tomb-chamber was built beneath the level of the other chambers. The Mastaba of Meraru-ka (also at Sakkâra) has no less than thirty-one chambers and passages appropriated respectively to the dead man, his wife, and his son.

of mud walls that marked the villages, the straight stems and waving plumes of the palm trees, and the vivid green of the clover fields, were the sole qualities of scenic value that the landscape possessed. The paths of trodden earth, the mud banks, the sandy roads, the desert hill-sides, the masses of broken stones and mounds of still more sordid matter, the bleached sands of

ENTRANCE TO MASTABA OF THY.

the desert, offered in themselves nothing which could delight, soothe, or satisfy the eye. The sole attraction of these arid and stone-strewn hills and plains is that which arises from the fact, that they contain the remains of the work of men now separated from us by an interval of 5000 years.

Before we left Cairo we made a pilgrimage to the barren site of the "City of the Sun," the On of the Bible, and the Heliopolis of the Ptolemaic period. All that remains of the great Temple where Re-Harmachis—the Sun-god, Re, identified with the local deity Harmachis—was worshipped, is the solitary obelisk, which is said to be the most ancient of all the existing obelisks in Egypt. The stone of which it consists is the red granite, quarried on the hills behind Syene (Assuân); and the bold hieroglyphics on the north side of its face are still clear and legible. The base of the obelisk, which measures 66 feet in height, has been uncovered from the earth which has risen around it, and the space thus excavated has been surrounded with a railing. The town itself was a religious centre, and the learning of its priests was so celebrated that Plato came thither to study their secrets.

"In Heliopolis," Strabo writes, "I saw the great houses in which the priests used to live; for this place, they say, was in ancient times an especial seat of the priests, who were learned men and versed in the laws of the stars. To-day both the men who formed this society and the arts which they practised have ceased to exist. When I was there, no one thus proficient was to be seen; there were only the officiating priests and the guides whose business it was to show strangers round the temple precincts. It is true that when Aelius Gallus, the præfect, sailed up the river into Egypt from Alexandria, a person named Chaeremon joined his company, on the ground that he was possessed of some such knowledge: but he was generally derided for an impostor and a charlatan. But besides the priests' houses, the lodgings of Plato and Eudoxus were to be seen. Eudoxus, it will be remembered, was Plato's companion on his journey hither; and these two lived in the company of the priests for thirteen years, as some persons say. For while the priests possessed an exceptional knowledge of the science of the heavenly bodies, they were very reluctant to impart their secrets to others: and it was only by dint of both time and assiduity that they could be prevailed upon to relate certain of their principles; and even then they kept most of them from their Greek visitors. These latter, however, made known the fraction of the day and night by which the solar year exceeds the 365 days of the calendar. But the Greek world remained ignorant of the fact that the solar year was longer in other respects also, until the later astrologers were placed in possession of the observations of the priests, through the interpretation of their notes into the Greek language. And even in the present day the astrologers have recourse to these observations of the Egyptian priests, and similarly to those of the Chaldaeans."[1]

Nor was Greece the only country that was indebted for its revised calendar to the priests of Heliopolis. The "Egyptian" calendar of Eudoxus served as the basis of the reforms which were carried out by Julius Caesar in B.C. 45, when the official

THE OBELISK AT HELIOPOLIS.

year of the Roman world had fallen two and a half months behind the solar year; and the Julian calendar thus introduced remained the standard of the civilized world, until the "new style" was adopted by Pope Gregory XIII. in 1582.

In Strabo's time the city itself had already become entirely deserted. While, however, the temple precincts had been allowed to remain in the mutilated condition to which they had been reduced by the mad sacrilege of Cambyses, the main fabric of the temple must have been complete; for he gives a full description of the arrangement and construction of its several parts. He mentions, also, that two of the obelisks which had escaped the violence of Cambyses had been conveyed to Rome. To-day the whole of the vast structure, with its avenue of sphinxes, its three

[1] xvii., C. 806.

successive pylons, its colonnaded court, its fore-court, and its shrine, has disappeared; and the obelisk that Usertesen, " King of Upper and Lower Egypt, Lord of the Diadems and Son of the Sun," set up " on the first festival of Set," four thousand years ago, stands solitary in the clover-fields.

CHAPTER XIII

RAILWAYS, SUGAR, AND FINANCE

From Cairo to Luxor by rail — Defective administration of railways — Its causes and results — Proposals to remedy this — Visit to a sugar-mill at Beliâneh — Work of the Egyptian Sugar and Land Company — Irrigation and sugar-crushing — The pumping station — The sugar factory — Processes employed — Crushing — Cleansing — Evaporation — Separation of sugar crystals from molasses — Sugar culture in Egypt — The Daïra administration — Private mills — Amount of private capital invested — Methods of the Daïra factories — Economy in working — Fall of prices — Destination of sugar export — Development of private enterprize probable — The Daïra administration to be wound up in 1905 — Extension of area available for sugar cultivation by Nile reservoir — Effect of fall of prices in cotton and sugar — Egyptian finance — Sir Elwin Palmer's views — Both industries safe — Other prospects of expansion of revenue.

WE left Cairo on the evening of February 6, 1899, by the 9.30 train. We had chosen to go up the Nile by rail instead of boat, in order that we might lose as little time as possible in moving from place to place. The advantages which the railway possesses over the steamboat, in point of speed and independence, are obvious, but at present railway travelling in Egypt is accompanied by certain considerable inconveniences, arising mainly from the defective administration of the railway system, to which allusion has already been made on more than one occasion. This train was timed to reach Luxor at 1.30 in the following afternoon; that is to say, it carries the traveller over the 417 miles, which separate the two places, at the rate of rather more than 25 miles an hour. A journey of the same length in England—say from London to Edinburgh—would be performed in half the time; and it is scarcely necessary to add that, with the exception of the service between Cairo and Alexandria, this rate of progression is considerably in advance of the speed attained by the majority of trains. The carriages of which this train was composed were in tolerable repair; nor was there any lack of accommodation, for J—— and myself had no difficulty in retaining undisturbed possession of a separate compartment during the night. Moreover, a sleeping-car of the *Compagnie Internationale* was attached to the train, for the benefit of those travellers who preferred its arrangements to the accommodation offered by the ordinary first-class compartments.

But this limited speed is a matter of slight importance in itself; nor do the Egyptian railways compare unfavourably in this respect with those of other eastern countries, or even with the railways of Australia and South Africa. The most serious inconvenience, which attaches to railway travelling in Egypt at present, arises from the fact that no adequate method has as yet been employed to exclude the sand of the desert from the interior of the carriages. After a few hours both seats and passengers are covered with this sand, and towards the end of the journey the condition of the carriages becomes almost unbearable. At the same time the arrangements for supplying food are quite insufficient; and the European traveller is compelled to carry baskets of provisions obtained from the hôtels, when he undertakes a journey of any length.

The defective administration of the Egyptian railways has produced results far more serious than any which are concerned with the convenience of the European passengers. The deterioration of the plant, and the insufficiency of the rolling stock, constitute a serious hindrance to the progress of commercial and industrial development; and as such they have evoked protests from all classes of the commercial community. There is a further reason which makes the subject worthy of consideration at the present time. The Railway Administration, being one of the mixed or International Administrations, affords a signal example of that necessity for the elimination of the International factor, which is becoming more and more apparent every day. The special evils produced in the present case by the system of International Administration, and the measures by which it is proposed to remedy these evils, are described by Lord Cromer in his last report. It will be remembered [1] that, under the Law of Liquidation (1881), the revenues of Egypt were divided roughly into two parts, of which one was assigned to the payment of the interest due upon the various debts, while the other was appropriated to defray the ordinary expenses of governing the country. The economic defect of this arrangement lay in the fact that Egypt was treated as a country incapable of industrial development; and while, therefore, every precaution was taken to secure the payment of the annual sums due to the European creditors, no provision was made for supplying Egypt with the funds necessary for the development of the sources from which these annual sums and the general revenue were alike derived.[2] And, as we have also seen, the instruments of the International authority, whether administrative or judicial, cannot under the existing arrangements be adapted to the requirements of the present situation, without recourse to the difficult and tedious procedure of diplomatic action. In the case in point, the profits of the railways, together with those of the telegraphs and port dues of Alexandria, were assigned by the Liquidation Commissioners for the payment of the interest on the Privileged Debt, and the administration of the railways was entrusted to an International Board. The results of this arrangement are thus summarized by Lord Cromer.

"In 1883, the first year of the British occupation, the gross receipts amounted to only £1,195,000. In fifteen years there has been an increase of 84 per cent. It is certain that this increase is due mainly to the growing prosperity of the country, and also in part to the individual efforts of those concerned in the management of the railways. It is in no degree due to the

[1] See chapter iv., p. 61.
[2] In 1887 a Reserve Fund was constituted; but this fund, which is under the control of the Caisse de la Dette, is insufficient—or insufficiently administered—to fulfil the purposes required. It is called the "General Reserve Fund," in distinction from the "Special Reserve Fund," which is at the disposal of the Egyptian Government.

system under which the railways are administered. That system, far from stimulating, has indeed materially retarded progress.

"The railways do not merely suffer from those defects—of which divided responsibility is perhaps the most notable—which are common to all systems of international administration. They possess some further defects which are peculiar to themselves. In the first place, the working expenses are fixed, by international arrangement, at 45 per cent. of the gross receipts. This proportion is low as compared to railways in other countries. Unfortunately, this is not the only evil. The Law of Liquidation, and the subsequent decrees which have received international sanction, make no adequate provision for capital expenditure on the railways. The proportion of the gross receipts which is at the disposal of the Railway Board, and which is only just sufficient for working expenditure and ordinary maintenance, is, strictly speaking, the only available fund from which money can be taken for the purchase of fresh stock, and in fact for all such expenditure as, under ordinary circumstances, is either charged to capital account, or exceptionally charged to revenue. The natural result has been that, whilst the country has been rapidly progressing the railways, being deprived of all power of expansion by the defective administrative system to which they are condemned, have, relatively speaking, stood still. The commercial community complain, with great reason, of the delays in the transport of merchandise. The Government lose money because they cannot provide the engines and waggons required by traders. At the same time, the members of the Railway Board, and in fact, I think, every responsible authority in this country, fully recognise the justice of complaints to which they are unfortunately powerless to apply any thoroughly effectual remedy."[1]

The condition of the rolling stock in 1898 is sufficiently indicated by a passage quoted by Lord Cromer in his preceding report. Here Mr. Robertson, the late President of the Railway Board, writes that the statement of the "working expenses" for

[1] Egypt, No. 3 (1899).

1897, as amounting to 43 per cent. of the gross receipts, is a "meaningless figure." He then continues: "An examination of the amounts spent on the purchase of rolling stock and rails during the last ten years shows a deficit of £E218,000 from the sum necessary to maintain these items in good order, owing to the insufficiency of the Budget for maintenance. The buildings have also been neglected, and the running repairs to engines are woefully in arrears owing to the impossibility of laying by an engine so long as it can move. These engines have, many of them, done three times the distance, without repairs, that they should have run for economy. The absolute quantity of the rolling stock is also quite inadequate to meet present wants. It was never abundant, and the increase during the last ten years renders it ludicrously insufficient."[1]

Lord Cromer introduces his account of the remedies proposed with the significant statement: "I have no hesitation in saying that, if the hands of the Egyptian Government were free in this matter, by far the best course would be to borrow at once about £E1,500,000, and thus place the railways in thoroughly good working order. The country would gain by this expenditure, and the increased receipts would certainly far more than cover the additional interest charged. As, however, this is impossible, the alternative adopted is to obtain annual grants from the General Reserve Fund, and to supplement these grants by an increased expenditure on maintenance on the part of the Railway Board itself. In this way it is proposed to spread an expenditure, amounting in all to £E1,330,000, over a period of five years (1899–1903). Of this sum £E980,000 will be furnished by the Caisse de la Dette from the General Reserve Fund, and the remaining third will come from the Railway Administration." As to the appropriation of these Funds, he writes: "This money will suffice to buy 2700 10-ton trucks, 200 passenger carriages, and 30 locomotives. It will enable steel to be substituted for iron rails over 550 kilom. of line, and 1500 kilom. to be properly ballasted."

[1] Egypt, No. 1 (1898).

Also, it will be possible to repair and improve some of the stations, and, where necessary, to strengthen the bridges in order to allow of heavier trains passing over them."[1]

As £E330,000 is to be spent during the current year (1899), we may hope that the more immediate defects of the Egyptian railways will be at once remedied. In February, however, they were still under the old régime, and we had left Cairo barely an hour before the engine broke down. There was no reason for alarm: on the contrary, the Arab engine-men and guard seemed to take the incident as a matter of course, but to us it formed an effective commentary upon Mr. Robertson's plea for the over-worked Egyptian engine. Moreover, it was unfortunate, for we had arranged to break our journey at Beliâneh, in order that we might visit a sugar-mill. When, therefore, we reached this station on the following morning, it was annoying to find that the short period at our disposal for this purpose had been reduced by the three-quarters of an hour lost through the breakdown.

Mr. Edmund Carver, to whose courtesy I was indebted for this opportunity of becoming acquainted with the details of the Egyptian sugar industry, was on the platform; and in a few minutes we were seated in a trolley, drawn by a donkey, on whose back an Arab rode. The mill belonged to the Egyptian Sugar and Land Company, Limited, and Mr. Carver was the chairman of the board of directors. The work of the Company, which had been started two years ago, he told us, consisted of two distinct operations. In the first place, it irrigated some 5000 acres of land, and in the second, it crushed the sugar-cane which was grown on part of the land thus irrigated. Fifteen miles of the two-foot rails upon which we were now travelling had been laid down; and on these rails the trucks ran which conveyed the cane from the fields to the factory, and the sugar from the factory to the railway station.

We went first to the pumping station. Here we saw a pumping plant capable of raising from four to five tons of water

[1] Egypt, No. 3 (1899).

from the Nile per second, and thus filling the system of main canals with sufficient water for the irrigation of the 5000 acres. The duty of the company is to maintain the water in these canals at such a level that the occupier of the land can bring the water on to his fields by gravitation—that is to say, by merely cutting the channels in which it can flow. From March to August, when the summer crops are being grown, the great pumps are steadily at work, and from August to March periodical supplies of water are provided in accordance with the requirements of the various crops. About one-third of the land thus irrigated is under sugar; the other crops which are grown are dhura, or maize, in the summer, and wheat and beans in the winter. In the spacious engine-room we saw the two driving engines and the great pump, and we went down from the floor to the mouth of the pipe through which the water is sucked in from the Nile. The machinery, which was supplied by Messrs. Ruston, Proctor & Co., of Lincoln, was placed under the charge of two European engineers—an Englishman and an Austrian—and some ten or twelve natives were employed, as stokers and otherwise, under their direction.

From the pumping station we spun over the rails through palm groves, fields of sugar-cane, and lands of varying cultivation, to the factory. In general the occupiers of the land were fellahin, but one comfortable house which we passed was pointed out to us as being the home of a European cultivator, a Greek. The factory or sugar-mill is, of course, considerably larger than the pumping station. The European staff numbers about twenty, of whom some ten or twelve are Englishmen. The most important of these are the manager, Mr. N. J. Sinnott, the chief and assistant engineers, and the chemical adviser. The number of natives employed is 400—men, women, and children; the men are paid at the rate of three piastres (7½d.) a day, and the women and children receive about half of this sum. They work in day and night shifts of 200 each; for the fact that the liquid extracted from the cane requires immediate treatment, and other considerations, make it necessary that the mill should work continuously during the period—about three months—in which the crushing for the year is effected. In this working year of three months, or thereabouts, 75,000 tons of cane can be treated, and 10 per cent., or 7500 tons of raw sugar on an average, can be extracted.

The entire process consists of four distinct operations. First,

FEEDING THE MILL WITH CANE.

the cane is crushed; second, the liquid thus obtained is purified; third, the purified liquid is reduced by evaporation to *masscuite* —a mixture of sugar crystals and molasses; and fourth, the crystals are separated from the molasses. As we passed through the mill, Mr. Carver explained the several stages of the process. But before we entered the factory, we went first to see how the crushing machines were fed. Here we found a busy throng of Arabs taking the cane from the trucks in which it had been brought from the fields, and placing it in layers upon the carrier, a continuous band which passes into the mill, and through the rollers of the crushing machines. We followed the band into the mill, where the successive machines were tearing the cane. The operation was effected, we were told, by the triple crushing process. The cane is passed through three successive machines. As it leaves the second of these it is *macerated*—that is to say, hot water is sprayed upon it from a pipe placed above the carrier. In all three machines liquid flows from the crushed cane, and the brown stream produced by their united action is passed through a strainer, which frees it from shreds of fibre, and then flows on for purification. This second operation is by no means simple. The brown stream is first pumped through a box containing fumes of sulphur. From this box it passes to the *limeing* tanks, where lime is added to counteract the acid properties of the natural juice of the cane. It is next pumped through high-pressure clarifiers, where its temperature is raised to 250° Fahrenheit, to the "continuous settlers," in which any matter in suspense is deposited. The clear liquor yielded by the settlers is passed through Taylor-filters, while the muddy settlement is forced through filter presses.

For the third operation the juice from both filters and presses is carried to the Lillie-evaporator. Here it loses about 70 per cent. of its original volume by the evaporation of the water. The liquid thus obtained is then boiled down in evaporating pans, until the sugar crystals actually appear, and the mixture of crystals and molasses called masseenite is formed. From the evaporating pans the masseenite is taken to cylindrical machines, in which it is constantly stirred by rotating arms, and allowed gradually to cool; and in the course of this process the crystals continue to absorb sugar from the molasses, and thus increase in size.

The fourth operation—the separation of the sugar crystals from the molasses—is performed by centrifugal machines, consisting of circular baskets of wire gauze, which revolve rapidly in fixed outer casings of iron. When the massecuite has been introduced into these baskets, the molasses are thrown off through the wire gauze into the outer casings and drained away, while the crystals are retained in the baskets, and dropped by a sliding bottom into a trough. From this trough the sugar, as we may now call it, is raked on to a continuous band by which it is carried up to the drying-room, where it is exposed to the air for a time, and then shot down through a wooden shaft into the packing-room below. Here it is packed into sacks, ready to be despatched by train to Alexandria or elsewhere.

Mr. Carver was an admirable guide. In spite of the intense heat and the deafening noise, he explained what was essential in each process clearly and fully. Perhaps the most remarkable feature was the manner in which the different sets of machinery were combined. In the course of a single day of twenty-four hours the juice was extracted from the cane, cleansed, and reduced to massecuite, and the sugar crystals separated from the molasses. Moreover, the greatest economy was exercised in all processes. Before we left the mill we paid a visit to the chemical laboratory, in which experiments were being conducted with the object of effecting further economies in the several processes.

The sugar crystals which are thus produced, and then exported from Egypt, are either used in the manufacture of preserves and sweetmeats, or they are converted by the refiners into the white sugar of the tea-table.

From the factory we passed on to a group of houses, or bungalows, where the manager, the chief engineer, and other officials of the company lived. They were pleasantly placed on the banks of the Nile, with a view across the river to the cliffs opposite; and I noticed that a tennis-court had been laid out, and that the loofah spread its graceful foliage over the walls by which the gardens were enclosed.

The cultivation of the sugar-cane in Egypt for export purposes, and not merely for local consumption, is an industry

of comparatively recent date; and at the present time nearly
the whole of the sugar export is produced by the Government
mills of the Daïra Administration. Apart from the Daïra cultivation it is difficult—if not impossible—to procure any exact
returns; but in the absence of this precise information, I give
such approximate figures as I have been able to obtain. These
figures will, I hope, be sufficient to enable the reader to form that
general idea of the industry as a whole, which is necessary to
enable him to understand the significance of the precise information afforded by the returns of the Daïra Administration.

In 1897[1]—to take a definite year—about 2,000,000 kantars,[2]
or 90,000 tons of sugar, were raised in Egypt. Of this amount
only 69,800 tons were exported. The value of this export
was £E634,518; and of this sum £E583,000 was paid for the
sugar produced by the Daïra Administration. It is obvious,
therefore, that in addition to the small amount which is locally
consumed, the exported sugar is furnished almost entirely by
the Government mills. These mills, which are erected at
various points on the Daïra Lands, are nine in number; while
private enterprize is represented by four large, and two or three
small mills. These latter are, however, mainly occupied in preparing sugar for local consumption and not for export. The
amount of capital which is invested in these private mills is
about £2,000,000, and of this amount one-tenth only is English.
To complete this general view of the position of sugar cultivation
in Egypt at the present time, it remains to add that all sugar
is obtained from cane, and that with the exception of a small
quantity grown in the Delta, this cane is exclusively produced
in Upper Egypt, where the area under sugar crop is being
gradually extended.

We may therefore take the returns furnished by the factories

[1] The crop for 1898 was exceptionally small—about three-fourths of this amount.
The decrease was due solely, however, to the fact that the cane was "nipped"
by the exceptionally cold weather experienced in the month of January in that
year (1898).

[2] Ninety-nine lbs.

of the Daïra Administration as representative of the results which may be obtained by scientific methods of production. Here, as in the cotton industry, the yield of the factories has been increased by improved processes of production, and by increased economy in working. The success which has followed the efforts of the Administration is these directions is shown by the fact, that the percentage of sugar obtained from the canes has risen from 9.38 in 1890 to 11.02 in 1897; while, on the other hand, the cost of production per 100 kantars has decreased in the same period from £E42.003 to £E33.174.[1] In addition to this percentage of sugar a small amount of alcohol and of molasses is also obtained from the canes. The general result of these economies is indicated by the following statement which appears in the "Commissioners' Report," issued in 1898. "In 1896," they write, "the factories had crushed 815,439 tons of cane, and produced 83,375 tons of sugar of all grades. This year (1897), 711,680 tons of cane have passed through our mills, and we have obtained 78,394 tons of sugar of all grades; that is to say, with 104,000 tons of cane less to crush, we have only a difference of 5000 tons of sugar in production."

At the same time the sugar industry, like the cotton industry, has been confronted by a fall of prices—a material fact "against which," the Commissioners write, "we are powerless." While in 1881 the Daïra sugar of the first grade realised 111 piastres (£1, 3s.) per kantar, in 1897 it sold for 43½ piastres (9s.).[2] In this same year, the average price realized by the Daïra sugar was 10s. 10d. per cwt. f.o.b. at Alexandria, as against the 12s. 8d. obtained in 1896. This was the lowest price which had been obtained during the last ten years, and the fall in this one year represented a loss of £E120,000 to the Administration.[3] In 1898, however, there was a slight rise in price—

[1] *Rapport présenté par Le Conseil de Direction de la Daïra Sanich, &c., Le Caire* (1898).
[2] Ibid. and *Tableaux Statistiques* (1898).
[3] Egypt, No. 1 (1898).

a circumstance which compensated in part for the deficiency of the sugar crop of this year. As regards the destination of the Egyptian sugar export, it is interesting to notice that during the last two or three years the United States has become the chief purchaser, while the export to England has rapidly fallen off. The increased purchase of the United States is attributed partly to the war with Spain, and partly to the tariff wars of the United States with France and Germany. Of the 69,800 tons of sugar exported from Egypt in 1897, 52,300 tons went to the United States, 9000 to England, 4600 to the Continent of Europe, while the remainder was sent to India and the Red Sea ports.[1]

Although at the present time the production of sugar for export purposes is almost entirely a state industry, two circumstances point to the development of private enterprize in the future. In the first place, arrangements have already been made for winding up the Daïra Administration in 1905; and in the second, the area available for the cultivation of the sugar-cane will be largely increased by the new Irrigation works in Upper Egypt.

The extent of the lands administered by the Daïra Commissioners has been reduced by annual sales from 504,901 feddans,[2] in 1881, to 304,988 feddans in 1896, and as the result of this process the Daïra debt has been reduced from £9,512,900 sterling in 1881, to £6,431,500 sterling in 1898.[3] Since 1896, the demand for the Daïra Lands has increased, and a contract was signed on the 21st of June 1898, under which, in Lord Cromer's words, "whatever lands belonging to the Daïra Administration remain unsold on the 15th October 1905, will pass into the possession of a Syndicate. The Government Administration will then cease to exist."[4]

[1] "Annual Report of British Chamber of Commerce" (1897).
[2] Feddan = 1.03809 acres.
[3] *Tableaux Statistiques* (1898).
[4] Egypt. No. 3 (1899).

Of the second of these circumstances it is sufficient to say here, that the creation of the Nile reservoir at Assuân, and the subsidiary dam at Assiût, will have the effect of placing 774,000 feddans of land, now served only by flood canals, under perennial irrigation. In other words, this immense area—to say nothing of lands reclaimed from the desert—will be rendered available for the cultivation of sugar-cane. These figures are contained in Sir William Garstin's Note, of 19th November 1897; and their significance will be understood, when we remember that the entire cultivable area of Upper Egypt consists at present of two and a quarter million feddans.

As cotton and sugar together constitute the bulk of the marketable produce of Egypt, it is impossible to leave this subject without some allusion to that "material fact," which, as we have seen, affects both industries alike—the fall of prices. The cotton crop has been doubled in the last fifteen years, yet its export value remains practically the same; the sugar export has been quadrupled, but the value of this export, instead of being quadrupled, has been doubled. Making due allowance for the increased purchasing power of the money thus earned by Egypt, this fall in prices nevertheless constitutes an adverse force which the Egyptian financier must be prepared to meet. Before I left Cairo, I was fortunate enough to ascertain the views of Sir Elwin Palmer on this subject. Referring to the facts as revealed in the admirable *Tableaux Statistiques*, which had been issued by him as Financial Adviser in 1898, I ventured to express the opinion that these facts seemed to endanger the future prosperity of Egypt. In reply Sir Elwin pointed out to me certain conditions which, in his opinion, were sufficient to render these industries secure, even supposing that the fall of prices should continue. In respect of the cotton industry, it was improbable that any further economies in production could be effected; the security of this industry lay in the fact, that Egyptian cotton, owing to its superior quality, would always be preferred to that grown in America or elsewhere. Cotton would continue to be cultivated in Egypt, therefore, even after prices had fallen so low as to render cultivation in America no longer profitable. In other words, so long as the civilized world continued to use cotton goods, the raw cotton of Egypt would find a market.[1] The sugar industry was also safe; because, apart from any future economies which might be effected in the working of the factories, the cane could be grown in Egypt at a less cost than in any other country. The two factors which together constituted this minimum cost were the fertilization of the fields by the natural irrigation of the Nile, and the system under which the fellâh, together with his wife and children, cultivated the cane on his own ground, and then sold it to the factory. The labour with which the sugar industry was thus supplied, through the voluntary efforts of the fellâhin, was economic in the highest degree.

Sir Elwin Palmer added a few words on the financial prospects in general. The revenue had shown in recent years a great expansion in the Customs, especially in tobacco and in legal receipts. This latter item, which was derived from the Mixed Tribunals and from the Mehkemeh, or Religious Courts, required explanation. It was not that the Egyptian Government was making money out of the administration of justice: for three-fourths of the receipts in question were derived not from litigious business, but from the registration of deeds. As the presence of the International factor prevented the Egyptian Government from taxing foreigners, except with the consent of the Powers, this registration of commercial processes in the Mixed Tribunals was a convenient device, by means of which the foreign residents were made to contribute to the expenses of the Administration. They represented, therefore, a source of revenue which would appear in the Budgets of other civilized countries under the heading of direct taxes, as the stamps or fees exacted in the case of the formation of a company or the sale of property.

[1] It should also be added that the Egyptian acre under cotton yields twice as much as the American.

These receipts, being the ordinary incidents of commercial development, were expanding, and would continue to expand, as the wealth and prosperity of the country increased. The railways also could be regarded as a national asset. The funds necessary for putting the rolling stock in order had been obtained, though they had not yet been expended; but when the proposed improvements had been effected, the Railway Administration would provide a valuable and increasing source of revenue.

CHAPTER XIV

LUXOR

Arrival at Luxor—Egyptian weather—Site of Thebes—The capital of the New Empire—Its monuments—Strabo's account of Thebes—The Colossi of Memnon—Explanation of the phenomenon—Advantages of Luxor—Wind and dust—Strabo's description of the Egyptian temple—His criticism—Comparison with the Greek temple—The deficiency of design in the Egyptian temple—Its significant features—Its vast size—The Pylon—The Polystyle Hall—The Egyptian Column—The Polystyle Hall at Karnac—The temple of Luxor—Sordid surroundings of the temples—The temples on the west bank—The Valley of the Tombs of the Kings—The Ramesseum—View of Luxor.

A GARDEN of orange trees and palms, an air clear and stimulating, like a draught of champagne, after the heat and dust of the railway—this and no more I noticed, as we crossed from the veranda to the dining-room of our hôtel at Luxor. At Cairo we had been both pleased and disappointed. January had been cold, and our rooms, in other respects all that could be desired, had been unprovided with fire-places. Unfortunately, our pretty sitting-room had a northern aspect, and the chilly mornings and evenings had almost robbed us of the use of it, when we required it most. The interest and beauty of mediæval Cairo had been marred by the blinding dust and evil smells of its streets. The biting wind, which was the regular companion of the bright sunshine, had made driving, and even walking, in the broad thoroughfares of European Cairo by no means pleasant. Moreover, many mornings had been cloudy, and on some afternoons rain had fallen. The monuments of ancient Egypt, which we had seen in the neighbourhood of Cairo, had scarcely approached—certainly they had not satisfied—the anticipations which had grown up in our minds out of the great things that we had read or heard about them. We had found the Pyramids shapeless accretions of stone, and the burial-ground of the Pharaohs a dusty wind-swept plateau, strewn with broken masonry, that lay in unsightly mounds across the monotonous banks of sand. At Sakkâra the generous vigour of the sun had been undiminished by the feeble wind; but even the tomb of Thy, a perfect example of its kind, had left upon our minds an impression wholly disproportionate to the anticipation raised by the enthusiastic accounts of the antiquarians.

We had not dared, therefore, to look upon our enjoyment of Luxor as assured. After these experiences, it seemed doubtful whether we should ever find that sunny, windless, palm-shaded Nile-land, where the old Greek tells us rain never fell but once within the memory of man, and that once, to foretell the coming overthrow of the Empire of the Pharaohs by the Persian Cambyses.[1] We had almost ceased to expect to find ruins or remains that could interest and delight, not merely the archaeologist and the student, but travellers like ourselves, anxious to observe, and eager to enjoy, the picturesque in one of its most characteristic and stimulating forms. We felt that for such effects something more was necessary than exquisitely mortared and polished surfaces, chased with innumerable figures and hieroglyphics. Should we find masses of sufficient dignity to present in themselves an appreciable feature in the landscape? And what would be the surroundings of these monuments? We knew enough of Egypt by this time not to expect any environment that could increase the artistic value of the forms themselves. All that we could hope was, therefore, that these surroundings would not be so utterly sordid as to prevent the ruins, however beautiful in themselves, from producing any sense of beauty in the mind of the spectator.

[1] "In the time when Psammenitus, the son of Amasis, reigned over Egypt, a mighty portent appeared to the Egyptians. It rained at Thebes of Egypt; where rain had never fallen before, nor has it fallen since up to my day, according to the men of Thebes."—HERODOTUS, iii. 10.

We know that here, if anywhere, we should find the realization of our hopes. Around us, on either bank of the Nile, were the remains of Thebes, the second capital of Egypt, the "populous No" of the Bible, and the "hundred-gated Thebes" of Homer. Originally the seat of the independent princes of the Thebaid, under the Middle Empire it became for a time the residence of the Kings of the united Egypt; but it was not until the New Empire had followed the expulsion of the Shepherd Kings that Thebes attained to its full grandeur. It was not merely the residence of the Kings who wore the double crown that symbolized the sovereignty of Upper and Lower Egypt—not merely the capital of the re-united Egypt—but it was the centre of Egypt when Egypt had become an Empire. As the capital of this Imperial Egypt, Thebes was magnificent with the wealth of subject states that stretched from the shores of the Caspian and the Ganges to the centre of Africa. The monarchs of the XVIII. dynasty include Queen Makere and Thutmosis III.; the XIX. dynasty —where the hitherto divergent chronologies of Mariette and Lepsius are separated only by a single year, 1,462-3 B.C.— includes the great names of Sethos I. and Ramses II. In this period the Egyptian capital, known to the civilized world through the literature of the Greeks as "Thebes of Egypt," spreading itself on either bank of the Nile, assumed the vast proportions which made it the rival of Babylon in the ancient world. The temples and tombs which form the sole remains of this Thebes lay around and about us. Within a stone's throw was the Temple of Luxor, the joint work of Amenophis III. and Ramses II.; a mile to the north lay the mighty assemblage of Karnac. Across the river were the Colossi of Memnon, rising from the plain, with the mingled Egyptian and Ptolemaic temples of Medinet Habu, and the beautiful ruins of the Ramesseum behind them; westward the hill temple of Queen Makere rested under the shelter of the Lybian range, which hid in its secluded valleys the tombs of the Kings and Queens.

The main characteristics of the site of Thebes are much the

254 THE REDEMPTION OF EGYPT

same now as they were when Strabo visited the place some twenty years before the birth of Christ. At this date the ancient capital of Egypt had long been deserted, and the only buildings that remained were temples and tombs. Its place had been taken by Ptolemais, lying a hundred miles to the north, which Strabo calls the "most important town in the Thebaid, and the equal of Memphis, being endowed with a constitution on the Greek model."[1] At this epoch, and during the succeeding cen-

THE COLOSSI OF MEMNON.

turies, the chief attraction which the site of Thebes afforded to the Roman visitor consisted of the twin Colossi of Amenophis III., styled the Colossi of Memnon. The spectacle of these huge figures on the west bank of the river, and the phenomenon of the plaintive note which issued at sunrise from the northernmost of the two, excited an interest in the Roman mind second only to the interest with which the Pyramids were regarded.

[1] xvii., C. 813.

The Ramesseum

"After the city of Apollo," Strabo writes, "is Thebes, or, as it is now called, the city of Zeus—

> 'That hath a hundred gates, each gate so vast,
> That ten-score men can pass with horse and car.'

'As Homer says; and he speaks also of its wealth—

> 'Nor all the wealth of Thebes,
> Egyptian Thebes, where each house hath its store.' [1]

And others say the like, making it the capital of Egypt. Even now the traces of its vast extent— it was eighty furlongs in length—are apparent. The remains are chiefly temples, and of these the greater part were mutilated by Cambyses. The collection of villages, where the present population live, lies partly on the Arabian shore of the river on the site of the ancient city, and partly on the opposite bank where the Memnonium stands. On this latter shore two colossal figures, each constructed out of a single block of stone, stand side by side. One is complete, but the second has lost its members from the throne upwards. They were thrown down, it is said, in an earthquake shock. The belief is that once every day an inarticulate sound, such as would be produced by a slight blow, issues from the part that remains on the throne and the pedestal. Now I myself was present on the spot with Aelius Gallus and his company of friends and soldiers, and heard the sound about the first hour of the day. But I have no means of saying with certainty whether it proceeded from the pedestal or from the figure, or whether it was produced designedly by some one of the persons who were seated in a circle round the pedestal. For in the absence of a known cause, any explanation is more credible than the supposition that the sound proceeds from an object thus constructed of stones.

[1] οὐδ' ὅσα Θήβας
Αἰγυπτίας, ὅθι πλεῖστα δόμοις ἐν κτήματα κεῖται.
Αἴθ' ἑκατόμπυλοί εἰσι, διηκόσιοι δ' ἀν' ἑκάστας
Ἀνέρες ἐξοιχνεῦσι σὺν ἵπποισιν καὶ ὀχεσφιν.

"Above the Memnonium there are about forty Royal Tombs in the caverns; they are hewn out of the rock, and their marvellous construction makes them worthy to be seen. In Thebes there are on certain obelisks inscriptions recording the wealth of the ancient kings, and how their empire extended as far as Scythia, and Bactria [Bokhara], and India, and what is now Ionia, and the full tale of their revenues, and of the army by hundreds of ten thousands. The priests of this place are said to have been especially learned and skilled in the laws of the stars. It is from them that we get the system of reckoning the days, not by the moon, but by the sun, for they added five days every year to the twelve months of thirty days; and, as the full natural year still exceeded this number of days by a part of a day, they added a further day to the years thus formed at intervals, when the sum of these parts amounted to a whole day."[1]

The genuine character of the vocal Memnon, which appeared incredible, or rather inexplicable, to Strabo, was subsequently established by the evidence of numerous Roman visitors; and the mysterious phenomenon continued to delight the Roman world until two centuries later, when the statue was restored by Septimus Severus on the occasion of his visit to Egypt. The remains of the upper part of the figure were erected upon the pedestal; but this restoration, which was effected by courses of sandstone blocks, caused the phenomenon to cease. Modern science accounts for both the original phenomenon and its cessation. The sound was caused by the expansion of the stone under the heat of the sun after it had contracted during the cold of the night—a process in the course of which minute particles would be thrown off the surface; and sounds similar in character have been heard more than once by travellers and scientific observers, proceeding from masses of stone or rock subject to the same conditions. When, however, the solid mass of the original figure was replaced by a composite, and therefore

[1] xvii., C. 815-16.

more elastic, structure, the effect of the expansion would be diminished and the sound would cease.

Although Strabo's account of the site of Thebes was written nineteen hundred years ago, it is only during the last twenty or thirty years that any material changes have been effected in its general aspect. By the joint exertions of the Department of Egyptian Antiquities and the Egypt Exploration Fund, the ruins of the temples are being freed from the accumulations of sand and débris which disfigured and concealed them, and the necessary measures have been taken both to preserve the existing monuments—tombs and temples—and to render them accessible alike to the scientific observer and the traveller. Under the stimulus of the tourist system established by Messrs. Thomas Cook & Son, the village of el-Kusûr,[1] or el-Uksûr, now corrupted to the familiar "Luxor," has flourished into a little town with three hôtels, and a quay, where tourist steamers and dhahabiyehs lie side by side with the primitive Nile boats.

The advantages which Luxor offers to the traveller are twofold. In the first place, there is no other centre from which so many groups of temples—and groups of such importance—may be visited. In the second, the broadening of the riband of fertile land which forms the valley of the Nile, and the comparative height of the ranges by which the valley is bounded on either side, unite to protect this neighbourhood of Luxor from those prevalent winds which elsewhere, driving the loose sandy soil in clouds of dust, constitute the great defect in the climate of Egypt. Not that Luxor is by any means free from this plague of mingled wind and dust. During the two weeks that we remained here, there were three days at least on which the plague of wind made any lengthy excursion practically impossible, and on one day the air was filled with so dense a cloud of sand that the opposite bank of the river was veiled as if by a

---

[1] The word *Kusûr* is the plural of *Kasr* (castle), which occurs in *e.g. Kasr en-Nil*. It means, therefore, the "castles"—the term applied by the natives to the ruins of the Temple of Luxor.

R

dense yellow fog. Still there were days enough, and more than enough, when no wind blew, when the light breeze was scarcely sufficient to temper the royal ardour of the sun; and on these perfect days we visited most, if not all, of the monuments of Thebes, before we passed southwards to Philae.

It is not my intention to give the reader any account of the details of these various excursions, but I shall endeavour to

THE AVENUE OF KRIO-SPHINXES AT KARNAC.

present the general results of my studies in such a form as may serve to illustrate some of the more characteristic features of the temple architecture of ancient Egypt. As a point of departure I shall take Strabo's description of the Egyptian temple. The particular example which he takes is the long since destroyed temple of Re-Harmachis at Heliopolis; but it is evident that the account is intended to serve as a general description, and the passage has a special value for us, since it embodies the impression which the sight of an Egyptian temple produced upon a European traveller in the Augustan age. He writes: "The plan of the construction of the Temple is as follows. At the entrance of the enclosure there is a stone pavement, about a hundred feet or less in breadth, and three or four times that distance in length, or in some places even longer. This is called the dromus, or avenue, and the word is so used by Callimachus when he says, 'This is the holy avenue of Anubis.' On either side a succession of stone sphinxes are placed, which extend the whole length of the avenue, at intervals of twenty cubits, or rather

TEMPLES AT MEDINET HABU.

more, from each other; and thus there is one row of sphinxes on the right hand, and one row on the left. After the sphinxes, there is a great propylon; then, as we advance, a second propylon, or even a third. There is no fixed number either for the propylons or for the sphinxes; they vary in the different temples, as do also the avenues in length and breadth. After the propylon, one or more, comes the temple. The forecourt is spacious and remarkable; the sanctuary is of corresponding dimensions, but it contains no statue—that is to say, there is no human figure, only a representation of one of the lower animals. In front of the forecourt, on either side, is the so-called 'winged entrance,' or propylon. It consists of two walls equal in height to the temple, which are at first separated by a space a little wider than the basement of the temple, but which rise with inclining lines to a height of fifty or sixty cubits. These walls contain reliefs of great figures which resemble the Etruscan figures, or those which are to be found on the most ancient buildings erected by the Greeks. There is also a hall of many pillars (polystyle), as at Memphis. Its construction is fantastic; for, apart from the fact that it contains many rows of pillars, and that these pillars are many in number and vast in size, it has neither beauty nor artistic quality; in fact, it is rather an example of wasted labour than a work of art."[1]

The term which I have translated "fantastic," in the above passage, is $\beta\alpha\rho\beta\alpha\rho\iota\kappa\acute{o}\varsigma$, that is, more literally, "outlandish." In applying this adjective to the polystyle[2] hall, which, with the exception of the pylon, forms the most characteristic feature of the Egyptian temple, Strabo pronounces a criticism which seems at first sight to be unduly severe: and it is only when we remember the rigorous harmony of the Greek temple, that we realize that such a verdict was natural, and indeed inevitable. As the Greek temple, now as then, affords the highest example of the form of building in question, no estimate of the æsthetic value of the temple architecture of ancient Egypt can be valid, unless it is based upon the standard established by this perfect form.

The germ of the Greek temple was the $\tau\acute{\epsilon}\mu\epsilon\nu o\varsigma$, or enclosure, which contained a representation or other emblem of the deity worshipped, with an altar of sacrifice in front; just as the germ of the mosque was the open-air prayer-enclosure. The statue, or emblem, was subsequently covered, or merely enclosed, by an oblong chamber—the sanctuary—called the $\sigma\eta\kappa o\varsigma$, or cella. The Greek temple in its fully developed form never ceased to retain the perfect unity of this simple original, and every new member

[1] xvii., C. 805-6.
[2] Termed "hypostyle" ($\dot{v}\pi\acute{o}$, $\sigma\tau\hat{v}\lambda o\varsigma$, "under" pillars) by antiquarians.

subsequently added was an enlargement or an embellishment of one or other of these two primitive elements—the enclosure and the cella. The erection of a portico before the entrance of the cella formed the first of these additions; and the cella was further extended in front by a πρόναος, or vestibule, and behind by an ὀπισθόδομος, or inner chamber, which was used as a treasury. The interior of the cella was sometimes divided into nave and aisles by two rows of columns. The temple thus developed, with its portico, vestibule, cella, and inner sanctuary, or shrine, was surrounded by columns; and the peristyle, as this environment was called, was raised by two or more steps from the ground.

Temple of Poseidon at Paestum.

The floor of the cella was sometimes also raised by steps above the peristyle; and the entire structure, cella and peristyle, was covered by a roof, which rested upon the columns of the latter. The various members of this roof were concealed, and the roof itself was dignified by the pediments which emphasized its slope at either end of the building; while the broad band of the entablature, which marked the transition from the roof to the columns of the peristyle, being identical on all four sides, still further enforced the sense of unity.

Moreover, the Greek architect was not always content with a structural perfection based upon exact material proportions. In certain temples the vertical lines and disposition of the columns of the peristyle, the horizontal lines of the exterior, and the vertical lines of the interior, were slightly modified, so that effects of light and shade, and other visual interferences, which would have caused an appearance of imperfection in the building as presented to the eye of the spectator, were corrected or removed. And thus by means of these optical corrections, this perfect form was presented to the senses, with its outlines undisturbed by any accidental effects of light and distance.

As compared with this absolutely harmonious structure, the Egyptian temple is a mere assemblage of courts and chambers—a fortuitous collection of members, which is only rescued from architectural chaos by its massive pylons and its central hall of many columns. For the rest, colonnaded forecourts, and lateral or rearward chambers, are added at will to the sanctuary, in complete disregard of any unity of design, other than such unity as is afforded by the construction of the main courts and pylons on a single axis.

The deficiency of design in the Egyptian temple is so marked, that it deprives the building of any claim to architectural merit as a single structure. Nevertheless, this deficient structure embraces individual members which are endowed with two of the most significant qualities that a work of architecture can possess—simplicity and greatness. In the pylon, in the central colonnade of the polystyle hall, and in the peristyle forecourt, these qualities were developed to a degree unattained by the works of any other people. Moreover, although the ruins of these temples afford us no sufficient means of forming any adequate conception of the effect produced by the conglomerate masses of which they were severally composed, we may be sure that each temple group would have produced a profound impression on the mind of any modern spectator, if only by reason of its mere vastness. In spite of its structural deficiency, the Egyptian temple, as a whole, possessed this quality of greatness; but it is only in its separate parts, where this greatness is united with simplicity of form, that

it affords us any characteristic manifestation of the art of architecture.

A few figures will serve to show the degree in which this dominant quality of greatness was developed. In round numbers the Ramesseum measured 600 feet in length, the Temple of Luxor 800 feet, while the great Temple of Ammon, at Karnac, spread its courts and pylons for 1200 feet from east to west. In comparison with these vast accretions of masonry, the Greek temple was a beautiful toy; and the 600 feet of St. Peter's at Rome, which serve to make that church the largest of Christian edifices, fall to a bare average. It is only in the secular buildings of Imperial Rome, in the Baths of Caracalla, and the amphitheatre of Titus, that the art of architecture can provide us with examples of uniform structures conceived upon so vast a scale. A striking illustration of the difference in the respective dimensions of the Greek and Egyptian temples is afforded by the Temple of Ramses III., which is included in the system of the great temple at Karnac. This temple of Ramses III. forms an insignificant adjunct to the great system in which it has been incorporated; nevertheless its dimensions—it measures 170 feet in length—would equal those of a Greek temple of average size. It has recently been cleared of débris, and been restored by the Department of Egyptian Antiquities, and thus restored, it affords a notable example of a homogeneously constructed Egyptian temple. But it is in the separate parts, and not in the structure as a whole, that we find those characteristic manifestations which embody the genius of Egyptian architecture. First among these commanding features is the massive structure by which the entrance was environed—the pylon. The conception out of which this remarkable structure grew, was that of two pyramids placed side by side, and united by a junction wall, which was pierced by the actual gateway.

The transition from the original conception of a pair of pyramids thus united to the pylon, or more correctly, pair of pylons, can be readily traced. The summits of the pyramids were cut down, the vertical lines were straightened, the truncated forms were elongated, and the two members were presented to the eye as a single structure by the line of the projecting cornice, which emphasized the union already effected by the junction wall. The pylon, thus developed, constituted an architectural form which united the qualities of simplicity and strength in a degree unattained by any other entrance structure. Nor did its vast proportions serve only to impress the senses of the worshipper as he approached the sanctuary of his god; its broad surfaces afforded

PYLON OF THE TEMPLE OF LUXOR.

space whereon the deeds of the royal builder of the temple, as well as other public records, could be appropriately engraved.

The front of the pylon of the Temple of Luxor—which I have selected as affording a characteristic example—is marked by the presence of the colossal statues of Ramses II.; while from the space in front there rose, on this side and that, twin obelisks. Of these latter one only remains; for its fellow was removed in 1831, and now stands in the centre of the Place de la Concorde at Paris.

Second to the pylon is the central hall of many pillars, which divided the court of assemblage from the sanctuary, and formed a

The Temple of Luxor

fitting transition from the light of day to the darkened chambers which formed the actual home of the god. The polystyle hall of the Temple of Luxor, raised by Amenophis III., was never completed. Of the three members—the deep lateral chambers or aisles, divided by a more lofty central avenue or nave—of which this hall consists, only one, the central avenue, was erected. It consists of seven pairs of columns, forty-two feet in height, which support the architraves of giant blocks, upon which the lofty roof was borne. The lips of the calix capitals, the most fragile portion of the column, are generally broken, but one or two remain sufficiently complete to present the contour of the perfect curve which united and yet separated the shaft from the abacus. It is difficult to estimate the æsthetic value of the interior of these polystyle halls; but, apart from any effect produced by the interior as a whole, they had the merit of affording a unique display of the one architectural member—the column—which attained absolute perfection in the hands of the Egyptian builder. The forms of the column reproduce generally, though not exclusively, certain familiar manifestations of plant life. In the temples of this period, that is to say, of the New Empire of which Thebes was the capital, the shafts were the single, or clustered, papyrus stem, and the capital, the bud, or the opening flower. Of these two common forms of pillar, the former, the clustered papyrus shaft with bud capital, is used in the lateral chambers of the polystyle hall, and also in the colonnade of the open courts

BUD CAPITAL.

while the latter, the papyrus column with calix capital, is employed to support the roof of the central avenue. And it is in the pillars of this central avenue that we find the supreme effort of the Egyptian architect.

The polystyle hall at Luxor lacks both its lateral chambers; but in the great Temple of Ammon, at Karnac, we have a complete and majestic example, alike of the chamber as a whole and of this central avenue. This great example measures 338 feet in breadth and 170 feet in length. The roof which covers this enormous area is carried by 134 columns, disposed in rows, which run from east to west. The two rows which form the central avenue consist respectively of six columns, which are roughly 70 feet in height and 12 feet in diameter. The column of the lateral chambers are 42 feet in height and 9 feet in diameter. The roof of the nave rested upon the architraves, supported by the columns of the central avenue in conjunction with the clerestory, which was carried on either side above the two inner rows of the lesser columns of the lateral chambers. The nave thus formed by the four central rows was 78 feet in height, while the lateral chambers were only 46 feet.

CALIX CAPITAL.

These figures enable us to form a rough conception of the appearance of the great polystyle hall at Karnac in the past. To-day the forest of pillars by which the central avenue was environed on either side is concealed by the masses of broken masonry which lie around it. The only sight that the spectator can command is the vista of Titan columns expanding high above his head into the generous circles of their broad calix capitals. Even thus

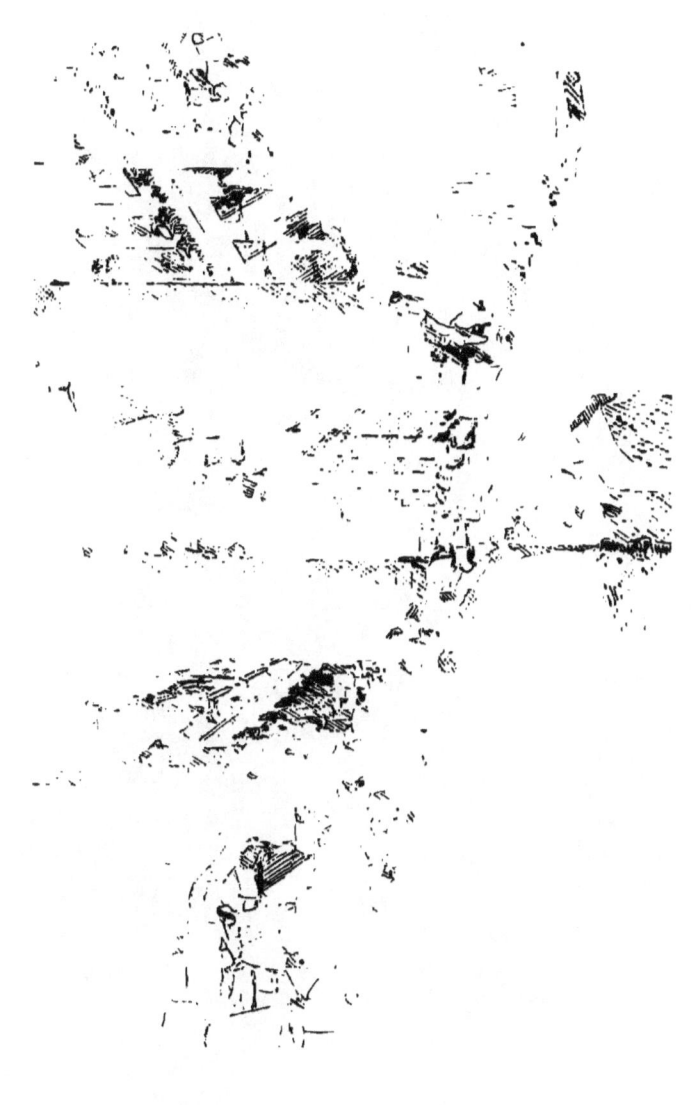

presented the columns of Karnac are sufficient to vindicate the claim of Ancient Egypt to the art of architecture. There is a charm in the scene which neither dust nor débris can wholly dispel. The sharp lines of the shadows which cross the columns the vision of the Lybian Hills rising above the palm trees by which the vista is closed, the chant of the Arabs who are clearing the soil from the basement of the temple —these are the significant accompaniments of the spectacle. Suddenly an Arab crosses the pathway, and standing erect for a moment forms a line of black against the whiteness of a massive shaft; and with the apparition there comes to the startled senses of the spectator a knowledge of the greatness which lies before him.

The Temple of Luxor is cast on a lesser scale than the vast pile of Karnac— the Throne of the World, as its priests proudly styled it. Nevertheless, the Luxor temple has a special interest which its giant neighbour does not possess. The present fabric retains traces of alterations which are typical of the changed uses to which the Egyptian temples were subjected in succeeding epochs. In the front

CLUSTERED PAPYRUS SHAFT.

court there are numerous colossal statues of Ramses II., the joint founder of the temple, and the most prolific builder of all the Pharaohs. The most perfect of these statues—though by no means the largest—measures 17½ feet in height from the pedestal. By the side of the king the queen is represented by a diminutive figure, which is typical of the inferiority of her sex. In its sanctuary is the shrine which Alexander the Great built for the reception of the Sacred Boat of Ammon. Indeed, the sanctuary itself was restored, or rather rebuilt by him, and it thus affords an illustration of the policy of recognizing the national religion, which the Macedonian conqueror of Egypt shrewdly adopted. In the passage which leads from the court of Amenophis III., through the polystyle vestibule towards the sanctuary, there stands an altar of stone, which still bears upon its broken front an inscription in Latin. It was dedicated to Augustus, "most great and most holy," in the age when the supreme ruler of the civilized world was held out to the subject races of the empire as the equal of the gods. A few paces beyond this altar there is a chamber which has undergone a significant transformation. The eight columns which supported the roof have been removed, and in the centre of the opposite wall there is a semicircular recess, which occupies the place of the original doorway, leading to the sanctuary of Ammon. On either side of the recess are two granite pillars, with Corinthian capitals; and in this recess, and the pillars thus disposed, we recognize the Coptic original on which the prayer recess of the mosque was modelled. The chamber thus transformed was used as a Christian church;

STATUE OF RAMSES II.

and in the faint remains of the frescoes, which covered the reliefs of its pagan walls, the flowing robes of saints and apostles can still be discerned.

SHRINE OF ALEXANDER THE GREAT.

As to the aspect which these monuments present to-day, it must be frankly admitted that their surroundings are sordid to a degree which almost baffles description. To find a parallel for the present appearance of the Temple of Luxor, we must

270   THE REDEMPTION OF EGYPT

imagine an English cathedral surrounded and half buried by some of those huge accumulations of waste matter from the collieries or iron foundries of North Staffordshire. Over the space which has been cleared round the basement of the Temple

ALTAR TO AUGUSTUS.

at the north-western corner, hang cliffs of accumulated refuse; and from these cliffs, whenever the wind blows, volumes of dust, heavy with the waste of the poultry-yard and all manner of indescribable filth, are poured over the Temple. Nor are the surroundings, in which the various temples of Karnac are set, much less degrading. The approach from Luxor, which leads through the avenue of sphinxes to the pylon of Ptolemy Energetes, is perhaps the sole instance in which these noble monuments are set off by any natural beauty in the landscape. Here the graceful stems and feathery plumage of the palms which rise on either side afford a fitting introduction to the marvels which lie behind the portal.

On the other side of the river the actual environment of the

CHAMBER TRANSFORMED INTO CHRISTIAN CHURCH.

monuments is less distasteful. The Lybian Hills rise here to a height of 1200 feet, and both in ascending to the Valley of Bibân el-Mulûk, or the "Tombs of the Kings," and in crossing the crown of the ridge by the path which leads back, by a precipitous descent, to the foot of the eastern escarpment, where lies the Temple of Dêr el-Bahri, the traveller may study certain characteristic aspects of desert scenery. The southern extremity of the valley, which the kings of the XIX. and XX. dynasties made their burial-ground, is closed by a natural amphitheatre of precipitous cliffs, crowned by a conical peak. In this curious spot the face of nature is alike brilliant and pitiless. Humble flowers push their leaves through the snow of the Alps, coarse tussock grasses cover the mountain wastes of New Zealand, succulent plants defy the deserts of South Africa. Here, there is neither blade of grass nor green leaf. The cliffs that should be grey are brown and orange; the slopes that should be covered with a mantle of green, are dazzling stretches of white sand. Barren it is, but not desolate; for the sun is shining in his

TEMPLE OF DÊR EL-BAHRI.

might, and down into the valley he pours a flood of light which makes the rocks and the sands laugh in the face of the traveller.

Apart from the fact that these Lybian Hills rise high enough to form an appreciable feature in the landscape, the immediate surroundings of the temples on the west bank, with the exception perhaps of the group at Medinet Habu, are less sordid. Beyond the fertile belt of irrigated fields, the sandy and rock-strewn wastes stretch to the foot of the range; but these wastes are at least light in colour, and free from the grosser impurities which have accumulated around the monuments on the eastern bank. The Ramesseum, I know, can look beautiful, though it lies in the desert. Once when I saw it, the level rays of the setting sun poured a flood of light alike over the brown masses of the temple and over the sands from which it rose, whilst the slopes of the Lybian Hills showed a background of delicate crimson against its tawny columns.

But a still fairer spectacle awaits the traveller as he returns

VALLEY OF THE TOMBS OF THE KINGS.

to Luxor. When he has turned his back upon the dazzling sands, and the red cliffs, and the brown masses of the monuments, and crossed the green fields to the grey sands that edge the Nile, a transformed Luxor meets his gaze. The sun is just sinking below the crest of the Lybian Hills behind him, and the eastern sky before him shows an opal blue which melts gradually into the deep crimson that gathers on the horizon. The Nile is glassy smooth, and from its lucid plain Luxor rises as beautiful as Venice. Over its sordid mounds and brown walls, over its square white-washed houses, and over the broken columns of its deserted temple, the Egyptian sundown has spread its magic colours. Beyond the glowing mass a line of emerald foliage meets the purple slopes of the Arabian Hills; in front, the Nile boats fringe the river-bank with masts and curving yards.

CHAPTER XV

ASSUÁN

From Luxor to Assuán—The first cataract—Elephantine—Syene—Philæ—Strabo's visit—His account of the Nilometer—Position of Syene under the tropic—The passage of the cataract—Journey to Philæ—Relation of Egypt with the desert tribes under the empire—The Christians of the Thebaid Visit to the quarries above Assuán—To the Nilometer—The Convent of St. Simeon—Harbour of Assuán *en fête*—Philæ—The Temple of Isis—Conception of the goddess—Introduction of worship into Greece and Italy—Roman buildings at Philæ—Captain Lyons's survey—The Nile reservoir—Scene on the east bank of the Nile—Dimensions of the dam—Other works for the irrigation of Upper Egypt—The dam at Assiút—Terms of the contract for construction—Deferred payment—International control makes this arrangement necessary—Estimated gain to Egypt from reservoir, &c.—Number of workmen employed at Assuán.

ASSUÁN lies 130 miles southward of Luxor, and it marks the boundary line where Egypt ceases and Nubia begins. The train by which we travelled left Luxor at eight in the morning, and deposited us, not indeed at Assuán, but near Assuán, at about half-past six in the evening. This was not rapid travelling, but on the other hand there were compensating advantages. In the first place, the line scarcely professes to be a passenger line at all; it is really a narrow-gauge military railway, constructed in 1898 for the purpose of conveying troops and material to Shellál, the point of embarkation for Wádi Halfa, at the time of the last Sudán expedition. At the present time its chief function is to bring up the metals for the Sudán railways, and to provide for the multifarious requirements of the great Nile reservoir. The front windows of our carriage commanded an unbroken view over a long line of trucks, laden with iron pipes, barrels of cement, and other materials, to the engine; and this circumstance, combined with the leisurely pace at which we travelled, gave us an excellent opportunity of studying the strange region through which we passed. Moreover, the sand of the desert was much less disturbed by this sedate locomotion, and comparatively little of it found its way through the windows of the carriage.

For the first twenty miles we were carried through irrigated lands, where the level of the green fields was broken by groups of palms. Then the cultivated area narrowed and the desert advanced, until the railway formed a line which sharply divided the green fields on the right, which lay between it and the Nile, from the yellow sands on the left. At Edfu, where the pylon of the Temple of Horus reared its massive front on the opposite bank of the Nile, the riband of green fields broadened, and once more environed us, but only to recede again before the advancing sands. Thirty miles beyond Edfu the railway leaves its constant companion, the Nile, and strikes through a spur of the Arabian Hills into the desert. Here broken cliffs closed threateningly on either side of the narrow line, and then opened to let it pass through broad spaces of radiant sands. At Ombos it joined the river again, and from this point it ran once more between the barren sands of the desert and the green strip that edged the river to the foot of the rugged hills that lie over Assuân.

The town of Assuân lies along the east bank of the Nile, opposite the Island of Elephantine. The stream of the Nile is here divided by islands and confined by rocky banks. At a point four miles above the town, where the promontory of Shellâl runs suddenly westwards, is the first cataract; and a mile above the cataract, just where the eastern channel of the river is forced westwards under this promontory, is the little Island of Philæ, with its famous Temple of Isis. The Island of Elephantine was held to be the limit of Egypt; and several circumstances united to give importance to this district, called Yebu, or "elephant land," by the ancient Egyptians, and Elephantine by the Greeks. In the first place, it afforded a station from which the movements of the Nile flood could be observed: in the second, it commanded

Philæ

the passage of the cataract and the trade routes to the interior, and in the third, the quarries in its neighbourhood provided the famous pink granite which was used by the later Pharaohs in the construction of the monuments. The town was originally built on the island itself, but subsequently a second town, known during the Greek and Roman periods as Syene, grew up on the east bank of the Nile, and this town is now known as Assuân. As comparatively few tourists ascend the Nile beyond this point, many steamers and dhahabiyehs are to be seen in the season lying off the river bank; and, indeed, the appearance of the river front, where the hôtel and public buildings are built, is almost European. The native population of Assuân is said to be about seven thousand in number, and the town is also a military station.

Under the Ptolemies the ancient Egyptian temples erected on the Island of Philæ were restored, or rather replaced, by the Temple of Isis; and during the subsequent Roman period the kiosk and other buildings, both sacred and secular, were added. When Egypt became a Roman province, in 30 B.C., the strategic importance of Syene was at once recognized. Cornelius Gallus, the first prefect of the new province, had been compelled, almost upon his arrival, to suppress an insurrection in Upper Egypt—caused by the Roman taxation—and to repel an invasion of the Ethiopians; and one of the three main divisions of the army of occupation was henceforward stationed at Syene. Moreover, since the introduction of the worship of Isis into the Graeco-Roman world, the temple of this goddess at Philæ had become a favourite place of resort for European travellers, who inscribed their names upon its walls as they did upon the pedestal of the vocal Memnon.

Among these travellers was Strabo, who continued his journey up the Nile from Thebes to Philæ. His account of Syene and the neighbourhood is both full and interesting; and in spite of the interval of nearly two thousand years which separates his epoch from our own, many of the features which he describes remain unaltered to-day.

"Syene is a city on the borders of Ethiopia and Egypt, and Elephantine is an island in the Nile, lying in front of Syene, half a furlong away, whereon is a city having a Temple of Knuphis, and a Nilometer—as Memphis has. The Nilometer is a well constructed on the banks of the Nile with regular stone work, on which the risings of the Nile—the highest, lowest, and the mean —are indicated; for the water in the well rises and falls with the river. There is a scale on the wall of the well which measures the height of the full flood and the lower levels of the stream; and by observing this scale information is furnished to the other inhabitants of Egypt. For by a comparison of the scale with the time in which the movements recorded on it occur, it is known that the flood is coming long before it arrives, and the fact is proclaimed beforehand. This forecast is useful to the cultivators in respect of the management of the water, and the embankments, and the channels, and other such matters; while it is useful to the authorities in respect of the taxes, for a higher flood signifies a proportionate rise in the revenue. In Syene also is the well which shows the tropical point of the sun, as this region lies under the tropic circle. For if we advance from our region—the region of Greece, that is—to the south, this is the first place where the sun comes exactly over our heads, and makes the index of the sun-dial cast no shadow at noon. And as it is overhead, it must cast its rays down to the water of the wells, however deep they may be; since we stand perpendicularly, and the wells are dug perpendicularly.

"There are three companies of Roman soldiers stationed here to guard the frontier.

"A little above Elephantine is the small cataract where the boatmen make a display for the entertainment of their superiors. The cataract is in the middle of the river. It consists of a rocky ridge, low enough up-stream to allow the water to pass over it, but ending in a steep face over which the water breaks, while on either side there is a stream near the shore which affords the best navigation. Taking this course, then, they rush down over the cataract and are thrust with their boat upon the line of rock, without suffering any harm themselves or injuring the boat.

"A little higher up the cataract Philæ appears. It has a mixed population of Ethiopians and Egyptians, and it is similar in formation and equal in size to Elephantine. There are Egyptian temples here, where the bird, which they call a hawk, is worshipped. . . .

"We came to Philæ from Syene by carriage, travelling for nearly a hundred furlongs through a remarkably level plain. All along the road, and on both sides of it, we constantly came upon abrupt masses of rock, resembling the Hermaea,[1] which are erected by the side of our roads. They were rounded and remarkably smooth, almost conical in form, and consisted of the black hard stone which is used for mortars. Sometimes a stone was placed upon another larger stone, and then itself carried a third stone; sometimes the stones lay apart by themselves. The diameter of the largest was not less than twelve feet, and they were all larger than the half of this. We crossed over to the island in a 'pakton,' a small boat constructed of interwoven wands, and looking as though it had been plaited. We stood in the water, or seated ourselves on some boards, and were thus easily carried across. Our fears were unnecessary, for there is no danger; unless, indeed, the ferry-boat is overloaded."[2]

Strabo also gives some account of the geographical position and general characteristics of the tribes that inhabited the regions southward of Egypt. He mentions the Troglodytæ, the Blemmyes, the Noübæ, and the Æthiopians above Syene; all of whom, he says, were neither populous nor warlike, and yet they were able formerly to harass the exposed frontiers of Egypt. And he dwells with pride upon the defeats which the Roman commanders had inflicted upon them, and upon the ease with which the frontier was then secured by a handful of legionaries.

[1] They were heaps of stones, placed under the protection of Hermes, which served to mark the road. In later times they were replaced by statues, or rather busts, of the god, standing on pillars.

[2] C. 817–18.

With the decline of the Empire, however, these desert tribes grew more daring. When Diocletian, at the end of the third century of the Christian era, had reduced the rebellion which had broken out in Upper Egypt—a rebellion in which the Egyptians of the Thebaid had been supported by the wild tribes of Æthiopia—he made a new disposition for the defence of the frontier. "With a view of opposing to the Blemmyes a suitable adversary," Gibbon writes, "Diocletian persuaded the Nobatæ, or people of Nubia, to remove from their ancient habitations in the deserts of Libya, and resigned to them an extensive but unprofitable territory above Syene and the cataracts of the Nile, with the stipulation that they should ever respect and guard the frontier of the empire. The treaty long subsisted, and till the establishment of Christianity it was annually ratified by a solemn sacrifice in the Isle of Elephantine, in which the Romans, as well as the barbarians, adored the same visible or invisible powers of the universe."[1]

As we had only a few days at our disposal for seeing both Assuân and Philæ, as well as the Nile Reservoir, it was necessary to avoid any waste of time. On the morning after our arrival, therefore, we crossed the sandy plain, and climbed to the crest of the range, on whose slopes lie the quarries from which the Pharaohs took their supplies of granite. The ridges which mark the lines of the ancient workings could still be distinguished, in spite of the sand which had gathered in the hollows; and here and there we came upon cartouches engraved upon rocks still unhewn, and rows of round holes, which showed where the chisel had prepared the way for the wedges, by which the cleavage was to be effected. We sat on the brow of the hill for a few minutes to enjoy the wide prospect which spread before us. The brown rocks and yellow sand of the desert stretched southwards from beneath our feet to the white buildings and the palm groves of the town; and beside the town the stream of the Nile sparkled, and then lost itself in the barren hills that close about

[1] Decline and Fall, chap. xlii.

the cataract. Then we descended to the plain again, and passing through the Mohammedan burial-ground and the Bishárin encampment, made our way back to the hôtel on the bank of the Nile.

In the afternoon we took a boat, manned by a crew of lively Arabs, and crossed to the island of Elephantine. We went ashore at the south-east corner, under the black polished cliffs, in the midst of which the Nilometer was constructed. After we had traversed the mounds of débris, which form almost the sole remains of the town of Elephantine, we returned to the Nilometer, and descended the narrow staircase which leads down to the level of the water. An inscription in Arabic and French

THE NILOMETER.

informs the traveller that "After more than a thousand years of neglect and forgetfulness," the work was restored in 1870, by the astronomer Mahmoud Bey, "one of the faithful servants of the Khedive Ismáil the Good, the Regenerator of Egypt." From the Nilometer we sailed up stream, among the round masses of black rock which protruded everywhere above the waters of the river, to a sandy bay on the west bank. About half a mile inland we could see the object of our quest—the brown walls of the ruined convent of St. Simeon, which rose on the crest of a sandy ridge. Between us and them long slopes of loose sand, very beautiful to look upon—for the sand of the desert here was almost as white and dazzling as snow—but by no means easy to walk over, as we soon discovered to our cost. When we had at length struggled over these slopes of shifting sands, we found the remains of a building, which must have formed a complete example of its class. The central building, which has two storeys, is surrounded by a high outer wall, and the space between this wall and the main building was partly occupied by a church, with nave and aisles, by rock-hewn cells, and by other structures. In the convent itself we found long corridors, with the cells of the monks opening from them, and on the east wall of the church the frescoes could still be distinguished. The lower portion of all the buildings alike were constructed of stone, but bricks of Nile mud had been used for the walls above, and for the arched roofs of the vaulted chambers. This convent is said to have been deserted by the Coptic monks as long ago as the thirteenth century; and the fact that a fabric constructed of such frail materials as these Nile bricks should have been preserved until now, affords a striking proof of the extreme dryness of the atmosphere of the Thebaid.

The existence of these ruined walls amid the white sands of the desert serves to remind us that the inhabitants of the Thebaid were early converted to the Christian faith. In the persecutions of the Christians which followed the edicts of Diocletian, this remote district is said to have suffered more than any other part of the Roman empire. According to Eusebius, it was no uncommon thing for as many as from ten to one hundred of its inhabitants to suffer martyrdom in a single day. These numbers, which Gibbon deems incredible, may partly be explained by the circumstance that the sequestered deserts and hidden valleys of the Thebaid afforded a convenient asylum for the refugees from all parts of Egypt.

As we sailed back down the river, we noticed many finely-cut cartouches upon the masses of black rock which projected from the east bank into the stream, and other signs of the handiwork of the masons of ancient Egypt. A pretty scene awaited us as we approached the quay. The granite hills which we had traversed in the morning were coloured by the rays of the setting sun to a crimson so vivid, that they seemed aflame; and the town and harbour beneath them were gay with bunting. The crowd of boats which edged the quay, the dhahabiyehs along the opposite bank, and two large steamers lying off the bank in front of the hôtel, were all alike decked with long streamers and bright-coloured flags. The occasion of the display, as we afterwards heard, was the news just brought by telegraph that a son and heir had been born to the Khedive Abbâs Hilmi.

The two following days we dedicated to Philæ. We went there by the military line which connects Assuân with Shellâl,

CONVENT OF ST. SIMEON.

thus avoiding the tedious ride by donkey through the desert, which forms the alternative. The station of Shellâl is just opposite the island, but before we crossed the narrow stream, we walked down the bank towards the promontory of Shellâl in order that we might see the island from the most picturesque point of view. I was the more anxious to secure this view, because, in two or three years at most, Philæ will cease to rise, as it does now, loftily above the waters of the Nile below, and its temples alone will appear above the broad plain of waters created by the giant weir a mile below. When I had finished my sketch, or rather sketches, for I made more than one, we returned to the station where we had left our luncheon-basket, and then crossed over to the island.

The construction of the Temple of Isis, which stands in the centre of the island, was commenced by Ptolemy Philadelphus and Arsinoë his queen, and continued by his successor Ptolemy Euergetes; while successive sovereigns decorated the temple walls with reliefs and embellished the interior. The beautiful colonnades, which run on either side of the outer court, were added at so late an epoch that they are sharply distinguished from the main fabric. The temple itself affords a characteristic example of the period in which Egypt was first subjected to the influence of Greek art and thought. Although the Egyptian forms are still preserved, the extravagant proportions of these forms are restrained, and the structure is at once more complete and more harmonious. At the same time the reduction of size has been accompanied by a more complete development of the several parts, manifested in particular in the delicacy and richness of the interior decorations. The colouring on the ceiling of the polystyle hall, and on the capitals of the columns by which the roof is supported, has been preserved in a remarkable degree; and the strange beauty which this shaded interior still possesses, enables us to form some definite conception of the bewildering loveliness with which such colouring must have invested the more magnificent chambers of the ancient temples.

Isis and her consort Osiris were the national deities of Egypt. "The Egyptians as a people," says Herodotus, "do not worship alike the same deities except Isis and Osiris—the latter they say is Dionysus—but these they all alike worship."[1] The earliest conceptions of these deities appear to have been very simple. Osiris was the god of the Nile; and it was he who had taught the use of the plough. Isis was the goddess of the earth, and to her inspiration was ascribed the cultivation of wheat and barley. Afterwards, when Egypt had been brought into relation with Syria and Persia, the original conceptions were modified by the

[1] ii., 42.

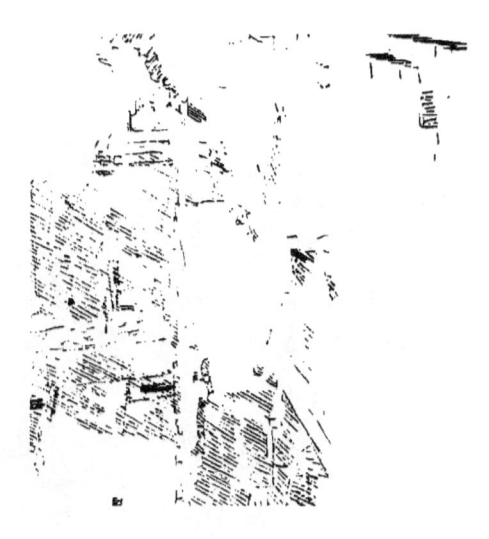

more spiritual influences of the East, and Osiris was identified with the sun and Isis with the moon. The worship of Isis was early introduced into Greece, where she was identified with Demeter, the beneficent goddess of the earth; and during the period of political and moral disturbance which followed the civil wars of Marius and Sulla, this worship appeared in Rome among a crowd of strange superstitions from the East. "The

CAPITALS AT TEMPLE OF ISIS.

brighter and gentler celestial forms of the Persian religion," says Mommsen. "did not so rapidly gain a footing in Rome as the wearisome, mystical swarm of the grotesque divinities of Egypt— Isis the mother of nature, with her whole train, the constantly dying and constantly reviving Osiris, the gloomy Serapis, the taciturn and grave Harpocrates, the dog-headed Anubis. In the year when Clodius emancipated the clubs and conventicles (696) and doubtless in consequence of this very emancipation of the populace, that swarm even prepared to make its entry into the old stronghold of the Roman Jupiter in the Capitol, and it was with difficulty that the invasion was prevented, and the inevitable temples were banished at least to the suburbs of Rome. No worship was equally popular among the lower orders of the population in the

THE KIOSK.

capital; when the Senate ordered the temples of Isis constructed within the ring-wall to be pulled down, no labourer ventured to lay the first hand on them, and the consul Lucius Paullus was himself obliged to apply the first stroke of the axe (704); a wager might be laid that the more lax any woman was, the more piously she worshipped Isis. That the casting of lots, the interpretation of dreams, and similar liberal arts supported their professors, was a matter of course. The casting of horoscopes was already a scientific pursuit; Lucius Tarutius of Firmum, a respectable and in his own way learned man, a friend of Varro and Cicero, with all gravity cast the nativity of kings Romulus and Numa, and of the city of Rome itself; and for the edification of the credulous on either side confirmed, by means of his Chaldean and Egyptian wisdom, the accounts of the Roman annals."[1]

Under the Empire the worship of Isis and Serapis became

ROMAN GATEWAY.

recognized, and in the time of Vespasian, scarcely more than a century after the Senate had issued a decree forbidding the private worship of the Egyptian goddess, a Temple of Isis was erected in the Campus Martius, and the cult subsequently spread from Italy into Gaul. It is not surprising, therefore, that the island which formed so venerable a seat of the goddess should have been decorated with buildings erected by successive emperors. And indeed, to-day the entire surface of the little island of Philæ

[1] Mommsen's "History of Rome," v. ch. xii. (Dickson's translation.)

is covered with the remains of these Ptolemaic and Roman buildings, through which the traveller threads his way by narrow passages paved with stone. Chief among these Roman buildings is the graceful kiosk which forms an architectural feature second only in significance to the temple of the goddess. In the reliefs with which the interior walls are decorated, the Emperor Trajan is represented in the act of worshipping Isis and Osiris. But both the interior decorations and the carving of the capitals of the columns have been left unfinished. The latest of these Roman additions is said to be the gateway erected at the north of the island in the reign of Diocletian. It should be added that in view of the possible effects which the Nile reservoir may produce on the antiquarian remains at Philae, a very complete examination of these remains has been made by the Survey Department of the Ministry of Public Works; and the results of the excavations, and of the observations which were then carried out, have been embodied in a very complete report prepared by Captain Lyons, the Director-General of the Department. In the course of this survey, accurate photographs were taken of the various buildings and of the characteristic features of the several structures; and copies of the report thus illustrated have been presented by the Egyptian Government to the museums of Europe and America.

But the antiquarian interest of Philae is overshadowed at the present moment by the vast work which is in process of construction a mile below it. To throw a bar of solid masonry across the Nile, and convert the Nubian valley into a lake, is a programme which sounds heroic, but is nevertheless being executed in sober earnest. The magnitude of the engineering task, and the splendid advantages which it promises to Egypt, invest the enterprize with an interest which appeals alike to the imagination and the reason. A week before we hurried down the sandy path which leads from the village of Shellâl to the reservoir works, the foundation-stone of the actual dam had been laid by the Duke of Connaught, and we knew therefore that sufficient progress would have been made to reveal something of the

ASSUÂN

engineer's design even to the eye of the uninitiated traveller. Our expectations were more than fulfilled. Although barely six months had elapsed since the preceding 1st of July (1898), when the five years' period allowed for the completion of the works had commenced to run, what seemed a considerable town had sprung up on the east bank of the river. Houses, offices, sheds, restaurants, shops, and a hospital had been built; lime-kilns, brick-kilns,

STEAM CRANES AT NILE RESERVOIR.

drying-sheds, and a powder magazine of solid stone had been erected. On this side and that, busy locomotives were hauling trucks of materials over the rails which had been laid down, and everywhere huge cranes raised their iron arms over jagged masses of rock. A courteous French engineer, to whom I had explained my errand, furnished us with an Arab guide, and thus directed we made our way to the summit of a convenient hill, and from this point of vantage the whole marvellous scene was spread before

T

us. Right across the sandbanks and rocks through which the waters of the Nile poured here and there in silver threads—right across the broken bed of the river from shore to shore—there stretched a huge trench; a trench so long that its farthest point disappeared in distance. On either side of the trench, mounds of sand and broken rock had been thrown up, and along the sides of these mounds black masses of Arab workmen gathered round the cranes and trucks, looking from this distance like swarms of ants. It was from this trench that the solid bar of masonry, which was to hold back the stream of the Nile in its most impetuous moments, would rise from foundations laid securely in the space thus excavated.

The actual dimensions of the dam are appropriate to the magnitude of the task which it will perform. The bar of masonry will measure in length 2156 yards, or about a mile and a quarter; a length which is about double that of the barrage below Cairo. The masonry at its crest will be 26.4 feet wide, and the base where it is laid deepest will spread over 82.5 feet; and from this depth it will rise 92.4 feet. This bar will be pierced by 180 under-sluices, fitted with gates; and when these gates are closed, the water accumulated in the Nubian Valley will be held up to a point 106 metres above mean sea-level, and 20 metres above the low-water level of the river itself. The volume of water which will be thus stored is estimated at 1065,000,000 cubic metres. When the gates are open, the surplus water will pass through the bar of masonry, or the supplies of water will flow from the reservoir to fill the summer canals of Upper and Middle Egypt. The dam itself will be furnished with three locks, and on the west bank of the Nile an artificial navigation channel, with a double lock, will be constructed, through which the Nile boats will pass up and down the river.

But the Nile reservoir forms only a part—an essential and important part, but still only a part—of the works now under construction for the purpose of supplying Upper Egypt with perennial irrigation. These works include also a dam and lock on the Nile at Assiût, a regulator and lock for the Ibrahimiyeh Canal, which supplies the fields on the Lybian shore of Middle Egypt, and the subsidiary works which are to assist in the distribution of the increased supply of water thus obtained. The dam at Assiût, which is to be 903 yards in length, will be similar in construction to the barrage below Cairo; that is to say, instead of being a solid mass like the dam at Assuân, it will be an "open barrage" of 111 bays, 16.5 feet in width, and furnished with regulating gates. And the function of this dam will be to hold

SITE OF THE NILE RESERVOIR.

up the Nile water, so that the Ibrahimiyeh Canal may be sufficiently supplied with water in the spring and summer.

The terms upon which Egypt is to acquire these important works are worthy of notice. The cost of constructing these works is estimated at a total of £2,000,000. Under the contract which the Egyptian Government made with Messrs. Aird & Co. on the 20th of February 1898, the works are to be completed within a period of five years, running from 1st July 1898; while, on the other hand, the Egyptian Government has bound itself to make annual payments of £157,226, in half-yearly instalments, for a period of thirty years, commencing on 1st July 1903. The essential points of this arrangement are—

(1) that the contractors provide the entire capital ; (2) that the Egyptian Government pay nothing until the works are actually completed ; and (3) that at the end of thirty years, after the completion of the works, Messrs. Aird & Co. will have been paid some 4¾ millions, or more than twice the estimated cost of the works in question.

It is obvious that such an arrangement for deferred payment is less desirable, from a financial point of view, than a ready-money transaction ; since, making due allowance for the interest saved on the capital sum, which would have been required for immediate payment, the Egyptian treasury will, in the end, pay considerably more than the ready-money cost of the work. The inability of the Egyptian Government to find the necessary funds for immediate payment is due, however, not to any deficiency in the revenues of Egypt, but to the control over these revenues which is exercised by the International Authority. At the very time when this contract was entered into, a fund sufficient for the purpose, and one which might have been most properly applied in providing the country with public works of this reproductive nature, was actually in existence. It had been accumulated by the successive economies resulting from the conversion of the Privileged Debt in 1890, and on December 31st, 1897, the value of the Egyptian stocks, in which these annual economies had been invested, amounted to £E2,767,000. Under the existing arrangement, this fund cannot be touched by the Egyptian Government without the consent of the Powers ; and the Nile reservoir thus affords another instance of the injury which is inflicted upon Egypt by the continued presence of the International factor. Under the given circumstances—that is to say, in the face of this inability of Egypt to employ her own accumulated capital—the arrangement was not only the best that could be made, but the fact that the Egyptian Government had the courage to make it, forms in itself a practical denial of the allegations by which this ungenerous policy is supported. For the retention of this and similar funds in the hands of the

Caisse de la Dette, can only be justified on the supposition that the power of Egypt to meet her obligations is decreasing. The evidence of the last fifteen years is in itself sufficient to make this supposition untenable; but the fact that the Egyptian Government are prepared to increase their liabilities to so large an extent, shows that they, at least, look forward to expanding revenues.

The details of the actual gain which is expected to result

A SAKÎYEH ON THE NILE.

from the construction of these new irrigation works in Upper Egypt, are contained in a memorandum by Sir William Garstin, enclosed in Lord Cromer's Report for 1898.[1] It will, however, be sufficient to give the main conclusions at which Sir William Garstin arrives, without entering into these details. In the first place, 774,000 feddans of "basin" land will be converted into

[1] Egypt, No. 1 (1898).

sifi; that is to say, the present system of flood irrigation will be superseded by perennial irrigation in this area. In the second place, as the result of this extension of the perennial system of irrigation, and generally of the water-supply of Egypt, the value of the annual wealth of the country will be increased by £E2,608,000; and in the third place, the State will derive an annual benefit from this increased wealth of £E378,400, while it will obtain an additional sum of £E1,020,000 from the sale of reclaimed lands. This estimate is a very cautious one; for, as Sir William Garstin points out, he has based his computations upon a year of "low Nile," and such years occur, on an average, only once in five years. Unless, therefore, the nature of the Nile should be suddenly altered, the figures of this estimate will be exceeded in four out of every five years.

At the time of our visit to the Nile reservoir there were, we were told, some 3000 Arabs and some 700 Europeans at work. Of these latter, the bulk were Italian stone-cutters. The work was to be continued through the summer, but in the hot weather the workmen would rest between 11 A.M. and 2.30 P.M., and the quarries would be covered with canvas screens. All the stone which was required for the dam was to be taken from the rocks around it; and the men were all paid on the system of piece work. Next year, it was expected that some 5000 Arabs, and more than 1000 Europeans, would be employed.

CHAPTER XVI

LOCAL GOVERNMENT AND THE CONDITION OF THE FELLÂHÎN

From Assuân to the Fayûm—Scene of the Nile reservoir of ancient Egypt—Herodotus's account of Lake Moeris—Strabo's account—Fertility of the district—The Labyrinth—The Mudir of the Fayûm—Local administration in Egypt—Representative institutions established by organic law—Legislative Chamber—General Assembly—Municipalities—Provincial and Town Councils—The Mudir central figure in provincial administration—Hassan Bey—His duties and functions—Relations of Mudir and Parquet—Industrial development of the provinces—Light railways—In the Delta—The Fayûm Light Railway Co.—Native Board of Management—Construction of markets in provincial towns and villages—Aspect of the Fayûm—The Fellâh—In the fields—At home—The indebtedness of the Fellâhîn—Proposals to remedy this evil.

WE left Assuân on Saturday, the 25th of February, and reached Medinet el-Fayûm a little before noon the next day. As the only train which would catch the Cairo express at Luxor passed Assuân at six o'clock on its way from Shellâl, it was necessary to make an early start; and the grey light of dawn was only just beginning to appear as we rode from the hôtel to the station. At five o'clock on Sunday morning we left the express at Wasta, the junction for the Fayûm. It was then quite dark, and some time elapsed before we could find any place in which to bestow ourselves and our luggage. Eventually we were taken to a room in which the station-master lay asleep. Here we saw our bags deposited in safety, but for ourselves we preferred the fresh air of the platform. The train for the Fayûm did not leave until ten o'clock, but our faithful tea-basket was with us, and with the aid of this and the remains of the provisions which we had brought from the hôtel at Assuân, we were able to provide a simple breakfast.

We had written beforehand to engage rooms at the Hôtel du Fayûm, and we found a stout Nubian, with a couple of Arabs, waiting at the Medinet station to take charge of our luggage. A friend from whom we had heard of the place had called it " a tolerable Greek inn"; and this description exactly fitted it. The street door opened directly into a large bare chamber, of which the sole furniture consisted of a billiard-table, and a number of small iron tables and chairs standing round the sides. One or two small rooms opened directly from this chamber, and opposite the entrance a staircase led to a balcony which overlooked the interior of the large room, and gave access to the bedrooms above it. The Greek proprietor, however, did all that he could to make us comfortable during the week that we remained under his roof, and the simple fare with which he provided us was by no means unpalatable. The hôtel stands in the centre of the town, on the bank of the Bahr Yûsuf, and it was alive with the stir and movement of the capital of a flourishing province.

Thanks to the railway, we had been thus swiftly carried from the scene of the engineering enterprize which is to furnish Egypt with its Nile reservoir to-day, to the site of the reservoir with which ancient Egypt was provided by the wisdom of the Pharaohs. This ancient reservoir was the natural basin enclosed by low hills, which, lying some fifteen miles westward of the Nile, and some twenty miles southward of Memphis, was known to the Greeks as Lake Moeris. The greater portion of this basin, which was roughly some thirty miles in diameter, once covered by the waters of Lake Moeris, now forms the fertile province of the Fayûm;[1] and the waters which once stretched over the entire area are now confined to the narrow lake called the Birket Karûn, which lies under the hills which form its south-western edge. Two accounts of this ancient reservoir have come down to us. The first was written by Herodotus, who saw it as it was more than four hundred years before the Christian era; the second,

[1] The word is said to be derived from the Egyptian *Phiom*, meaning "lake." *Moeris* is connected with the Egyptian me(r)-wēr, *i.e.* the "great canal."

Strabo's account, describes its appearance four centuries later, that is, at the time of his visit in 24 B.C. A comparison of these two accounts, separated by so wide an interval of time, enables us to form some idea both of the process by which this basin was first utilized for the storage of the surplus water of the Nile flood, and of the subsequent changes by which the area of the reservoir was first contracted, and then the water contained within this contracted area became gradually insufficient for the useful purpose which it had originally been made to serve.

When Herodotus visited the neighbourhood of Lake Moeris, the inhabited area was confined to the slope of the eastern ridge of the basin. Here, on the edge of the lake, which extended from this point alike to the north and south, was the "City of Crocodiles," and a vast building styled the Labyrinth, which, with its twelve halls, constructed and roofed of massive stones, surpassed the Pyramids in marvellousness. The circumference of the lake, he says, was 3600 stades, but this distance—more than 400 miles —seems incredible, even if we allow for the indentations of the coast-line. The fact that the lake was artificial was shown by the presence of two pyramids, 600 feet in height, which rose 300 feet above the level of the water, and were crowned by colossal statues in stone. The water of the lake was not the result of any natural source, for the neighbourhood was absolutely rainless, but it was brought from the Nile by a canal. "For six months it floweth inwards into the lake, and for six months it floweth outwards into the Nile again." In addition to the canal the lake had an independent and subterranean vent, by which its waters were carried off into the Lybian desert, westward of the range of hills at the back of Memphis. Underneath the colonnaded halls of the Labyrinth there were a series of subterranean chambers containing the tombs of the kings, who had constructed the edifice, and those of the sacred crocodiles. These subterranean chambers Herodotus was not permitted to inspect, but all that was above ground he saw, and the twelve peristyle halls, enclosed by a wall, constituted, together with the adjacent pyramid, a work of superhuman vastness.[1]

At the commencement of the Roman period the appearance of the country had considerably changed. The capital of the district was no longer situated by the side of the Labyrinth on the eastern ridge, but it lay twelve miles westward, and between it and the Labyrinth stretched the most fertile and highly-cultivated lands in Egypt. The Ptolemaic town, which had replaced the former "City of Crocodiles," had been named Arsinoë in honour of the Queen of Ptolemy Philadelphus, and its inhabitants are said to have numbered at one time as many as 100,000 persons. To-day its remains can be seen in the black and sordid mounds which cover the high ground lying northward of Medinet. The Arsinoite district is described by Strabo as exceeding any other district in Egypt in beauty, fertility, and cultivation. "It is only in this district," he says, "that the olive trees come to perfection; here they are large, and produce both oil and fruit, and the oil is of excellent quality when it is properly treated; and if the trees are neglected they yield an abundance of oil, which, in this case, however, is spoilt by its smell. The rest of Egypt is destitute of olives, with the exception of the gardens of Alexandria, which are able to furnish the fruit of the olive, but do not avail for the production of olive oil. Among the other products of the district are a considerable quantity of wine, corn, beans, and all manner of podded plants." Writing of the general appearance of the lake, he says that "it resembles the sea in size and in colour, and that its shores are obviously identical with those of the coast." And he describes the manner in which it fulfilled its function as a Nile reservoir in the following terms. "Lake Moeris," he writes, "is capable, by reason of its size and depth, of receiving the overflow of the Nile flood without allowing the water to inundate the inhabited and cultivated land. Afterwards, as the flood subsides, it returns the surplus water by the same canal through the second of the two mouths, but at the same time the

[1] II. 148-150.

lake and the canal together retain a volume of water sufficient to fill the irrigation channels. The movement of the water is natural, but there are gates at both mouths of the canal by means of which the engineers regulate the flow of water both inwards and outwards."

Strabo also adds that the Labyrinth and the Pyramid-tomb of its royal founder stood near these gates. He, like Herodotus, compares the Labyrinth to the Pyramids, and he gives a full description of the system of buildings of which it consisted. He also gives an interesting account of a visit which he paid to the sacred crocodile kept in the lake by the priests. Through the good offices of an influential friend he had an opportunity of seeing the quarters in which the animal was kept, and the manner in which it was fed.[1] From this time (24 B.C.) onwards the land of the district was rapidly reclaimed; and it is said that by the second century of the Christian era the area of the lake had contracted to its present dimensions, and the ancient Nile reservoir had ceased to exist.

It is obvious that the Fayûm is not deficient in antiquarian interest. And, in fact, apart from the Pyramids and the remains of the Labyrinth and of the other lesser structures of the ancient Egyptian period, the mounds which cover the sites of the towns of the Ptolemaic and Roman periods in this district have yielded a rich harvest of papyri. But it was the interests of the present and not those of the past that had attracted me to Medinet. I wished to see something of the efforts which were being made to benefit Egyptian agriculture – apart from the irrigation works — and to improve the condition of the Fellâhîn. Moreover, the town itself, as the capital of a Mudîrîyeh, and one of the lately established municipalities, afforded a convenient example of the working of the system of local government.

On the morning after my arrival I called upon the Mudir, Hassan Oassif Bey; and when I had explained that I was anxious

---

[1] C. 809-812.

to learn something of the system of provincial administration, he courteously invited J—— and myself to take tea with him on the following Wednesday afternoon, in order that we might discuss the subject more at leisure. Before, however, I give the reader the benefit of the very interesting information which I thus obtained, it will be convenient for me to describe the main outlines of the system of local administration in Egypt as a whole.

For purposes of local administration, Egypt is divided into fourteen Mudiriyehs or provinces, which are further subdivided into districts. The towns of Cairo, Alexandria, Damietta, the Suez Canal towns—Port Said and Ismailiyeh—and the districts of Suez and el-Arish, are placed outside of the provincial system, and endowed with separate administrations, municipal and otherwise, over which a governor presides. And apart from these governorships, twenty municipalities, or "local commissions," have been established for the management of the larger native towns; and in one of these latter—Mansûra—a special municipality, with extended powers, was created in October 1898. These native municipalities are important, because it is in them we must look for the first signs of the development of self-government in Egypt. It is true that more imposing representative institutions are in existence, but the Legislative Council and the General Assembly, established, in accordance with the recommendations of Lord Dufferin, by the organic law which was promulgated by the Khedivial decree of May 1st, 1883, appear up to the present only to have served the somewhat doubtful purpose of ventilating the crude opinions of the leaders of Mohammedan sentiment. Of these two bodies, the first, the Legislative Council, consists of thirty members, of whom fifteen, including the president, are nominated by the government, and the remaining half are delegates elected in the provinces. It meets once a month, and its members are paid sums calculated to cover the expenses which they may incur in attending these meetings. The special function of the Council is to discuss the financial and legislative proposals of the government; but its powers are wisely restricted to the discussion of such actual measures as may be proposed by the government from time to time; and the recommendations they put forward have no binding force, since the legislative authority of the state is exclusively vested in the Council of Ministers and the Khedive. The General Assembly is constituted of the members of the Legislative Council, with the addition of the six ministers and forty-six members elected under a system of popular representation. The Assembly must meet at least once in every two years; and under the terms of the organic law by which it was created, no new direct personal or praedial tax can be imposed by the Executive without its consent. The important power with which this body is thus invested has been inoperative up to the present, since the financial policy of the Egyptian Government has been hitherto directed towards the removal of the financial burdens of the native population; but this power is in itself sufficient to rescue the Assembly from political impotency in the future. Its members, like those of the Legislative Council, receive a small sum, which is calculated to cover the expenses incurred by them in coming to Cairo on the rare occasions when it is convoked.

But, as I have remarked before, it is the local administrations, and not these chambers, which exhibit progress in the direction of self-government. Medinet, being the capital of the Mudíriyeh, as well as a municipality, is the seat both of a Provincial Council and of a Town Council. The Provincial Council consists of three *ex-officio* and of two elected members. The former are the Mudir, who presides, the Inspector of Public Works for the province, and the Irrigation Inspector. The remaining two members are elected by the votes of representatives from every village in the Mudíriyeh, and these delegates are themselves elected by all qualified persons in each village—that is, by practically all the men, with the exception of any who may have been convicted of crime. The functions of this council are merely consultative; it discusses and suggests in matters concerned with irrigation, agricultural roads, &c., and these suggestions, embodied in its resolutions, are reported to the appropriate Ministry—the Ministry of Public Works, Finance, &c., in Cairo. The Town Council consists of the same elements, but it is rather larger. The *ex-officio* members are the Mudir, the Public Works Inspector, and the Sanitary Inspector; and the Inspector of the Ministry of the Interior is entitled also to attend the council if he desires, but he has no vote. The elected members are four in number. The business of the council is to make arrangements in such matters as drainage, lighting, sweeping, and watering the streets, and local improvements such as the provision of public gardens, supplies of drinking water, and other conveniences. The funds which are at the disposal of the Town Councils vary with the size of the municipality, and range from £E400 to £E2500. They are supplied by the government, and not by local taxation; and the decisions of the council must be submitted to the Executive Council of the Ministry of the Interior, and approved by this Central Board before they can be put into effect. As in the Provincial Council, the Mudir presides, and it is by him that the decisions of the Town Council are executed when they have been approved by the Central Board.

The new Mansûra municipality has less restricted powers, and the council consists of eight elected members, in addition to the same *ex-officio* members. In the first place, it can levy optional taxes on imports and exports, in addition to the funds provided by the government; and in the second, its decisions are valid without being submitted for the approval of the Ministry of the Interior. But here again, progress is barred for the present, by the conflict of authorities in Egypt. "The privileges conferred on Europeans by the Capitulations," says Lord Cromer, "stand in the way of any considerable extension of the municipal system. No tax payable by all the inhabitants can be imposed without the consent of the Powers. In an exceptional case, such as Mansourah, it may be possible, after much labour and discussion, to obtain the consent of each individual European to the imposition of a tax, but the difficulties in the way of any general application of the optional system of taxation are obvious." [1]

The Mudir is the central figure in the system of local administration, of which these representative bodies form part. As the title (Mudir) signifies, he is "the man who turns everything round." The primary duties of the Mudir are to protect the lives and properties of the inhabitants of the Mudíriyeh, and to receive and forward the taxes. In addition to this he has certain restricted powers of summary jurisdiction; and in virtue of these powers he is able to assist the irrigation officers by punishing offenders who may break their regulations, and he can also protect the agricultural roads and other works of public utility in the province.

But I think that I had better let the Mudir of the Fayûm speak for himself, only remarking that Hassan Bey had spent several years in England, and spoke English with perfect ease, and that he, like the Khedive, had adopted the European fashion of limiting himself to one wife. He received us in the large drawing-room of his official residence, the Mudíriyeh, and gave us afternoon tea in the English manner. It is scarcely necessary for me to add that the same enlightened views and accomplishments are not to be expected in all members of the class of provincial governors of which he formed so pleasing an example.

"The Mudir," said Hassan Bey, "represents the executive power of all the Ministries; he is responsible for the public safety, he collects the taxes, and remits them to the Finance Ministry, and, on the other hand, all public funds for the purposes of local administration are remitted through him, although the officials can draw their salaries directly from the Ministry if they so desire. Besides being President of the Provincial and Town Councils, I am also President of the 'Family Council,' which, acting under the direction of the Religious Courts, appoints executors, &c., in cases of intestacy. I also preside at all meetings for the sale of Government lands, &c. I have power, as

[1] Egypt, No. 3 (1899).

President of a Council of three notables, to punish 'contraventions' (petty offences) against the regulations for the management of the Nile banks, by as much as two months' imprisonment; and in the case of offences against the agricultural roads I can punish by myself."

In respect of the work of the Town Council, Hassan Bey said that Medinet, like other centres of population, had been visited by the cholera in '95, and by the fever in '97; and in view of these outbreaks his attention had been especially directed to the subject of sanitation. He had caused the houses, with their imperfect drainage, bordering upon the canal, to be pulled down, and the *birkets*, or pools of standing water, had been filled up. In speaking of these matters the Mudîr said that the average length of Arab life would be about forty-five years, but that this low average was due mainly to the heavy mortality among the children. If, however, this disturbing factor were removed, the average would rise to between sixty and seventy years.

In response to an inquiry from me, Hassan Bey replied that there was no difficulty now in collecting the taxes. "The Fellâhîn," he said, "know now both when they have to pay their taxes and the exact amount; they need not pay until the twenty-fifth of the month, on the first of which the taxes are legally due. If they do not pay then, they are warned, and told that they must pay within forty days. If they fail to pay within this period, their property is sold by public auction, and in order to make any connivance on the part of their neighbours impossible, the government has power to purchase itself, if necessary. But of course," he added, "my most important duty is to provide for the safety of the public. If any crime is committed in the Mudîrîyeh, the preliminary inquiry is made by me, and the evidence thus collected is forwarded to the Public Prosecutor at Cairo. If he considers it sufficient, he submits it to the Court; but if it appears insufficient, fresh evidence is obtained. If the Parquet [1] are not satisfied with the evidence, nothing more can be

[1] See Chap. ix. p. 178.

done until the representative of the Public Prosecutor has conferred with the Mudir, and if the Mudir and the Public Prosecutor then disagree, the case must be reported to the Ministry of Justice."

The defect in this system—a defect which is engaging the attention of the Government at the present time—consists in the

NATIVE POLICE.

fact, that the Mudir is unable under the existing arrangements to avail himself of the professional knowledge of the Parquet in the earliest stage of the inquiry. In theory, the efforts of the police, of the prosecuting counsel, and of the Mudir, as the provincial representative of the Executive, are directed at one and the same object—to secure the conviction of the criminal; but in practice the Parquet appear to have aimed rather at exposing any

U

deficiencies in the evidence provided by the Mudir, than at assisting him and the police in their investigations. If, on the other hand, the criticisms and objections of the Parquet were offered to the Mudir before the evidence of the preliminary inquiry was completed, the results of this inquiry would then, whether sufficient or insufficient, at least represent the joint results of the efforts of both Mudir and Parquet. As it is, the whole blame of any failure to bring a criminal to justice is borne by the Mudir and the police, and the authority of the Mudir is liable to be needlessly weakened.

In reply to an inquiry respecting the position of the Shêkhs, Hassan Bey informed me that they were elected by the men of their respective villages, but that the election was approved by the Mudir before it became valid. He added that the Arabs were revengeful, and that therefore, in order to prevent disturbances, he advised the Shêkhs in his province to punish promptly, and not to let any quarrel or offence stand over.

The improvement of the system of local government is being accompanied by the development of the industrial resources of Egypt. The great agency in this development is, of course, the irrigation system; and, as we know, great works are being constructed, and large sums of money are being spent, for the purpose of bringing this system to perfection. But apart from this all-important work of supplying Egypt with water, other lesser agencies are being employed to assist and stimulate the efforts of the cultivator. Perhaps the most important of these lesser agencies is the construction of Light Railways in suitable districts. An instance of the use of such railways has already been presented by the sugar plantations at Beliâneh. But the system is most advanced in the populous plains of Lower Egypt. In the Delta there are three companies already at work, and by the end of 1898 a total of 207 miles had been opened by them for traffic. Of these three companies, the Mansûra-Matariyeh line, which connects the fishing towns of Menzaleh and Matariyeh with the Government railways at Mansûra, is rather a "feeding" line than an agricultural railway; and it appears to suffer commercially from the competition of the water carriage afforded by the adjacent canal. Of the two agricultural railways, properly so called, one is French and the other English. The French company, the *Société des Chemins de fers Économiques* serves the province of Sharkieh and parts of the provinces of Kalyûb and Dakaliyeh: while the Delta Light Railways Company serves the provinces of Behêreh and Ghabiyeh. Both of these companies are prosperous; and it was the success of the light railways in the Delta that stimulated the introduction of the system into the Fayûm.

I had been happy in learning something of the official aspects of an Egyptian province from the Mudir of the Fayûm, and I was equally fortunate in securing industrial information from Mr. W. O. Joseph, the Managing Director and Chief Engineer of the Fayûm Light Railways Company. Mr Joseph's acquaintance with the Fayûm had commenced eleven years ago, when he came into the neighbourhood as an Assistant-Inspector of Irrigation. At that time there were no roads, and in order to supply this deficiency meetings were held at the suggestion of Major Brown (now Inspector-General of Irrigation for Lower Egypt), and it was proposed to levy a voluntary tax on the land of the district, in order to raise funds for the construction of agricultural roads. There were now some 300 kilomètres of these roads in the Mudiriyeh, and fresh roads were being made every year as they were required. The cost of these roads, which are constructed of earth without any covering of metal, Mr. Joseph said was about £30 per kilomètre. Five years ago Mr. Joseph had proposed the construction of tramways: but nothing had been done until the concession now held by the Fayûm Light Railway Company had been obtained in May 1897. The concession was in itself remarkable as being the first which had been granted by the Government to a native syndicate.

This company, which has a capital of £180,000, is managed by a Board of Directors, who are all natives. Two, however, of these are Government delegates, and Mr. Joseph has a seat on the Board as Managing Director. The bulk of the capital, Mr. Joseph said, had been subscribed by the Copts at Assiût, and the remainder by the local landowners and millowners. The assistant engineer, Mr J. C. Day, and the rest of the staff employed in the construction of the line were Europeans; the plant, the rolling stock, and the permanent way had been manufactured in England. The total length of the railways which had been sanctioned by the concession was 146½ kilomètres; and at the present time (March 1899) 8 kilomètres had been laid, 60 kilomètres were ready for laying, and would be in working order within six weeks, while the whole line would be ready for the cotton crop in September. As the Government had guaranteed a return of 3 per cent. on the capital invested, the company was under the control of the Ministry of Public Works. The maximum charges both for passengers and goods had been fixed by the Government, and were practically identical with the corresponding charges on the Government railways. Each train was bound to be provided with carriages of two classes for passengers, and in this and other respects the interests of the public were carefully safeguarded by the provisions of the concession. The main industrial advantage which the railway would confer upon the cultivators of the Fayûm was the reduction of the cost of transporting produce from the outlying districts to Medinet. When the line was in working order, the company would draw its supplies of native employés from the Bûlâk "shops," and from the schools at Cairo.

Since I have spoken of these agricultural railways as constituting an important agency in the industrial development of Egypt, it will be convenient for me to say a few words in this place with reference to an auxiliary enterprize, which promises to perform a considerable service to the native producers in the provincial towns and villages. This enterprize is the construction of cattle markets, and markets for general produce, in 120 centres in Upper and Lower Egypt. In June 1898 a concession was granted by the Egyptian Government authorizing the

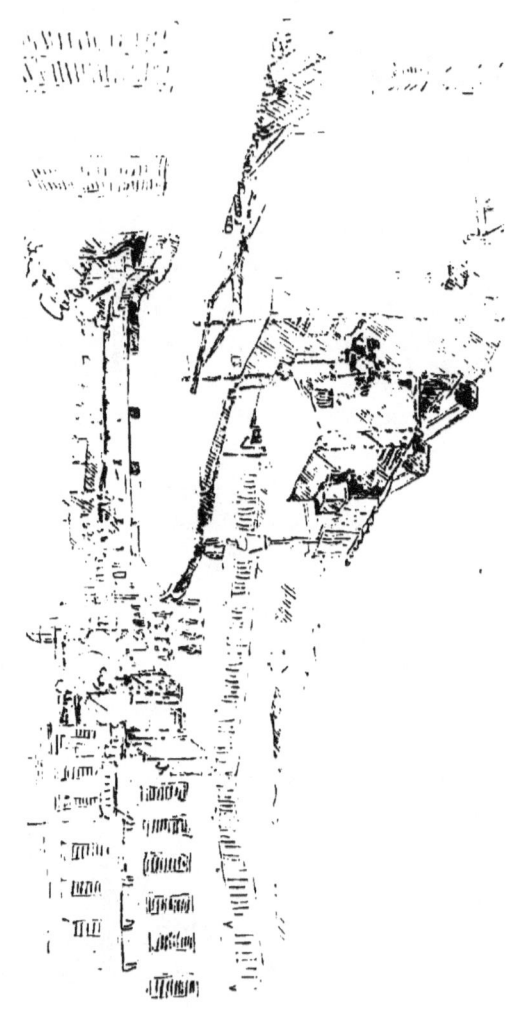

concessionaires to construct and manage these markets, and to collect tolls and rents from the persons who should use them. This concession, which runs for thirty years, has been acquired by a company, called the Egyptian Markets, Limited. The structures which the company erect consist of sheds with a framework of wood and roofs of red tile, with rows of stalls for cattle, and shops for general produce; and the whole market so constructed will in each case be surrounded by a railing of steel fencing. The population which will be benefited by these markets is estimated to number more than 6,000,000, and the markets are held once in every week. The tolls which the company are authorized to collect are fixed by the Government; they are very light, but the markets are held so frequently and are so numerously attended, that it is expected that they will yield a gross annual revenue of £100,000. Under the terms of the concession the Egyptian Government receives a substantial percentage of this revenue, and at the end of the thirty years the markets themselves will become the property of the State. Notwithstanding, however, the liberal share in the profits which the Government has thus secured, it is expected that the undertaking will prove sufficiently remunerative to the shareholders. I was informed that the capital required, some £200,000, had been subscribed ten times over in Egypt, and that, in addition to the European residents, the native Egyptians of all classes—including the fellâhin—had eagerly come forward to take shares in the company.

During our stay at Medinet we had various opportunities of exploring the town itself and the surrounding country. The aspect of Medinet is peculiar, and, I believe, unlike that of any other town in Egypt. The supply of water by which the Fayûm is irrigated is brought from the Nile by the Bahr Yûsuf, a partly artificial and partly natural channel which connects with the Ibrahimiyeh Canal. The picturesqueness of the "City of Fayûm" is due to the presence of this river, which flows through the centre of the town, where it is crossed by numerous bridges. The railway station, the Mudiriyeh, the Government school, and other official buildings lie to the south, but many of the newer and more imposing houses have been built on either side of the river. On the bank, opposite the Hôtel du Fayûm, there were in particular some handsome private houses, which were occupied by wealthy natives—landowners, merchants, and millowners; but the bulk of the population were housed in the narrow and crowded streets which lay to the north. The chief industry of

THE NATIVE PLOUGH.

the town is cotton-ginning, and the tall chimneys of the mills, which were built on the outskirts of the town, could be seen from the hôtel rising above the houses on the opposite bank. The capital which is employed in these mills belongs mainly, I was informed, to Copts and Syrians.

The principal crops grown in the fertile district, of which this town is the capital, are cotton, wheat, barley, and maize; and in addition to these, figs, oranges, the native apricot called mish-mish, prickly pears, onions, beans, bersin or clover, a little sugar, and a few olives and dates, are cultivated. Grapes are also grown, but they are not cultivated with sufficient skill to serve for the production of wine.

In the course of a visit which we paid to the remains of the statues of Amenemhet III. at Bihamu, we passed through a characteristic stretch of this "lake-land" country. We left Medinet mounted on donkeys, and attended by the tall Nubian from the hôtel; and when we were once free of the town we turned into one of the new agricultural roads. It was almost the width of an English highway, with a fairly hard surface, and it was carried over the canals by level bridges of wood. At first we met groups of the Fellâhin, who were bringing their produce into Medinet for the market which was being held on this day; but afterwards, as we got further from the town, fellow-passengers grew rare, and everybody seemed to be at work in the fields. The crops, we noticed, were corn, still green, but just breaking into ear, beans, bersin, onions, and figs growing about eight feet high, but leafless at this time of year, and further on we came across a walled garden of prickly pears. The country was perfectly flat, but its surface was pleasantly varied by these crops, and traversed in all directions with canals and irrigation channels, and here and there the landscape was broken by groups of palms. The animals which we noticed in the fields and villages were camels, buffalo, oxen, sheep, goats, and the ubiquitous donkey; and more than once we came upon strange groups in which the incongruous forms of the larger animals were curiously mingled with the men, women, and children. As we approached the goal of our journey the appearance of the country improved; the trees were finer and more luxuriant, and the streams and water-courses were larger and more numerous. Here we seemed to see something of the original lake-land, which had been gradually won from the waters of Lake Moeris.

On such journeys, and especially when I sat sketching, I was able to see something of the fellâh, as he appears in his native fields. More than once when I was thus engaged, a native would offer, of his own accord, to do me some slight service. On one occasion he spread his loose cloak, so that I might light my pipe in spite of the wind. When I was sketching in the native quarters of Cairo, and again at Luxor, I had found the native

AN ARAB SHEPHERD. (*Photo. by Mrs. Kay.*)

people civil enough. The donkey boys of Cairo, in particular, took an interest in my work, and I often heard a long-drawn *kwais* (good) from one or other of the group which had been patiently watching me. But in Cairo and Luxor, and in fact wherever there were tourists, the performance of any service, however slight, was invariably accompanied by a demand for bakshish. But here, where the native had not yet been demoralized, such small services proceeded from the natural *bonhomie*, which is a pleasing trait in the Arab character. At Luxor, also, I was able to see something of the Arab at home. I was indebted for this opportunity to a native gentleman of that place, to whom I had presented an introduction from a friend in Cairo. This gentleman provided me with a guide, who was able to take me into some of the characteristic dwellings of the native

GATHERING PALM FIBRE.

inhabitants. The dwellings of the very poorest class I found to consist of huts of Nile mud grouped round a diminutive courtyard, and both houses and courtyard were enclosed by a high wall of the same material. The huts appeared to be used only for sleeping in cold weather, and the real dwelling-place was the courtyard, where the men and women and children were seated on the ground, in the company of a calf, a goat, and numerous poultry. In another dwelling, which belonged to people of a rather better class, I found the house itself built of brick, but the walls of the courtyard, with the ovens for baking, and the circular receptacles for stores of corn and other food, were all built of mud. To this house a guest-chamber was attached, in a separate building; and it is characteristic of Arab hospitality that this guest-chamber was provided with a European bed, and was in fact far better furnished than any other part of the house.

Although the readjustment of the burden of taxation, and the abolition of the corvée (with the exception of service for the preservation of the Nile banks), has done much to improve the condition of the fellâhîn, the great mass of this class still remain miserably poor. The main cause of the poverty of the Egyptian cultivator is the exorbitant rate of interest which he pays upon the advances made to him by the money-lenders on the security of his crops. His land is productive, and he and his family live economically, but so long as the bulk of his profits are intercepted by the money-lender, there is little chance of his rising in the scale of civilization. To assist a class so backward and helpless as the Egyptian fellâhîn, is a difficult matter; since any interference with the economic action of the law of supply and demand might only intensify the evil which it was intended to remove. Nevertheless, certain tentative steps are being taken, with the approval and co-operation of the Government, for the purpose of supplying the fellâhîn with the necessary advances, at a moderate rate of interest.

The producers who require to borrow money consist of three classes. There are, first of all, the very rich, who come to Cairo to effect their loans. Secondly, there are the moderate men, who are not yet in debt, or only slightly in debt, but who cannot afford a journey to the capital; or could not even then obtain advances except by mortgaging their lands. And thirdly, there are the very poor, who wish to borrow quite small sums. The ordinary rates at which the two latter classes can borrow from the Greek usurers, range from 20 to as much as 40 per cent. per annum. The National Bank of Egypt has adopted two schemes, which are intended to provide for the needs of each of these two classes. The first scheme, devised with the assistance of one of the sub-governors, Mr. F. T. Rowlatt, consists in the establishment of a system of correspondents in various provincial centres. These correspondents have no authority to bind the bank, but they forward particulars of the proposed loan, and of the position of the borrower, to the bank at Cairo. When the loan is repaid, the correspondent is paid a commission. The sums thus advanced are £100 and upwards. At the present time, I was informed, such correspondents had been appointed at Zakâzik, Benisuêf, Sohag, Keneh, and other places in Upper Egypt.

The second scheme is directly intended to benefit the fellâhîn, and it has been devised by the governor of the bank, Sir Elwin Palmer. It provides for (*a*) advances up to £20, carrying an interest of ¾ per cent. per month, or fraction of a month, and repayable in the month of October: (*b*) advances up to £100, on the same terms, but repayable in five years, in the month of October. In the case of these latter advances, a mortgage is required. The interest to be paid on these advances is fixed at 9 per cent. per annum; and the scheme is being tried as an experiment in the district of Bilbêis, in the province of Sharkieh. An agent, approved by the Government, will forward lists of the advances required, together with the certificates of the tax collectors, relative to the properties of the several applicants. Such agents are to receive ½ per cent. on the 9 per cent. interest, as remuneration. A list of the loans thus effected will be forwarded by the bank to the Government; and then transmitted to the tax collectors, who will inscribe the particulars of the loans on the *wirde*[1] of the several proprietors.

---

[1] The *wirde* is the description of the property for purposes of taxation, showing the amount of the land tax, and the time when it is payable, which is furnished to each proprietor by the tax collector.

Each applicant must agree, as a condition of the loan, that his first payments made to Government shall be considered as payments on account of his loan, and not on account of the taxes. The interest and the capital will be thus collected by the Government tax collectors at the same time as the taxes, and the collectors will receive for their services $1\frac{1}{2}$ per cent. on the 9 per cent. interest. The actual interest received by the bank on these advances will amount therefore to only 7 per cent.

I have given a somewhat full account of these schemes, because the actual details serve to illustrate the difficulties of the situation. In particular, it will be noticed that extreme care has to be exercised in securing the bank against losses on the small loans. Moreover, it is by no means certain that the fellâhîn will be willing to take advantage of these opportunities of borrowing money at a reasonable rate; and it is only proposed, therefore, to introduce Sir Elwin Palmer's scheme at present into a single district. If it is found to work successfully, it will, of course, be extended. At the same time, these careful proposals are evidence of the earnest consideration which is being given to this difficult problem by the English advisers of the Egyptian Government.

CHAPTER XVII

THE DEVELOPMENT OF THE SUDÁN

The loss and recovery of the Sudán—Now depopulated and devastated by Mahdist tyranny—Condition of Sudán in 1882—Stewart's report—Present condition—Darfûr and Kordofán not yet recovered—Administration of provinces already occupied—Dongola province—Sir William Garstin's report on Sudán—Description of Khartûm—The Blue Nile and the White Nile contrasted—Egypt's immediate interest centres in the marsh area around Lake No—The weed barrier called "sudd"—Factors in the annual Nile flood—Effect of the sudd on the water-supply of Egypt—Enormous loss of water by evaporation in the marsh area—Possibility of diminishing this loss by preventing the river from "spilling" the water-supply of the Great Lakes—Clearance of sudd first operation—Climate of Sudán and its depopulation are obstacles to industrial development—Railway construction—Line from Wâdi Halfa to Khartûm—Proposed line to connect the Nile Valley with the Red Sea coast—Best route viâ Gedâref and Kassála—The "granary of the Sudán"—Little scope at present for private enterprize—Reasons for this—Pumping stations—Telegraph construction—The Gordon College.

Up to the end of last year there remained one failure which marred the otherwise successful record of British administration in Egypt. The possession of the former provinces of Egypt in the Sudân by an uncivilized and hostile power not only involved a direct loss of prestige, but it constituted a perpetual menace to the water-supply of Egypt, and drained her resources by the heavy military expenditure necessary for the protection of the southern frontier. Englishmen were sore too. The thought of the Sudân recalled one of the most bitter and tragic episodes in contemporary English history. There is nothing unusual in the loss of a life, or the ruin of a reputation. In the annals of Imperial administration such sacrifices to party considerations or national exigencies are only too common, but the case of Gordon was different. He went solely at the call of duty to fulfil a mission, which was thrust unsought upon him. The reasons which led to his abandonment were so sordid, the results were so immediate, that even 'the man in the street' felt his personal integrity diminished by an abuse of patriotism so absolutely shameless; and of the two countries England was more profoundly relieved by the news of Omdurman than Egypt.

It is no part of my purpose to tell the story of the abandonment and recovery of the Sudân,[1] but it is impossible to understand the present condition of this remarkable country without taking a hurried glance at the past. The events which took place between the outbreak of the rebellion in 1883, and the conclusion of the Sudân Agreement of January 19, 1899, fall naturally into three periods. In the first of these (1883 to 1885) the followers of the Mahdi gained possession of the Sudân; in the second (1885 to 1896), the Egyptian army was reorganized, and Egypt fought on the defensive; and in the third (1896 to 1898), Egypt assumed the offensive, and recovered possession of the greater part of her lost provinces. By "Egypt," of course, is meant the joint force composed of the Egyptian army, officered and organized by Englishmen, and the British troops which engaged from time to time in the various Sudân expeditions. The first period was marked by the destruction of General Hicks' force on November 5, 1883, in Kordofân; by the defeat of General Baker near Tokar, in February 1884; by the failure of the Nile Expedition, the fall of Khartûm on January 26, 1885, and by the evacuation of Dongola by the British troops in June 1885. These disasters were relieved by the victory of General Stewart at Abu Klea on January 17, 1885, and the splendid defence of "M'Neill's zareba," on March 22nd of the same year. During the second period the town of Suâkin and the Egyptian frontier at Wâdi Halfa were successfully defended against the attacks of the Dervishes. The Egyptian frontier force, which was formed in

[1] As the Sudân was closed to travellers last winter, the writer was unable to proceed to Khartûm. The facts given in this chapter are based entirely on official publications, to some of which his attention was drawn by Sir Reginald Wingate.

THE DEVELOPMENT OF THE SUDAN 319

1885, under General Grenfell, was at first supported by a British force at Assuân; but this latter was withdrawn in 1888. From that time onwards the task of defending Egypt against the attacks of the Khalifa Abdullah el-Taishi, who had succeeded the Mahdi in 1885, was successfully performed by Egyptian and Sudanese troops. A determined attempt to invade Egypt, in which the forces of the Khalifa were led by Wad el-N'jumi, was repelled by the victory of Toski on August 3, 1889, in which the Dervishes and their leader were destroyed by the combined forces of General Grenfell and Colonel Wodehouse at a point some seventy miles north of Halfa. The victory of Toski was followed by the establishment of an advanced post at Sarras, and henceforward the southern frontier of Egypt was free from Dervish outrage. In 1891 Suâkin was similarly relieved from the harassing attacks to which the garrison had hitherto been exposed by a successful advance upon Tokar, in which the Dervishes, under Osman Digna, were heavily defeated at Afafit. In 1892 General Kitchener succeeded Sir Francis Grenfell as Sirdar. Under the new Sirdar the work of training and organizing the army was steadily pursued, until Egypt was at length provided with a force of fighting men sufficiently reliable to enable her to commence offensive operations against her barbarous and difficult foe. In these offensive operations of the third period railway construction played an important part, and in the final effort the local forces were "stiffened" by the presence of British regiments. The several steps of the unbroken advance by which the English and Egyptian flags were finally raised over the walls of Gordon's ruined palace at Khartûm are these. In 1896 Dongola was occupied; in 1897 Abu Hamed was captured, Berber was occupied, and Kassâla was taken over from the Italian Government; in 1898 the battle on the Atbara, fought on April 8, prepared the way for the final and overwhelming defeat of the Khalifa's forces on September 2 at Omdurman.

The provinces which have been thus recovered by so great an expenditure of life and treasure, after many years of continuous effort, are devastated and depopulated regions. The Sudân is at its best a sparsely populated and inhospitable country; and to-day its original deficiencies have been intensified—first by the long years of Egyptian misrule, and then by the barbarous tyranny of the Mahdi and Khalifa. Such a country is not likely to pay the bare cost of its administration for many years to come; nevertheless this dearly-bought and expensive possession is necessary to the safety of Egypt, and it contains certain possibilities of future development, which, slight as they are, ought not to be altogether disregarded. Some idea of the normal capacity of the country can be gathered from the following extract, which is taken from Lieutenant-Colonel Stewart's report[1] on the Sudân in 1882. Under the head of "Trade, Commerce, and Manufactures," he writes: "Although at present, owing to the rebellion, the trade of the Sudân is almost at a standstill, in ordinary times it is considerable, and shows rather a tendency to increase.

"For trade purposes the country may be divided into three districts, each connected by roads with Egypt or the Red Sea.

"The first district includes the basins of the White and Blue Niles, with their tributaries, and also the eastern portion of the province of Kordofân. This district is connected with Egypt by the Nile Valley, and with the Red Sea by the Berber-Suâkin road. The great grain-growing districts of Karkotsch are also connected with Suâkin by a road passing through Guedaref and Kassâla. Khartûm, situated at the junction of the Niles, is the centre of this district.

"The trade consists chiefly of gum, ivory, ostrich feathers, tamarind, senna, hides, hippopotamus hides, gutta-percha, honey (fallen off), doora (kind of millet), salt (local trade), rhinoceros horns, indigo (small quantity), musk, palm-oil, and a vegetable fat used in scents.

"The second district includes the Darfûr and western districts of Kordofân. This district is connected with Egypt by the long

[1] Egypt, No. 11 (1883).

and toilsome road from Kobbé to Siout, known as the 'Road of the forty days' march.'

"In former years the track along this road formed an outlet not alone for the Darfûr, but also for the trade of the Wadai, Bagirmi, Bornu, and other districts further west, amounting, I am told, to over 100,000 kantars. Large quantities of salt and nitre were also exported to Egypt from the plains over which the road passes. Of late years the trade along it has, however, greatly fallen off, partly because the road was closed for some time to prevent the export of slaves, and partly because the Sultans of the Wadai, Bagirmi, &c., frightened by the never-ending conquests of the Egyptian Government, had forbidden all communication with Darfûr, so that the trade of these districts was diverted on to the northern road leading from Lake Tchad to Mourzoukh and Tripoli. The salt trade was also stopped by order of the Government in Egypt, as it interfered with the salt monopoly.

"At present only some two or more very large caravans leave Kobbé annually in September and January for Siout. On arrival at Siout they have to pay transit dues.

"The trade consists mainly of gum, ostrich feathers, ivory, ebony, and hides.

"The third district is that of Abyssinia, with its export centre at Massowah. Coffee, wax, and honey are the chief articles.

"By an order given some years ago, the White Nile was completely closed to traders. This was done to put a stop to the slave trade along that river. Although, of course, the order greatly hampers trade, still, for the above reason, it should be maintained.

"The natural result of the order is that the Equatorial trade has become a Government monopoly.

"Of other products, cotton, sufficient for local consumption, is grown in the districts of Berber, Sennâr, Kassála, and Ghedariff (or Gedâref).

"Tobacco culture has of late sprung up about Sennâr, and is, I hear, succeeding admirably.

"The tax is at present 200 piastres the feddan (acre), or

about 4 piastres per oke (3 lbs.). Probably, were this tax removed, the revenue would greatly benefit.

"All the districts south of Khartûm, between the Niles, and also about Karkotsch and Ghedariff, are celebrated for their corn-growing capacity, and may be said to be the granary of the Sudân. Were easy communications opened with the sea, there can be little doubt that a considerable export trade in grain would spring up. At present grain is allowed to rot in the ground in those districts, while it is perhaps at a famine price at Suâkin and Jeddah.

"*Manufactures.*—None, except a kind of light cotton cloth made at Dongola, and called 'tamur.'

"The import trade is mostly manufactured cotton goods, cutlery, &c.

"Transit dues are levied at Berber, at the rate of four piastres per camel-load on all articles passing through to Egypt, either *viâ* Korosko or Suâkin.

"Dues on all imports up the Nile Valley, at the same rate, are levied at Siout."

The second of these three districts—Darfûr and Western Kordofân—has yet to be reduced. Kordofân is a barren plain, or rather series of plains, which rise gradually towards the south, where they reach in some cases an altitude of 2000 feet. At present it is absolutely devoid of water, but the south-western district is said to be provided with a fine soil which might be rendered highly productive by irrigation. The surface of this vast barren plateau is broken here and there by low hills, and checkered with patches of thorny scrub, while stretches of cultivated land appear at rare intervals. Darfûr lies westward of Kordofân. It is broken by a central range—the Marra range—which stretches for a hundred miles from north to south, and then curving, runs for sixty miles westward. The country to the north and east of this range is as barren as Kordofân; but the mountainous and central region, where isolated peaks rise to 6000 feet, is fertile and well-populated. The slopes of the hills in this district are cultivated in terraces, and in the fields and gardens, corn, fruits, and vegetables are grown. The country to the west and south of the mountains is less fertile, but it is preserved from the barrenness of Kordofán by the presence of the "Khors," or deep valleys, where the water, which collects in the rainy season, can be found throughout the dry season a few feet below the surface.

In the remaining two districts distinguished by Colonel Stewart, the joint English and Egyptian administration has now been established; and the present characteristics of these districts are described in the report on the Sudán, which has just been written by Sir William Garstin. Before, however, I refer to this report, I shall present the reader with the totals of the respective Sudán budgets for 1882 and 1899. As the taxes are a rough indication of the cultivated area and population, a comparison of these figures enable us to form some estimate of the disastrous effects produced by the intervening fifteen years of Mahdist rule. In 1882 the revenue amounted to £E503,672, and the expenditure to £E600,444, showing a deficit of £E96,771. The estimated revenue for the present year is £E51,500, and the estimated expenditure is £E383,272, showing a deficit of £E331,772, which will fall upon the Egyptian treasury.

That portion of the Sudán which has been already recovered is divided, for purposes of administration, into the five first-class provinces, or mudiriyehs, of Dongola, Berber, Khartúm, Sennár, and Kassála, and the three districts of Fashoda, Suákin, and Wádi Halfa. Of these provinces, Dongola was organized in 1897; and some interesting particulars of its condition are mentioned in Lord Cromer's report[1] for 1898. In January 1897 the population had been reduced by Dervish misrule to 58,000 inhabitants, of whom 40,000 were women and children; but in the course of the year it was increased by the return of 19,000 persons, with 6000 adult men among them. At the same time the cultivable area was returned at 79,000 acres, and of this area

[1] Egypt, No. 1 (1898).

less than 20,000 acres were actually in cultivation. Moreover, the export of dates, which constitutes the chief wealth of the province, had diminished proportionately to the decrease of population. An English officer, styled mudir or governor, has been placed in charge of each province, and he is assisted in the work of administration by two English inspectors. These provinces are each further divided into districts, or mamûriyehs; and the mamûrs who are in charge of them are in general native military or police officers. The subordinate officials, placed under the direction of the mudirs and mamûrs, are in all cases natives. The supreme military and civil control is vested in the Governor-General of the Sudân, who is appointed by Khedivial decree on the recommendation of the British Government, and can be removed only by Khedivial decree with the consent of the British Government.[1] This office is at present held by Lord Kitchener of Khartûm.

Sir William Garstin, in his report on the Sudân, gives an account of the appearance of the country on the banks of the Nile and its tributaries, noting the towns and villages, and describing the inhabitants and industrial possibilities of the various districts. For descriptive purposes he divides the country thus traversed into three regions: the Nile, between Abu Hamed and Khartûm; the Blue Nile, from its junction with the White Nile at Khartûm to the borders of Abyssinia; and the White Nile, from Khartûm to Lake No.

Of the site of Khartûm and the junction of the White and Blue Niles, he writes:—

"Eight kilomètres up-stream of Omdurman the Blue and White Niles unite, forming the low tongue of land on which Khartûm was built. Just below the junction the well-cultivated island of Tuti is situated. The Blue Nile surrounds this last on two sides, one channel going to the east and the other running along the southern shore of the island towards the White Nile. At this point the difference in the colour of the two rivers is very

[1] Sudân Agreement, Art. III.

marked, the azure blue of the Blue Nile forming a vivid contrast to the yellowish-brown water of the White Nile. The line separating the two currents is visible for a long way down the stream. In flood, the velocity of the Blue Nile being much the greater, the water of this river pushes that of the White Nile across to the Omdurman shore.

"On the northern face of the tongue of land above mentioned, the town of Khartûm (latitude 15° 36′ 38″ north) was built. It is now a complete ruin, not a single building having been left standing by the Dervishes, who, however, fortunately spared the gardens and fruit trees. The work of rebuilding the town is being pushed on with great activity; the Governor's palace, built on the site of the old one, has made considerable progress, and work has also been started on the Gordon College and the new Government offices. Broad streets and roads have been cut and levelled through the ruins of the old town, and trees have been planted along these.

"The frontage on the Blue Nile is unrivalled as regards aspect, and obtains the full benefit of the prevailing north wind. Behind this, however, more especially in the direction of the White Nile, there are portions of the town which lie very low. Although all depressions are being filled up as far as is possible, it is to be feared that when the two rivers are in flood the subsoil water will approach very near to the surface of the ground, and malarious fevers may in consequence result."[1]

The two rivers, which thus unite at Khartûm to form the main stream of the Nile, are absolutely unlike in character. The waters of the Blue Nile descend rapidly from the Abyssinian plateau in a deep and narrow channel, carrying with them an abundance of fertilizing matter gathered from the mountains and forests which form its watershed. Sometimes it flows in a shallow stream, at other times its banks can scarcely contain the volume of water which it pours impetuously between them. The White Nile, on the other hand, flows with a broad and sluggish stream

[1] Report on the Sudân, Egypt. No. 5 (1899).

between low banks, and the volume of its waters varies but slightly, since it is fed by the constant supplies afforded by the Great Lakes of Central Africa. The country which surrounds the Blue Nile and its affluents, that is to say the districts of Gedâref, Sennár, and the eastern part of the Gezireh—as the country enclosed between the fork of the Blue and White Niles is called —afford the richest prospects in the Sudân. The region through which the White Nile passes is a succession of desolate and fever-stricken swamps, behind which low and treeless plains stretch in endless monotony. The White Nile flows southward for, roughly, 450 miles to Fashoda, where it curves westwards to its confluence with the Sobát, and running from this point due east and west joins the Bahr el-Ghazâl at Lake No, 610 miles from Khartûm. From Lake No it flows southwards to the Great Lakes, being henceforward distinguished as the Bahr el-Jebel.

The immediate interest of Egypt in the Sudân centres in the desolate region of swamps and grassy plains, which is formed by the confluence of these streams and their several affluents. The Bahr el-Jebel, the Bahr el-Ghazâl, the Sobát river, and the El-Zaraf, are all alike blocked, to a greater or less extent, by the barrier of dense, tangled water-weeds, known as the "sudd." The possibility of improving the water-supply of Egypt depends upon the removal of the sudd. The weed-barrier does not in itself affect the volume of water which the Nile discharges at Assuân in any appreciable degree, but the removal of the barrier, and the consequent opening up of these several rivers to navigation, is a condition precedent to an operation by which, in Sir William Garstin's opinion, Egypt's summer supply of water may be augmented by an increase of 50 per cent. It is incorrect to suppose that the weed-barrier, or the marsh region as a whole, has a beneficial effect upon the Egyptian water-supply; for this supposition is based upon the assumption that the obstacles thus presented have the effect of "holding up" the supplies of water which produce the Nile flood. As a matter of fact, Sir William Garstin points out, the closure of the river by sudd has no direct effect upon the volume of water which the Nile discharges at Assuân. He writes: "It is the Sobát, the Blue Nile, and the Atbara (not the White Nile) which form the ruling factors in the production of the annual Nile flood. The three first, being mountain torrents dependent on the rainfall of a vast area, rise rapidly, and, having a heavy slope, cause the sudden and excessive rise which early occurs in the river levels. The White Nile, on the contrary, has a steady and constant supply, which is controlled by the natural regulators formed by the rocky barriers over which it passes as it issues from the Great Lakes. This constancy of supply is a most important fact, and upon this entirely depends the possibility of any scheme for increasing the water-supply of Egypt by the permanent removal of the sudd."[1]

It is not, therefore, by the mere removal of the sudd that Egypt will reap the benefits which the recovery of the Sudân, and the consequent control of the Upper Nile, have placed within her reach. Briefly, Sir William Garstin believes that the vast area of swamps to the south of Lake No causes an enormous loss of that constant supply of water which the White Nile draws from the Great Lakes. The water which is thus "spilt"—to use his own expression—over this vast area is subjected to a rapid process of evaporation: and the amount of water which is thus lost yearly he estimates at a total of 12,175,000,000 cubic metres, equivalent to 33,356,000 cubic metres per day. "What is really required," he writes, "if an increase in the supply is to be obtained, is that the lost river should be formed artificially into a river again by regulating its section and augmenting its velocity and its discharge. This can only be done by preventing it from spilling over into the different side channels and marshes, and confining its volume to one main artery. If this be possible, the immense mass of water annually lost by evaporation, &c., will flow steadily to the north in a single stream, and the summer supply of Egypt be increased by the amount thus gained."[2]

Before, however, any definite scheme for the realization of this

---

[1] Report on the Sudân.   [2] Ibid.

object can be proposed, it is necessary that the whole of the marsh area should be surveyed, and that an effective method of confining the stream of the river within the banks of its channel should be discovered by experiment. The remoteness of the region, and the fatal character of its climate, will make such operations both difficult and costly; and many years must elapse, in Sir William Garstin's opinion, before these preliminary and essential observations can be concluded. In the meantime, even before these operations can be commenced, one river at least must be cleared of sudd, so that a navigable channel may be provided by which the steamers and boats of the surveyors can reach the scene of their operations. Sir William Garstin selects the Jebel river as most suitable for this purpose, and he believes that the work of clearing the sudd could be effected without any great difficulty, if a suitable apparatus were provided. "This apparatus," he adds, " owing to the flexibility as well as the tenacity of the weed-barrier, should 'tear it from below rather than cut it.'"

It remains to discuss the prospects of industrial development which the Sudân affords. At the outset two dominant facts appear, which make it plain that, for the present at least, any such enterprize must be restricted within very narrow limits. These facts are the dangerous climate, and the depopulation of the country under Dervish rule. The extent to which both the population and the cultivated area of the Sudân have been reduced can be roughly gauged by the smallness of the estimated revenue for the current year;[1] the malefic nature of the climate is only too notorious, but if further evidence of the deadliness of the malaria, by which the Sudân is infested, were needed, it would be found in the recommendations with which Sir William Garstin concludes his report. The troops which garrison the posts on White and Blue Niles must, he says, be lodged in huts which are raised on piles above the surface of the ground. Of the English and Egyptian officers, who are charged with the duty of

[1] See p. 323.

administering these districts, he writes that "their chance of preserving health will lie in yearly absences from the malarious tracts. Such leave rules should be granted them as will permit of their annually visiting Europe; at the same time they should receive salaries sufficiently liberal to enable them to avail themselves of this privilege."

Nevertheless there are two methods by which the conditions of this inhospitable and desolate Sudân may be appreciably improved. The first is the construction of railways, and the second the erecting of pumping stations upon the river banks for the irrigation of the more fertile districts. For the present there is a break of some 200 miles between the terminus of the Egyptian railway at Shellâl and the commencement of the Sudân railway at Wâdi Halfa. This break, which is due to the difficulty and cost of constructing a line along the rocky banks which enclose the Nile between the first and second cataracts, is covered by steam navigation. The Sudân railway, which starts thus at Wâdi Halfa, leaves the Nile, which here makes a wide sweep to the west, and strikes southwards across the desert for 371 kilomètres to the Abu Hamed. From this point it follows the Nile to Berber, 205 kilomètres further south, and then reaches the banks of the Atbara river, thus covering a total distance of 616 kilomètres from Wâdi Halfa. Here the Atbara bridge, opened on August 26, will carry the line across the river, and thence southward to Khartûm, which lies 336 kilomètres up the Nile. The actual distance to be traversed by the railway is, however, somewhat less[1] than the course of the Nile, and it is expected that the line will reach Khartûm by the end of the current year (1899). When railway communication has thus been established between Egypt and the capital of the Sudân, it is then proposed to connect the Nile Valley with the Red Sea. The railway which is to effect this purpose is to be constructed, not from Berber to Suâkin, but from Khartûm to Abu Haraz, Gedâref, and Kassâla, and thence to some point not yet determined on the coast.

[1] 187 miles.

The advantage of this more circuitous route lies in the fact that it will "tap" the rich wheat-producing districts which form the "granary of the Sudân." The first section of this line—from Khartûm to Abu Haraz, a distance of 122 miles—will be undertaken so soon as the railway to Khartûm has been made, and it is hoped that it will be constructed in the course of next year (1900). One immediate object which will be thus achieved is to render the ample food-supply of Gedâref available at Khartûm and Kassâla. At present, owing to the absence of any sufficient means of transport, there is a great difference in the price of grain at these places. "A short time ago," Lord Cromer writes, "almost famine prices ruled at Omdurman, whilst at Gedâref grain was so plentiful as to be well-nigh unsaleable. As I write, the price is P.T. 160 (£1, 12s. 6d.) per ardeb (300 lbs.) at Omdurman, and P.T. 22 (4s. 6d.) per ardeb at Gedâref. At the latter place the price is expected to fall to P.T. 10 (2s.) when the new crop, which is almost ripe, is harvested.

"I should add that Kassâla is now being supplied with grain from Gedâref, the current price being P.T. 48 (9s. 10d.) per ardeb. When the Kassâla crop is gathered, it is expected that the price there will fall to P.T. 22 (4s. 6d.) per ardeb."[1]

In discussing the question of the part which can be played by private enterprize in the construction and management of railways in the Sudân, Lord Cromer decides[2] that for the present at least, this important instrument in the development of the country must remain in the hands of the Government. Private enterprize is undesirable, in the first place, because "the elements are wanting to enable any conditions of sale to be settled which would be alike acceptable to the Government and the shareholders in the undertaking." Until some definite information on the industrial capacity of the Sudân has been acquired by independent observation, such enterprizes would be purely speculative. In the absence of such independent observation, neither the Egyptian nor

---

[1] Egypt, No. 3 (1899).
[2] *Sub voce* Sudân Railway Extension. Egypt, No. 3 (1899).

the Sudânese authorities are prepared to accept the responsibility of providing the data, on the strength of which the public would be invited to subscribe the necessary capital.

In the second place, the difficulty of finding labour and employés which private employers would experience, constitutes an "insuperable obstacle." The present Sudân railways, Lord Cromer points out, have been constructed and worked exclusively by military labour, and it is doubtful whether on this account alone any other system could be introduced, until the country has recovered from its present condition of depopulation.

At present, therefore, the only field for private enterprize in the Sudân is the construction of irrigation works on a small scale. Both in the Gezireh, and in the district of Gedâref, and on the banks of the Nile between Berber and Khartûm, the land is sufficiently fertile to warrant the construction of irrigation works on a large scale; but a generation or more must pass before the population will have sufficiently increased to justify the expenditure of public money necessary for such works. On the other hand, private enterprize might be usefully employed in the erection of pumping stations in these districts. "There can be no objection," Sir William Garstin writes, "even at present, to the erection of pumping-stations by private individuals or societies at different points along the Blue Nile. Were the sites for these stations carefully selected and within easy reach of large villages, such as Wad Medani, Rufaa, &c., it is probable that a considerable increase in the cultivation of valuable crops would ensue. The chief difficulties to be overcome would be the excessive height to which the water must be lifted, and the possibility of the river falling to a very low level in the early summer."[1] And similarly of the Nile between Berber and Khartûm, he writes that "the erection of pumping-stations would materially assist the return of prosperity to the people." He adds, moreover, that these operations would have no injurious effect upon the water-supply of Egypt.

[1] Report on the Sudân.

The telegraph system by which Khartûm has been placed in direct communication with Cairo and Europe, will be extended more rapidly than the railways. The line which is to connect Khartûm with Abu Haraz, Gedâref, and Kassâla, is already being constructed by a detachment of the Royal Engineers; and it is proposed to carry a second line from Abu Haraz to Sennâr, and thence to Abba Island on the White Nile, and so southwards to Fashoda and the Sobât river. In connection with this work it is interesting to read Lord Cromer's statement, that "an arrangement has been made as to the rates to be charged on through telegrams passing over the Sudanese and Egyptian lines in the event of telegraphic communication being established with South Africa."[1]

I do not think that I can find a more suitable conclusion to this chapter, in which I have endeavoured to gather up the most salient facts in the present condition and future prospects of the Sudân, than is afforded by a brief mention of the Gordon College at Khartûm. The necessary funds for the erection and endowment of this institution were provided in the main by the spontaneous liberality of the English public, but contributions from Egypt also helped to swell the total sum of more than £100,000 which was thus rapidly collected. The impulse which prompted Lord Kitchener to ask for this gift for the rebellious people whom he had subdued, and the generous response which England gave to his request, are in harmony with the best traditions of the Anglo-Saxon race; nor could any means more fitting to perpetuate the spirit of Gordon have been devised. The object of the Gordon College is, in Lord Kitchener's words, "to give the most practical, useful education possible to the boys for their future in the Sudân."[2] The condition of the country and of its inhabitants being what they are, it is obvious that an education framed on these lines must for the present be restricted to the most elementary subjects of instruction—that is to say, to such subjects as are taught in the primary schools of Egypt.

[1] Egypt, No. 3 (1899).   [2] Ibid.

But whether the instruction be confined to the merest rudiments of useful knowledge, or all the sciences of Europe be taught, if only the Gordon College can infuse something of the spirit of the man whose name it perpetuates into its alumni, it will prove a potent factor in the regeneration of the Sudân. For the spirit of Gordon was obedience to the ideal of duty—that Anglo-Saxon ideal which Mr. Kipling has expressed in his " Song of the English ":

> " Keep ye the Law—be swift in all obedience.
> Clear the land of evil—drive the road and bridge the ford :
> Make ye sure to each his own
> That he reap where he hath sown,
> By the peace among our peoples let men know we serve the Lord ! "

THE END

Printed by BALLANTYNE, HANSON & Co.
Edinburgh & London

www.ingramcontent.com/pod-product-compliance
Lightning Source LLC
Chambersburg PA
CBHW032015220426
43664CB00006B/259